Exploitation as Domination

NEW TOPICS IN APPLIED PHILOSOPHY

Series editor
Kasper Lippert-Rasmussen

This series presents works of original research on practical issues that are not yet well covered by philosophy. The aim is not only to present work that meets high philosophical standards while being informed by a good understanding of relevant empirical matters, but also to open up new areas for philosophical exploration. The series will demonstrate the value and interest of practical issues for philosophy and vice versa.

PUBLISHED IN THE SERIES

The Politics of Social Cohesion
Immigration, Community, and Justice
Nils Holtug

Not In Their Name
Are Citizens Culpable For Their States' Actions?
Holly Lawford-Smith

The Inheritance of Wealth
Justice, Equality, and the Right to Bequeath
Daniel Halliday

Exploitation as Domination

What Makes Capitalism Unjust

NICHOLAS VROUSALIS

OXFORD
UNIVERSITY PRESS

Great Clarendon Street, Oxford, OX2 6DP,
United Kingdom

Oxford University Press is a department of the University of Oxford.
It furthers the University's objective of excellence in research, scholarship,
and education by publishing worldwide. Oxford is a registered trade mark of
Oxford University Press in the UK and in certain other countries

© Nicholas Vrousalis 2023

The moral rights of the author have been asserted

First Edition published in 2023

All rights reserved. No part of this publication may be reproduced, stored in
a retrieval system, or transmitted, in any form or by any means, without the
prior permission in writing of Oxford University Press, or as expressly permitted
by law, by licence or under terms agreed with the appropriate reprographics
rights organization. Enquiries concerning reproduction outside the scope of the
above should be sent to the Rights Department, Oxford University Press, at the
address above

You must not circulate this work in any other form
and you must impose this same condition on any acquirer

Published in the United States of America by Oxford University Press
198 Madison Avenue, New York, NY 10016, United States of America

British Library Cataloguing in Publication Data
Data available

Library of Congress Control Number: 2022939691

ISBN 978–0–19–286769–8

DOI: 10.1093/oso/9780192867698.001.0001

Printed and bound in the UK by
Clays Ltd, Elcograf S.p.A.

Links to third party websites are provided by Oxford in good faith and
for information only. Oxford disclaims any responsibility for the materials
contained in any third party website referenced in this work.

For Efi

Contents

List of Figure and Tables	ix
Preface	xi

Introduction	1
Main Arguments of the Book	1
Summary of the Book	5
How to Read this Book	8

PART I. BACKGROUND

1. Theories of Exploitation	11
1.1 Introduction	11
1.2 The Generic Account	12
1.3 Conceptual Speciation	15
1.4 Teleological Theories	16
1.5 Respect Theories	22
1.6 Freedom Theories	29

PART II. THEORY

2. Domination at Work	37
2.1 The Non-Servitude Proviso	38
2.2 Justifying the Proviso	43
2.3 Reproducible Exploitation	45
2.4 Implications for Capitalism	48
2.5 The Role of Money	53
2.6 Forms of Domination	55
2.7 Domination, Alienation, Reification	59
2.8 The Presence and Relevance of Exploitation Under Capitalism	62
3. How Exploiters Dominate	66
3.1 Metrics of Exploitation	66
3.2 Vulnerability and Domination	72
3.3 Masters, Billionaires, Offers, Kidneys, Surrogacy	76
3.4 Against the Vulnerability View	81
3.5 Against the Fairness View	84
4. Structural Domination in the Market	92
4.1 The Structure of Structural Domination	93

viii CONTENTS

4.2 Structuration = Regulation	98
4.3 Defining the Regulation Function	100
4.4 How Capitalists Dominate	101
4.5 Capitalism Entails the State	103
4.6 Capital's Agentlessness	105
4.7 Modes of Capitalist Exploitation	109
4.8 The Cage's Girth	111

PART III. APPLICATIONS

5. Capitalist Exploitation: Its Forms, Origin, and Fate	117
5.1 The Problem of Subsumed Labour	118
5.2 Definitions	118
5.3 Capital Without Wage-Labour	121
5.4 Capital Before Wage-Labour	124
5.5 Capital After Wage-Labour	132
5.6 The Case Against Market Socialism	134
5.7 How Capitalists Dominate	138

6. Exploitation and International Relations	142
6.1 Domination in International Relations	142
6.2 Colonial and Liberal Imperialism	144
6.3 Globalization and International Exploitation	149
6.4 Resistance and Working-Class Internationalism	155

PART IV. ALTERNATIVES

7. The Emancipated Economy	167
7.1 Against Unconditional Basic Income	168
7.2 Ambiguities of Property-Owning Democracy	170
7.3 Trepidations of Workplace Democracy	174
7.4 'Liberal Socialism:' The Hybrid Model	179
7.5 The Black Box of the State	182

| *References* | 185 |
| *Index* | 193 |

List of Figure and Tables

List of Figure

4.1. Regulated domination	96

List of Tables

1.1. Enclosure	17
4.1. Vertical and horizontal exploitation	111
5.1. Relations of production	119
5.2. Skillman's taxonomy	126
5.3. How capitalists dominate	139
6.1. Who dominates whom (full logical partition)	150
6.2. Who dominates whom (instrumentalist partition)	150
6.3. Mode of surplus-extraction	152
7.1. Exploitation under POD and WD	179
7.2. Banking structure under market socialism	181

Preface

This book argues for two claims: that exploitation is unjust because it constitutes enrichment through the domination of others and that capitalist relations between consenting adults are inherently exploitative in that exact sense. This argument explains how exploiters dominate, how capitalists exploit, and therefore how capitalists dominate. The book's aim throughout is to change the conversation from contemporary theories of exploitation whose focus, almost invariably, is on harm, coercion, or unfairness. I argue, instead, that exploitation is a distinct injustice. So, in developing the domination-based alternative, I engage in dialogue with competing economic, social, and philosophical theories of exploitation.

Philosophers are famously prone to dogmatic slumbers. I am therefore grateful to Richard Arneson for awakening me from mine. Arneson's generous and open-minded intelligence has taught me a great deal about how to do philosophy in general, and political philosophy in particular. Along with G.A. Cohen, Arneson is one of the most interesting and demanding intellectual interlocutors I've had. The influence of both Arneson and Cohen is, I think, palpable throughout this book.

In trying to decipher my own thoughts about exploitation, I have drawn strength from the unflinching conviction of two comrades, John Filling and A.J. Julius. John subscribed to many of the ideas in this book before I came to have them, which gave me confidence when we agreed—and sometimes when we disagreed. I'm also grateful to A.J. for long peripatetic discussions on the main topics discussed here. I've learned so much from him that he bears responsibility for many errors and omissions in this book!

Much of the book was written during sabbaticals at Princeton University (2015–16), where I spent ten months as a Laurance S. Rockefeller Visiting Fellow, and Aarhus University (2018–19), where I spent ten months as a EurIAS/COFUND Fellow. I should like to thank the University Center for Human Values at Princeton and the Aarhus Institute of Advanced Studies for providing academic environments maximally hospitable to curiosity-driven research. I am also grateful to the Institute of Political Science at Leiden University for allowing me to take time off teaching and to the School of Philosophy at Erasmus University Rotterdam for enthusiastically supporting

xii PREFACE

my research since I arrived here in 2019. The Dutch Organization for Scientific Research (NWO) provided generous funding for this research as part of its Vidi grants scheme (016.Vidi.185.213).

Special thanks to Axel Gosseries, Eric Boot, and Tim Meijers for organizing book manuscript workshops at Aarhus, Louvain-la-Neuve, and Leiden, and to all workshop participants: Fritz Gillerke, Manuel Valente, Mirjam Muller, Louis Larue, Pierre-Etienne Vandamme, Juliana Mesen Vargas, Andreas Schmidt, Ben Ferguson, Titus Stahl, Dimitris Efthymiou, Annelien de Dijn, Paul Raekstad, Enzo Rossi, Dorothea Gaedeke, Sara Amighetti, A.J. Julius, Dan Halliday, Danielle Wenner, and Gabriel Wollner.

For helpful and incisive written comments on parts of this book, I should also like to thank: Dick Arneson, Luc Bovens, Paula Casal, Ruth Chang, Simon Cotton, Amitava Dutt, Ben Ferguson, Marc Fleurbaey, Pablo Gilabert, Dan Halliday, Faik Kurtulmus, Alex Kirshner, Niko Kolodny, Ben Laurence, David Leopold, Claudio Lopez-Guerra, Harry Papadopoulos, Harry Platanakis, Charlie Post, Christian Schemmel, Gil Skillman, Lucas Stanczyk, Annie Stilz, Roberto Veneziani, Kate Vredenburgh, Andrew Williams, Stuart White, Gabriel Wollner, Allen Wood, Naoki Yoshihara, Tamara Yugov, and Matt Zwolinski, as well as three anonymous reviewers for Oxford University Press.

This book is dedicated to my beloved wife and comrade Efi Papadodima, whose inexhaustible reserves of curiosity, courage, and good humour always fuel mine.

The book reworks published material, as follows. Chapter 1: 'Exploitation: A Primer.' *Philosophy Compass* (2018) https://doi.org/10.1111/phc3.12486 (accessed 15 Nov 2021). Chapter 2: 'Exploitation, Vulnerability and Social Domination.' *Philosophy & Public Affairs* 41 (2013): 131–157; 'Socialism Unrevised: A Reply to John Roemer on Marx, Exploitation, Solidarity, Worker Control.' *Philosophy & Public Affairs* 49 (2021): 78–109. Chapter 3: 'How Exploiters Dominate.' *Review of Social Economy* 77 (2019): 103–130; 'Exploitation as Domination: A Response to Arneson.' *Southern Journal of Philosophy* 54 (2016): 527–38. Chapter 4: 'Structural Domination and Collective Agency in the Market.' *Journal of Applied Philosophy* 37 (2020): 40–54. Chapter 5: 'Capital without Wage-Labour: Marx's Modes of Subsumption Revisited.' *Economics & Philosophy* 34 (2018): 411–438. Chapter 6: 'Imperialism, Globalization, and Resistance.' *Global Justice: Theory, Practice, Rhetoric* 9 (2016): 69–92. Chapter 7: 'Public Ownership, Worker Control, and the Labour Epistocracy Problem.' *Review of Social Economy* 78 (2020): 439–453.

Introduction

The exploitation of human by human is a globally pervasive phenomenon. Slavery, serfdom, and the patriarchy are part of its lineage. Guest and sex workers, commercial surrogacy, precarious labour contracts, sweatshops, and markets in blood, vaccines, or human organs are contemporary manifestations of exploitation under capitalism.

What makes these exploitative transactions unjust? And is capitalism inherently exploitative? This book offers answers to these two questions. In response to the first question, it argues that exploitation is a form of domination, self-enrichment through the domination of others. On the domination view, exploitation complaints are not, fundamentally, about harm, coercion, or unfairness. Rather, they are about who serves whom and why. Exploitation, in a word, is a dividend of servitude: the dividend the powerful extract from the servitude of the vulnerable. In response to the second question, the book argues that this servitude is inherent to capitalist relations between consenting adults; capital just is monetary title to control over the labour capacity of others. It follows that capitalism, the mode of production where capital predominates, is an inherently unjust social structure.

This chapter precisifies the two title questions, about the injustice of exploitation and the exploitativeness of capitalism, provides some conceptual signposting, and summarizes the main arguments of the rest of this book.

Main Arguments of the Book

Social cooperation, in general, involves agents making claims on each other's labour contribution. The copy of the book you are reading involves hundreds of hours of labour contribution in terms of editing, typesetting, printing, and distribution, as well as thousands of hours of thinking and writing on the part of the author. By reading this book, you consume a share of the net social product—the vast array of books, shoes, cars, and computers—produced in the world economy in a year, as well as a share of the social labour that went into

---

Exploitation as Domination: What Makes Capitalism Unjust. Nicholas Vrousalis, Oxford University Press.
© Nicholas Vrousalis 2023. DOI: 10.1093/oso/9780192867698.003.0001

2 INTRODUCTION

producing it. That you can lay a *claim* to the fruits of this vast division of labour is a gigantic achievement of advanced social cooperation on a global scale.

The question that exercises philosophers who have thought about the division of labour is the nature and rational justification of any given *de facto* claim to alien labour, the labour performance of others. During long stretches of humanity's career, claims to the exercise of alien labour capacity were not typically based on rational justification. Under slavery, feudalism, and the patriarchy, for example, the claim maker receives a share of the claim recipient's surplus product—the product in excess of what she needs to subsist— by directly controlling her productive purposiveness. The feudal lord, for example, directly controls the serf's labour capacity, which enables him to unilaterally appropriate her surplus product. That claim to the serf's labour performance is based on the lord's might only. The realization of that claim therefore constitutes exploitation, the unilateral extraction of labour flow through power over others. It follows that feudal might makes feudal right, in the sense that a superordinate's power determines the subordinate producer's ends and work practices, as well as the social institutions that define and regulate these practices.

There is overwhelming consensus among social historians that the European absolutisms of the 16th and 17th centuries originate in an attempt to shore up such feudal exploitation by centralizing the power of lords in the hands of the state. Capitalism, feudalism's successor, does away with feudal might, and thereby with feudal right, by instituting the primacy of contract and by introducing the legal fiction of the labour contract. Early defenders of capitalism, such as Montesquieu and James Steuart, conceived these institutions as establishing a stable and rational equilibrium between juridical equals. But although they were right that capitalism changes the *content* of the subordination relation between the producer and her conditions of production, they failed to note how its subordinating *form* survives in the institutions of the labour market. Capitalist might makes capitalist right, in the sense that it is still a superordinate's power that determines the subordinate producer's ends, work practices, and the disposal of her final product. But what made this change of content possible?

Modernity ushers in the idea that no human is morally superior to any other. It follows that no claim to the labour performance of others can be rationally justified if it involves might making right. The revolutions of the 17th and 18th centuries that abolished feudalism and established the primacy of contract imprinted this idea of free consent by juridical equals into the structure of the states they founded. Thereafter, control over the productive purposiveness of others was theoretically represented as a consensual and mutually beneficial relationship between equally situated commodity owners: labour and capital. The upshot was that a claim to the producer's labour performance no longer amounted to military or political power, but rather to ownership of commodities and money. This is what enabled classical political economy, under the influence of Adam Smith and David Ricardo, to represent the labour contract not as a power relation between persons, but as a relation between mere things—the objects of contractual agreement between capital and labour. The capitalist mode of production could only enjoy its prodigious growth under such a mystified representation, only half enlightened and half true.

For it turns out that the represented universality of free and equal property owners does not preclude *economic*, contractual control over alien purposiveness. Rousseau and Kant recognized this fact in their discussions of citizenship, as did Hegel, Marx, and Mill. Capitalism, they argued, emancipated individuals in exchange only, such that the irrational subsumption of the individual survived in production. Recent years have seen a revival of this argument. Social democrats like John Rawls and Thomas Piketty have criticized mounting economic inequality on grounds of violating basic precepts of rational justification. But they have not attempted to connect that criticism to the nature of surplus extraction under capitalism.

This book reaffirms that connection. It represents the extraction of surplus from the labour of others as a central feature of exploitative social relationships. It then argues that capitalism is exploitative in that sense: for all its pretensions to freedom and equality—of having superseded might-makes-right—capitalism remains a system of unfreedom and inequality. To make good on these ideas, the book develops an account of exploitation, argues for its cogency, and applies it to capitalist social structure. More precisely, the book defends the following four theses.

First, unjust abuse of power—domination—is unilateral control over alien purposiveness. Undominated action, on the other hand, is action that reflects the agent's own purposiveness through independence of the ends of others. Applied to work, domination is unilateral control over the productive purposiveness of others, that is, over their labour capacity.

Second, exploitation is a dividend of servitude, the servitude of having to respond to the extractive ends and dispositions of the powerful. This dividend, I will argue, is cashed out in terms of *unilateral labour flow*: exploitation is power-induced unreciprocated service to others. The most general form of exploitation in the contemporary world, the exploitative appropriation of

4   INTRODUCTION

money, is exploitative precisely when and because it represents unilateral control over human labour capacity. Capital, I further argue, is a subset of such control: it is monetized title to alien surplus labour. These arguments restore the centrality of subsumed labour to complaints of exploitation, without presupposing controversial claims about the determination of prices or a labour theory of value.

Third, structural domination is a useful and coherent notion. I will argue that structural domination is a triadic relation between dominators, dominated, and third parties contributing non-contingently to the perpetuation of that dyad. I will then show that exploitative structures confront dominated humans with a double bind between altogether abstaining from social interaction and being subjected to the powerful. This double bind pervades work under the capitalist mode of production. Much like patriarchy and white supremacy, capitalism is a cage.

Fourth, the capitalist cage has global girth. Its instances are varieties of—largely obsolete—colonial imperialism and—regrettably nonobsolete—liberal imperialism. Imperialism, I will argue, is not only a coherent and useful concept but is also indispensable to understanding some of the institutions of contemporary globalization and their exploitative aspects. Emancipatory globalization, by contrast, would preserve the global interdependence wrought by capitalism, but without the concomitant encagement.

Compared with other contemporary philosophical treatments of exploitation, this book has three distinctive features. First, it shows that there is a plausible account of the nature and injustice of exploitation that is distinct from the liberal theories currently on offer. To develop this distinctive view, I draw upon contemporary debates among liberals, republicans, feminists, and socialists about the nature and place of power in the just society. I then put the theory to work in developing and defending a novel account of exploitation.

Second, the conceptual apparatus deployed in the book is, in principle, applicable to all forms of exploitation, from slavery to patriarchy to sweatshops to guest workers to reproductive labour. I will flag these cases when they are relevant. However, the book's principal focus is on economic relationships. Economic relationships are voluntary and uncoerced contractual relationships that are typically mutually beneficial. Such relationships make exploitation a philosophically interesting concept and give exploitation complaints their distinctive moral bite. The book does not discuss the state or the justification of state authority, although the theory it defends has important implications along both dimensions. I will flag these implications when necessary.

Third, the book engages in dialogue with contemporary social and economic theory. Three chapters of the book address topics in social theory directly: Chapter 5 discusses the nature and origin of capitalist exploitation, while Chapter 6 discusses the relationship between exploitation and international relations. This engagement supports the attempt, in Chapter 7, to sketch what a non-exploitative, democratically emancipated economy might look like. The unifying thread throughout is the critique of capital as monetary title to alien purposiveness.

A final methodological caveat. This book develops an account of exploitation, argues for its cogency, and shows that it is endemic to capitalism. But capitalism is not *actually existing* capitalism. To focus on contemporary capitalist institutions would needlessly complicate the exposition and arbitrarily restrict its scope and applications. For this reason, I steer clear of real life examples in the first part of the book, operating instead with a simple and general model of capitalist reproduction, which I introduce in Chapter 2. The latter part of the book, Chapters 5–7, takes up salient features of actually existing capitalism.

Summary of the Book

The book has four parts. Parts I and II are conceptual. Part I provides a conceptual map of the philosophical terrain. More precisely, Part I discusses different candidates for the 'exploiter' predicate and the kind of claim they make to the social surplus. Part II defends an account of domination that draws upon liberal, Kantian, republican, and recognitional accounts for its justification. More precisely, Part II argues that to dominate others is to treat them as servants. The powerful so treat the vulnerable by unilaterally subjecting their purposiveness to their own. Exploitation is the dividend the powerful extract from this servitude; it is the unreciprocated labour or effort they receive by converting the vulnerable into their servants. This argument explains how exploiters dominate, how capitalists exploit, and therefore how capitalists dominate.

Parts III and IV engage in dialogue with social theory. Part III applies the theory developed in Part II, taking up contemporary debates on the origin of capitalist transactions, international trade, and global justice. More precisely, Part III studies the historically specific form of claim-making inaugurated by the capitalist mode of production and its implications for capitalist globalization. Part IV discusses non-exploitative alternatives to the social predicament

6 INTRODUCTION

discussed in Part III, connecting them with the contemporary debate on market socialism and economic democracy. I now summarize the argument of each chapter.

Chapter 1 reviews the recent literature by painting a broad-stroke picture of the conceptual landscape on exploitation. It distinguishes between three species of exploitation theory: *teleology-based*, *respect-based*, and *freedom-based* accounts. Each class of theory is organized around an exploiter-archetype. Teleogical theory takes its archetype from the feudal lord and monopolist; respect theory from the rentier and the patrimonial capitalist; freedom theory from the capitalist and banker who unilaterally subsume the purposiveness of the direct producer. The chapter addresses the implications of each theory, paving the way for the arguments that follow.

Now, this book is about how power converts the service of others into servitude. As a matter of logic, servitude presupposes dominion. So what is dominion? What kinds of transactions, in general, does it censure? And what is the character of these transactions under capitalism?

Chapter 2 offers provisional answers to these questions. It argues that domination is violation of the requirements of rightful individual freedom: subjection of purposiveness to the choices of others. Applied to work, such subjection entails unjust unilateral control over the productive purposiveness of others. The chapter introduces the Non-Servitude Proviso, which grounds the subjected-purposiveness idea on a number of possible justifications: Kantian, republican, and recognitional. Now, exploitation is what happens when unilateral control over labour capacity translates into unreciprocated labour flow. With the help of a simple economic model, the chapter applies the Proviso to capital and discusses its implications for 'clean' capitalist accumulation. Capital, I argue, is a monetized claim to unilateral control over alien labour capacity.

Chapter 3 argues that exploitation is a dividend of servitude. It does this by extending, refining, and defending the domination conception of Chapter 2. The chapter kicks off by arguing that what makes exploitation unjust is that it constitutes domination-induced unilateral service to others. After rebutting John Roemer's influential critique of surplus labour, it shows that exploitation is cashed out in terms of labour time or effort. The chapter then criticizes competing contemporary accounts of exploitation, the vulnerability view and the fairness view. It argues that they fail to do justice to the servitude dimension and to account for important counterexamples.

Chapter 4 draws upon debates among feminists, republicans, and theorists of power to argue for the cogency of the idea of structural domination. It then applies that idea to capitalist economic structure. The chapter defends a definition of structural domination as *regulated* domination: any given instance of domination is structural just when it involves a triadic relation between dominator, dominated, and regulator—any social role that contributes non-contingently to the reproduction of the dominator–dominated dyad. The chapter then illustrates two general ways in which capitalist transactions between consenting adults evince structural exploitation. The first involves vertical authority relations between capitalists and workers—the standard labour-market case canvassed in Chapter 2. The second involves horizontal market relations between workers in different (and possibly democratic) firms. These two cases illustrate the difference between a hired and an unhired servitude, the dividends to which constitute exploitation.

Chapter 5 studies capitalist economic structure through the lens of historical sociology. It kicks off by exploring the idea of capital—as monetary title to subsumed labour—through a series of historical examples. It then extends the model of capitalist accumulation introduced in Chapter 2 by asking how exploitation becomes possible under capitalism and what historically specific forms it takes. Sophisticated answers to these two questions—of origin and form, respectively—have been provided by Karl Marx in volumes I and III of *Capital*. This chapter studies Marx's answers, drawing extensively upon the contemporary debate on the origins of capitalism. It then shows how that debate can shed light on discussions about precarity and the 'gig economy', as well as on post-capitalist democratic futures, including contemporary discussions on market socialism and the democratic firm.

Chapter 6 extends the account of exploitation already developed to international relations. If the argument of the foregoing chapters is sound, then exploitation is a form of domination—the activation of the extractive dispositions of the powerful. And if states can exploit states, then states can dominate states. The domination of one political community by another is called imperialism. This chapter argues for the cogency of that notion and applies it to capitalist globalization. It shows that there is a useful and defensible distinction between colonial and liberal imperialism and argues that resistance to imperialism does not, in general, entail a right to national self-determination. Such a right, it turns out, draws its justification from a broader internationalist commitment to resisting domination.

Chapter 7 discusses alternatives to capitalism. It sketches three important theories of the non-exploitative economy: unconditional basic income (UBI), property-owning democracy (POD), and workplace democracy (WD). It argues that only POD and WD are eligible candidates for the abolition

8 INTRODUCTION

of exploitation. POD does better in attenuating horizontal exploitation, the exploitation of one economic unit by another, whereas WD does better in attenuating vertical exploitation, the exploitation of workers by bosses or owners. It is therefore possible that a hybrid theory could do better than each taken by itself. This hybrid theory, variously travelling under the names 'liberal socialism' and 'democratic socialism', recommends worker control plus a strongly predistributive form of public ownership. The chapter concludes by outlining a pressing dilemma for advocates of socialized production, the socialization dilemma between statism and—what I will call—the labour epistocracy.

How to Read this Book

Readers already familiar with the philosophical landscape on exploitation can jump straight into Chapter 2. Chapters 2 and 3 jointly constitute the book's conceptual nervous system. Readers uninterested in conceptual neurology, or primarily interested in social theory, can read Chapters 2 and 4. Readers primarily interested in the economics and sociology of exploitation can read Chapters 2, 5, and 7; those primarily interested in international relations, globalization theory, or global justice can read Chapters 2 and 6.

PART I
BACKGROUND

1

Theories of Exploitation

This chapter reviews the recent literature by painting a broad-stroke picture of the conceptual landscape on exploitation. It distinguishes between three species of exploitation theory: *teleology-based* (including harm and mutual benefit), *respect-based* (including mere means, force, rights, and fairness), and *freedom-based* (including vulnerability and domination) accounts. Each theory is organized around an exploiter-archetype. Teleogical theory takes its archetype from the feudal lord and monopolist and is largely limited to them; respect theory takes its archetype from the rentier and the patrimonial capitalist; freedom theory from the capitalist and banker who unilaterally subsume the purposiveness of the direct producer. The chapter addresses the implications of each theory, paving the way for the arguments that follow in the rest of the book. The chapter also argues that one influential contemporary account of exploitation, due to Alan Wertheimer, is best interpreted along the lines of the freedom account.

1.1 Introduction

Social interactions can be modelled and evaluated in light of their effects on persons. These effects can be *negative-sum*, *zero-sum*, or *positive-sum* in the relevant metric—whether welfare, goods, capabilities, or some molecular combination thereof.[1] Call the relevant metric 'stuff'. A negative-sum interaction between persons involves a negative-sum total of stuff. Suppose A shoots B. The gun backfires, harming both A and B. This interaction is negative-sum. A zero-sum interaction is one in which the sum of stuff is zero: my stuff gain is your exact loss. Finally, a positive-sum interaction involves a *surplus* of stuff over and above the sum total enjoyed in the noninteraction baseline.

Exploitation theory is largely concerned with the control and distribution of the surplus from positive-sum transactions. Such transactions are particularly

---

[1] On the metric of distributive justice, see Arneson (1989), Cohen (1989, 2011), Dworkin (2000), and Sen (1992).

Exploitation as Domination: What Makes Capitalism Unjust. Nicholas Vrousalis, Oxford University Press.
© Nicholas Vrousalis 2023. DOI: 10.1093/oso/9780192867698.003.0002

12   THEORIES OF EXPLOITATION

interesting when mutually consensual and beneficial. Contrast theft: both exploitation and theft are forms of unjust taking, but theft is necessarily involuntary and zero-sum. Exploitation, by contrast, need not be involuntary[2] and is sometimes positive-sum. Indeed, it is precisely the mutually beneficial and consensual nature of capitalist transactions to which defenders of capitalism usually appeal. They argue that human productive power, however measured, has increased by more than ten-fold since industrialization began (Gordon 2012). It is, therefore, undeniable that vast stretches of humanity have benefited from the establishment and growth of capitalist institutions, especially the rule of law and private property. But it is equally undeniable that this growth has been concomitant with appalling misery, degradation, and unfreedom. One goal of this book is to explain the nature, grounds, and forms of that unfreedom.

Political economists have recently caught up with ordinary moral consciousness on these matters. They note how, by breeding and exacerbating economic inequality, the enforcement of capitalist private property can engender unfreedom (see Atkinson 2015, Piketty 2014, Stiglitz 2012). In other words, the complement to contemporary inequality is a series of practices that look like excellent candidates for exploitation: guest and sex workers, zero-hour and precarious contracts, sweatshops, commercialized reproductive labour, financialization (the selling of high-risk financial packages to the poor), and imperialism. The sheer pervasiveness of these presumptively exploitative practices in our world makes the study of exploitation topical. The rest of this chapter introduces concepts central to that study.

1.2 The Generic Account

In its colloquial uses, the expression 'exploitation of human by human' suggests receiving too much in return for too little, and doing so illicitly. I begin by nailing my colours on a platitude: A exploits B only if (1) A benefits disproportionately, (2) from a social relationship with B, (3) by taking advantage of B, where A and B may be individuals, groups, or social classes. This section draws some contours of the concept of exploitation by discussing each clause (1)–(3) individually, beginning with:

---

[2] 'Need not': slavery is exploitative but involuntary.

(1) *A* benefits disproportionately.

(1) says that exploitation involves benefit to the exploiter relative to some nontransaction baseline. Without this stipulation, it is impossible to distinguish between acts of exploitation and mere *attempts* to exploit. So when an attempt at exploitation succeeds, we can be certain that *A* has benefited from her interaction with *B*, no matter how short-lived or trivial the benefit. A further relevant distinction is that between an *exploitative act* and an *act of exploitation*. Suppose *A* offers to rescue *B*, a drowning child, in return for $1 million. *A*'s behaviour—the attitudes and dispositions it betokens—is exploitative. But it may not result in an *act* of exploitation if *A* immediately rescinds the offer.[3] This distinction is important, not just because it implies that exploitings are not dispositions but also because it suggests that making someone exploitable or treating her as such is a distinct injustice from exploiting her. I will return to this distinction in Chapter 2.

The second necessary condition for exploitation is disproportionate benefit:

(2) from a social relationship with *B*

For *A* to exploit *B*, *A* must benefit from meaningful interaction with *B*. Suppose that *A* benefits from good weather and *B* suffers from bad, but they live on separate islands, never to interact with each other. The resulting inequality between *A* and *B* will never be the outcome or cause of exploitation. On the theory defended in this book, a social relationship is any relation between agents representable in a true and complete social science. Social relationships contrast with the logically stronger concept of *structural* relationships, which I discuss in Chapter 4.

We can get more out of (2) if we stipulate that the social relationship must be reproducible across time. A set of negative-sum interactions, for example, is not indefinitely reproducible for an economy as a whole. At some point, the set of exploitees will become incapable of reproducing their own subsistence and their exploitation will become impossible.[4] Moreover, a zero-sum interaction is unlikely to be reproducible for very long. If my gain is your exact loss, then sooner or later you will catch on and either start resisting me, or, if that option is ineligible, drop out of interaction altogether. Both options make exploitation

---

[3] This is discussed by Wertheimer (1999, pp. 209–10), who also distinguishes between *ex ante* and *ex post* benefit.
[4] In Chapter 2 I offer a more precise definition of reproduction.

14 THEORIES OF EXPLOITATION

more difficult. An interesting theory of exploitation will therefore interpret (2) as at least allowing for positive-sum interactions. In what follows, I assume that such interactions involve reproducible production of a *surplus*, such that the exploitee produces more than she needs in order to survive and the exploiter lays a claim to that surplus. A theory of exploitation must explain the *source* of such claims,[5] as well as their *form*.[6] I discuss the source of claims to the surplus in Chapter 2 and their form in Chapter 4.

Claims (1) and (2) do not, alone, suffice for exploitation; if they did, then nearly every human transaction would be exploitative. We need a further condition, one that provides some normative leverage to (1), the idea of disproportionate benefit. So to exploit B, A must benefit from a social relationship with B:

(3)   by taking advantage of B.

When A exploits B, A takes advantage of B, that is, B's whole person. Many philosophers have noted that this implies a distinction between exploiting a person and exploiting her features or circumstances.[7] Exploiting someone's dribbling weakness in football, for example, may not amount to exploiting *her*. One might infer from this that A exploits B's whole person just when A takes advantage of enough sufficiently important features of B, features that are central to B's person, her life or well-being. However, this would get things the wrong way around; the concept of exploitation itself gives us better guidance.

To exploit a whole person—as opposed to her mere features—amounts to treating that person *as* her mere features, that is, to treating her as less than *she* is. So, for example, to exploit someone sexually is to treat her as if she were her genitals; to exploit a manual worker is to treat her as if she were her body; to exploit a mental worker is to treat her as if she were her brain, and so on. To exploit, on this view, is not to use a feature which, in virtue of its importance, is tantamount to *using the person who has it*. Rather, to exploit is to use a person as if *she* were her feature, that is, the feature she has. It is relevant, here, that the term 'exploitation' was first applied to humans—as the term's *object*—by Saint-Simon (Bazard 1831) and was meant to reflect precisely this subject–predicate inversion: the treatment of humans as things.

---

[5] Under feudalism, for example, the feudal lord lays her claim to the surplus on the basis of military or status power. Under capitalism, she does so on the basis of commodity ownership.

[6] The feudal lord's irrational claims to the surplus are sometimes formally presented as claims of divine right, the capitalist's claim of property right.

[7] See, for example, Goodin (1987) and Wood (1995).

How do you so treat a person? The answer given in this book is that you do it by taking these mere features that constitute the agency of another as vehicles for the advancement of your ends or, what amounts to the same thing, by treating an alien purposiveness as if *she* were that feature which serves your ends. A person is reduced to the hands and legs and brain and genitals that serve you. Whole-person exploitation therefore entails a kind of canine hierarchy of overdog and underdog, body and limb, master and servant.

But this is as far as conceptual analysis will take us. In order to make progress, we need a normative theory. We must, in other words, attend to different theoretical ways in which (3) has been understood. To focus intuitions, consider:

Pit—A and B are alone in the desert. A finds B lying at the bottom of a pit. A offers B costless rescue, on condition that B works for A for $1/day for the rest of her life. B accepts.

This transaction is paradigmatic of exploitation: if *Pit* does not instance exploitation, then nothing does. The trick is to figure out precisely what makes the transaction between A and B unjust. The rest of this chapter discusses different accounts of what makes such exploitation unjust.

1.3 Conceptual Speciation

The bare bones of the generic concept of exploitation in (1)–(3) have been fleshed out in at least three distinct sets of theories: *teleological, respect,* and *freedom* theories. These theories cover the whole ethical terrain, from consequentialism to virtue ethics to deontology. Each theory, moreover, corresponds to a distinctive kind of exploiter, a peculiar kind of 'archvillain'. I now review these archetypes.

According to teleological theories, exploiters either block possibilities for Pareto-improving cooperation or benefit from such institutional bottlenecks. The paradigmatic exploiter here is the feudal lord and the monopolist. According to respect theories, on the other hand, exploiters fail to treat exploitees with equal concern and respect. The paradigmatic exploiter here, in addition to feudal lords and monopolists, is the rentier and 'patrimonial capitalist'[8] who gains from background unfairness. Finally, according to freedom theories, exploiters

---

[8] The term is introduced and discussed in Piketty (2014).

16　THEORIES OF EXPLOITATION

unilaterally subsume the purposiveness of others. The paradigmatic exploiter here—other than feudal lords, monopolists, and patrimonial capitalists—is the capitalist and banker who gains from the subordinate pecuniary position of another.

In terms of the conceptual platitudes set out in section 1.2, teleological theories take claim (3) to entail that the exploitee has been harmed, or that the exploiter has undermined possibilities for mutually advantageous trade, or has failed to reciprocate in kind. Respect theories take (3) to entail that the exploitee has been illicitly forced to perform an act, has been used as a mere means, or has been treated unfairly. Finally, freedom theories take (3) to entail that the exploitee's vulnerability has been improperly taken advantage of, that her autonomy has been compromised, or that she has been dominated for the dominator's benefit.

I discuss these three sets of theories separately, beginning with teleological views. Readers familiar with such theories can jump to section 1.5.

1.4 Teleological Theories

1.4.1 Exploitation as harm

Harm is at the centre of many liberal theories of exploitation. I here follow Feinberg (1987) in understanding harm as setback to interests. If you punch me, then my well-being drops relative to a counterfactual situation in which you do not. I am therefore worse off relative to that baseline. On the *harm view*, A exploits B if and only if A benefits:

(4)　by causing harm to B.

Clearly, (4) does not complete the set of sufficient conditions for exploitation. Suppose A and B participate in a race, in which A wins and B loses. B has no complaint of exploitation; it would be inaccurate for B to say to A: 'you're exploiting me', *even if* A is cheating. Harm is not only insufficient for exploitation but also unnecessary.[9] Consider:

Enclosure—A and B live in the commons, earning 5 widgets each (first row of Table 1.1). Upon reading Robert Nozick, A has an idea. A will enclose the

---

[9] Buchanan (1984) defends necessity.

TELEOLOGICAL THEORIES   17

Table 1.1 Enclosure

	(payoff$_A$, payoff$_B$)
Pre-enclosure	(5, 5)
Post-enclosure with sweatshop contract	(100, 6)
Post-enclosure equality	(53, 53)

commons and hire B as a labourer on a sweatshop contract: B will work all day, producing a surplus of 96 widgets. A will not work at all. Of the surplus, A will get 95 widgets and B will get 1 (second row of Table 1.1). The options in the feasible set are as set out in Table 1.1.

Intuitively, *Enclosure* is exploitative. Indeed, the fact that there is a third possibility in the feasible set, that of sharing the surplus equally (third row of Table 1.1), heightens the sense that A exploits B. But if harm is defined relative to the pre-enclosure baseline, then it cannot be a necessary condition for exploitation. For B is better off under a sweatshop contract and is therefore not harmed relative to pre-enclosure. She *is* harmed relative to post-enclosure equality, but that is not how harm has been defined. So when harm is defined in terms of the pre-transaction situation, exploitation need not involve harm. Feinberg (1987) plausibly infers that exploitation is a non-harm-based 'free-floating evil'.[10]

Now, some philosophers believe that harm *per se* says nothing about injustice. A may harm B with B's consent, as when B freely engages in some form of masochism. What matters, they say, is nonvoluntary or nonconsensual harm. Partisans of this view claim that harm to others *just* is nonconsensual harm, and nonconsensual harm is presumptively unjust. This sort of harm, they say, completes the definition of exploitation (see, for example, Benn 1988). So, according to the *consent view*, A exploits B if and only if A benefits:

(5)   by causing nonconsensual harm to B.

What counts as genuine consent? Some forms of presumptive consent are unfree, as when someone puts a gun to your head and forces you to sign a cheque. Other forms of consent are irrational, as when a self-loving person signs her own death sentence under the influence of drugs. Yet other forms of consent are uninformed, as when you sign a piece of paper which,

---

[10] Feinberg's inference is cogently criticized by Wertheimer (1999, chapter 9).

18 THEORIES OF EXPLOITATION

unbeknownst to you, authorizes in your execution. The operative idea here is that of *free, rational, and informed* consent.

This redefinition does not, however, support (5) as a sufficient condition for exploitation. Suppose someone punches you in the street, and runs away with your purse. The interaction meets the conjunction of conditions (1), (2), and (5), but does not count as exploitation. Theft and exploitation, I have already argued, are distinct injustices.

Nor does nonconsensual harm furnish a necessary condition for exploitation. The *Enclosure* case shows that the social surplus can be shared extremely unequally even if all parties benefit, and *even if all parties consent to a sweatshop contract*. That contract still seems exploitative. Consider a related example:

> *Charlotte and Werther*—Charlotte is deeply in love with Werther, whom she leaves wholly indifferent. Charlotte gives away all of her livelihood to impress Werther, who is flattered and amused by her courtship. Werther takes Charlotte's gifts without reciprocating, and without discouraging her advances.

In this instance of unrequited love, Werther and Charlotte effectively agree that Charlotte be impoverished and Werther be enriched, in the relevant metric. Werther exploits Charlotte. If this is correct, then Charlotte is exploited through her own free, rational, and informed consent.[11] In light of these difficulties, why not just shift the baseline for harm, from pre-enclosure to complete equality? The only principled way to do this is by appeal to a harm-independent criterion, such as fairness, rights, or domination. I will discuss each of these criteria in the sections that follow.

I provisionally conclude that (nonconsensual) harm does not furnish a necessary or sufficient condition for exploitation. More generally, it is unlikely that failures of consent or voluntariness will help us understand exploitation. For the latter is objective, in the sense that it has to do with the mind-independent nature of the social relation between transactors and the set of justifications for engaging in it. The mental states of the agents, of course, help determine the rate at which A is willing to buy and B is willing to sell, as well as the concomitant formation of a surplus product. Any transaction that falls within the margin of agreement—a price lower than the buyer's reservation price, but greater than the seller's—will be mutually consensual and beneficial. It does not follow, however, that such a transaction is not exploitative.

---

[11] This conclusion is cogently defended by Feinberg (1988) and Wood (1995).

Now, a teleologist might retort that exploitation is unjust not because it harms, but rather because it is inefficient, or blocks possibilities for Pareto-improving trade. According to this teleological theory, the exploiter's archetype is the monopolist and his ilk.

1.4.2 Exploitation as failure of reciprocity

Anti-monopolists construe exploitation as a form of nonreciprocity, such that *A* benefits:

(6)   by receiving something from *B*, without giving an equivalent in return.

What is an 'equivalent'? According to the marginal productivity theory, advocated by many neoclassical economists,[12] only competitive markets reward 'factors of production' (land, labour and capital) in proportion to their 'contribution' to production. Contribution to production is measured by a factor's marginal productivity, that is, the amount of output created by the addition of an extra unit of that factor to production.

On the marginal productivity view, exploitation is failure to reward in proportion to marginal product. Restrictions on free trade, as well as monopolies, will therefore violate (6) and lead to exploitation. A relevant question arising is: what do owners of capital contribute to production? Owning stuff, as such, is not a productive activity. Yet all that capitalists do, *qua* capitalists, is own. Productive activity, by contrast, is carried out by labour (including idea-generation, the management and organization of production, etc.). The pro-capitalist response is that capitalists take risks with their money, and therefore deserve a reward for doing so.[13]

But advocates of the marginal productivity theory need to ask a prior question: why would anyone be entitled to a reward for risk if *what she risks with* was not hers in the first place? (Arneson 1981, Cohen 1988) I may create wonders by stealing your coat, or by renting it out for profit, but I am not thereby entitled to what value I earn, add, or contribute to the coat. In other words, if capitalist private property is theft, then no reward legitimately accrues to it. The marginal productivity theory therefore either is unconvincing or

---

[12] The idea originates from Clark (1902).
[13] This argument is disparaged by Marx (1976, pp. 738–46), who discusses the idea that profit is a reward for abstinence. In a similar vein, Alfred Marshall (1890) wryly mentions Baron Rothschild's 'reward for waiting'. See also Rawls (1971, p. 272).

20 THEORIES OF EXPLOITATION

resolves into the question of the moral legitimacy of private property, *on the theory's own terms*. I will address the latter question in section 1.5.

There are other ways in which (6) can be satisfied, which do not presuppose the marginal productivity theory. Suppose A gets B to pay for all the drinks, and A never does. Then their transaction satisfies (6). Likewise, when A gets B to work for A, or to give birth for A, or to have sex with A, without giving anything back, A benefits at B's expense. What is the *metric* of benefit, on this variant of the reciprocity view? One of Marxism's enduring legacies to exploitation theory is a set of definitions based on the *unequal exchange of labour* (UE). On this definition, A exploits B if and only if A extracts unreciprocated labour flow from B.[14] The rest of this section discusses this interpretation.

Marx's (1976) account of exploitation entails unequal exchange of labour, in this sense. That is, Marx's allusions to the worker 'working *gratis* for the capitalist', or performing 'unpaid labour' are central to his charge of exploitation of workers by capitalists. According to Marx, a part of the working day is spent by workers working on their own subsistence, which they receive in wages. Suppose that the worker's wage is worth 6 hours of labour time.[15] The capitalist is not, however, going to let the worker walk away with only 6 hours of labour time worked. If she did, there would be no reward for private risk-taking and therefore no livelihood for the capitalist. The capitalist therefore writes it into the worker's contract that she will work for 12 hours a day, such that her wage buys her consumption goods worth 6 hours of labour. She therefore works gratis for the capitalist for 6 hours a day.[16]

Now suppose that B produces stuff in an 'early and rude state of society', as Adam Smith called it, without nonlabour inputs. Suppose, further, that A appropriates a portion of that stuff. This appropriation is an instance of unequal exchange of labour: there is an unreciprocated net transfer of labour time from one party to another. Some philosophers attribute to Marx a 'technical' notion of exploitation, according to which unequal labour exchange is not only a necessary, but also a *sufficient* condition for exploitation. It is doubtful that Marx held such a notion.[17] But whatever Marx thought, the content of the attribution is implausible. For gift-giving implies unequal exchange, but no

---

[14] I discuss UE extensively in Chapters 2 and 3, where I draw upon John Roemer's early theories (Roemer 1982), to show that labour is indispensable to any defensible theory of exploitation.

[15] This assumption leads to the *transformation problem*, the problem of transforming labour *values* into *prices* (see Cohen (1988) and Roemer (1982) for discussion). Roemer's unequal-exchange definitions were invented precisely to circumvent this problem, without affecting the crux of Marx's theory.

[16] Marx defines the *rate of exploitation* as the ratio of unpaid (6 hours) to paid labour (6 hours) which is, in this example, 100 percent. See Marx (1992, chapter 18) for discussion.

[17] For vindication of these doubts, see Arneson (1981) and Geras (1986).

one thinks (even systematic) gift-giving exploitative. If B freely[18] decides to pass on stuff to A, the resulting inequality in labour consumption across A and B need not be objectionable. So UE is not, as such, a sufficient condition for exploitation.

One boon for UE-type definitions is that they can handily operationalize the concept of exploitation. Suppose S represents the difference between the amount of labour B expends to produce the net product and her subsistence bundle, such that S is proportional to the surplus product. Beneficial advantage-taking can now be interpreted as the benefit A extracts:

(7)   by consuming a commodity bundle that embodies S.[19]

Now, for much the same reasons as before, (7) cannot complete the set of sufficient conditions for exploitation: B might, for example, freely pass over the surplus to A.

So what does complete the set of sufficient conditions? A final teleological account I will consider says that exchange is exploitative just when it undermines possibilities for mutually advantageous or Pareto-improving trade. Some philosophers (Gauthier 1985, Van Donselaar 2009) claim that exploitation is a form of parasitism along these lines. When nonworkers appropriate the fruit of workers' labour, for example, the former exploit the latter. Such parasitism is unjust because it violates a putative requirement that agents not obstruct mutually beneficial transactions, or transactions to which they have no transaction-independent claims.

As it stands, this theory is untenable. Its major premiss implies, implausibly, that sick and disabled nonworkers who benefit from redistribution from the able-bodied thereby exploit the able-bodied. This may be 'parasitism' in the technical sense of that term, but it is not exploitation.[20] More generally, exploitation is not necessarily harmful, based on monopoly power, or incompatible with Pareto improvements. The feudal lord and the monopolist are not the only candidates for the 'exploiter' predicate, so we must expand our theoretical vision.

I now explore to another species of exploitation theory, broadly based on an account of respect.

---

[18] 'Freely': not by dint of domination, coercion, or force. The mere necessity of this qualification shows that the attribution to Marx of a 'technical' account of exploitation as naked unilateral labour flow is absurd.

[19] Note that A and B can stand for classes, instead of individuals. Moreover, 'consuming' labour refers to the consumption bundle the agent *can* afford, given her wage and price level.

[20] See section 1.5.1. Wolff (2010) criticizes the identification of parasitism with exploitation for similar reasons. In Chapter 3, section 3.1.1, I discuss a revised version of this theory, which is, I think, more palatable.

22 THEORIES OF EXPLOITATION

1.5 Respect Theories

Respect theorists hold that what completes the set of sufficient conditions for exploitation is the treatment of others as mere means or as less than equals. The disposition to so treat another is objectionable, on this view, because it violates Kant's formula of humanity, or something like it: 'So act that you use humanity, whether in your own person or that of another, always at the same time as an end, never merely as a means' (Kant 1996, p. 80). Sample (2003) offers an influential defence of this view, as do Rawls (1971) and Dworkin (2000). Broadly speaking, these respect theorists take their archvillains to be rentiers, patrimonial capitalists, and other structural beneficiaries from background injustice. The rest of this section builds on this generic Kantian view, with an eye to capturing the injustice specific to exploitation complaints.

1.5.1 Exploitation as forced nonreciprocation

Some liberals and many socialists maintain that exploitation constitutes treating others as mere means insofar as it involves performance of *forced*, unpaid, surplus labour (see, for example, Reiman 1987 and Peffer 1990). This philosophical matchmaking between liberalism and socialism, Kant and Marx, has the exegetical advantage that it accords with much of what Marx says about the worker's 'degradation to a mere means' under capitalism, through subjection to the 'silent compulsion of economic relations' (Marx 1976, p. 899). The force-inclusive definition also resonates with widely held intuitions about the putatively involuntary nature of exploitative interactions. This section shows that matchmaking on the basis of the force-inclusive definition is bound to fail.[21]

---

[21] It bears noting that force and coercion describe distinct events. To be forced to F is to lack a reasonable or acceptable alternative to F-ing. Coercion involves force, in the relevant sense, when A puts a gun on B's head and asks for B's money. But the converse, from force to coercion, does not hold. The wind can force, but it cannot *coerce*; coercion personalizes force. This distinction sheds light on the following contentions in economic and historical sociology. Most historical economic formations since antiquity generate surpluses through social cooperation. In all of these formations it is a small part of society, one class, that has direct access to, and control over, the surplus. In ancient societies, for example, it is the slaveowners who control and appropriate the surplus created by slaves. There are, at the same time, priests, politicians, and states, all of whom absorb a portion of the surplus. These are meta-parasites, parasites parasitic on the class exploiting the direct producers (see Anderson (1974) for an influential overview of the historical literature). Under feudalism, serfs produce the surplus, which the feudal lords control and consume. Serfs spend a part of their time working for themselves, and another part working for the feudal lord. Under both slavery and feudalism, the *mode of exploitation* is direct coercion (see Cohen (1978), chapter 3). Capitalism is like slavery and feudalism in that the surplus is appropriated and largely consumed by one class, namely capitalists, in conjunction with

RESPECT THEORIES 23

It is widely held that propertyless workers under capitalism are forced, by their economic circumstances, to work for *some* capitalist or other (see Cohen 1988 and Chapter 4). And it is the *forced* nature of the unilateral labour transfer between capitalists and workers that makes, or breaks, the case for (capitalist) exploitation. According to this *force-inclusive view* of exploitation, *A* benefits:

(8) by getting *B* to perform forced, unreciprocated, surplus labour.

(8) combines the surplus-extraction idea in (7) with the state enforcement of propertylessness under capitalism. I now show that (8) provides neither a necessary nor sufficient condition for exploitation. I consider sufficiency first.

Societies with welfare states generally provide for the sick and disabled. Those welfare beneficiaries receive a net transfer of labour time from able-bodied taxpayers. And these able-bodied taxpayers are, in turn, forced—because coerced by the state—to engage in these net transfers. It follows, by the force-inclusive definition, that the welfare state is a system in which the disabled poor exploit the able-bodied rich. More precisely, consider the following argument:

(8a) Exploitation is forced, unreciprocated labour transfer.

(8b) In any welfare system with progressive taxation, some rich able-bodied people are forced to engage in unreciprocated labour transfers with poor *disabled* people.

So (8c) The disabled poor exploit the able-bodied rich.

This argument shows why liberals and socialists, all constitutively opposed to a conclusion like (8c), are ill-advised to affirm the force-based definition (8a). More precisely, if (8b) is granted, then either (8a) must be false or liberals and socialists must rethink their commitment to the welfare state, among other things.

---

some meta-parasites. This is to say nothing about the moral status of that appropriation, which, unlike slaveowning and serfdom, may be entirely justified. But, in contrast to both slavery and feudalism, the capitalist mode of exploitation does not involve coercive surplus extraction. No capitalist is permitted, by law, to coerce someone into working for her. And if the law is properly enforced, as it is in many capitalist countries, then workers have formal control over their own labour power. The existence of trade unions and welfare states, moreover, makes such control modally robust, that is, accessible to workers across nearby possible worlds. I discuss these issues further in Chapter 5.

24   THEORIES OF EXPLOITATION

Now, this argument *by reductio* might seem like a boon for right-libertarianism. It is not, for right-libertarians cannot affirm (8a) either. Consider this argument:

(8a)   Exploitation is forced, unreciprocated labour transfer.

(8d)   Under capitalism, some poor *able-bodied* people are forced[22] to engage in unreciprocated labour transfers with rich able-bodied people.

So (8e)   The able-bodied rich exploit the able-bodied poor.

Nozick (1974, pp. 253–4) realizes that, if claim (8a) is granted, then at least some proletarians—able-bodied people with zero net wealth—will be exploited by capitalists. They are, after all, forced (by their economic circumstances) to transfer net labour time to the rich able-bodied. (8e) follows. Nozick balks at this conclusion and proceeds to disavow its major premiss. What this dialectic shows is that the force-inclusive definition is a plague on *all* your houses: socialist, liberal, or libertarian. So (8) cannot provide a sufficient condition for exploitation.

What about (8) as a necessary condition for exploitation? Consider a variation on an example due to Roemer (1996):

> *Two Plots—A* and *B* own different plots of land. They have identical utility functions that are increasing in stuff consumed. If they do nothing, then their land will magically generate an equal amount of stuff, such that they both enjoy an equal level of utility. Now, *A* offers *B* work on *A*'s land, which is much more productive than *A*'s when worked on by human hands. If *B* accepts *A*'s offer, *B* will produce *N* stuff and consume a small proportion of *N* (sufficiently large, say, to compensate for the disutility of labour, if any). *A* will then consume the residual, without working at all. *B* accepts the offer.

Roemer argues, plausibly, that this sort of transaction is exploitative. But *B* is forced neither by her economic circumstances nor by third parties, to enter into the transaction.[23] Hence force does not furnish a necessary condition for

---

[22] Note that, unlike the rich able-bodied in (8b), the poor able-bodied in (8d) are *not* coerced. It is therefore easier to object to (8b) than to (8d). Liberals and Marxists are therefore *less* well-placed to affirm the force-inclusive definition than right-libertarians, like Nozick.

[23] *A* is forced to *F* if and only if *A* *F*s and there are no reasonable or acceptable alternatives to *F*-ing. What counts as a reasonable or acceptable alternative to *F*-ing may vary with time, the general conditions of social development, and so on. Yet *Two Plots* seems to refute the force-inclusive definitions however 'reasonable' or 'acceptable' are defined (see Elster (1982) and Cohen (1995)). Roemer argues

exploitation. Kant and Marx are a match made in heaven, but, *pace* generations of liberals and socialists, that heaven does not include the force-inclusive definition.

I now consider two alternative and more promising respect-based theories.

1.5.2 Exploitation as a rights violation

A distinctive respect-based explanation for the injustice of exploitation, of a more explicitly Kantian pedigree, invokes rights. One such view, due to Steiner (1984), fixes the benefit baseline in (1) in terms of the absence of rights violations. That is, A exploits B if and only if A benefits from a transaction with B, where the benefit is greater than what A would have obtained had there been no violation of B's rights. In the *Pit* case, for example, B is entitled to costless rescue, which A fails to provide. A proceeds to benefit illicitly relative to that baseline. In so doing, A exploits B. So advantage-taking is here interpreted as A benefiting disproportionately:

(9)   from a violation of B's rights.

Yet (9) fails as a necessary condition for exploitation. That is, there are cases where no Steinerian rights violations occur, yet A exploits B. It seems not to matter, for example, *how B* found themselves at the bottom of the pit. All that matters is that they are there and that it is presumptively unjust to ask for money in return for help, at least as long as the would-be rescuer sacrifices nothing of comparable moral significance. Or consider a more explicit case of rights-forfeiture, where B has forfeited her rights against being helped nonexploitatively:

> *Ant and Grasshopper*—Grasshopper spends the summer months singing, whereas Ant spends all her time working. When the winter comes, Grasshopper needs shelter, which she presently lacks. Ant has three options: she can do nothing to help Grasshopper, she can offer costless shelter, or she can offer costless shelter on condition that Grasshopper signs a sweatshop contract.

that what is wrong with the *Two Plots* example is injustice in the distribution of assets. Distributive injustice provides the necessary and sufficient condition for unjust exploitation. I return to this view in section 1.5.3.

26 THEORIES OF EXPLOITATION

It is plausible to think that, by dint of her irresponsible behaviour, Grasshopper forfeits a right to nonexploitative satisfaction of her winter needs. Ant's offer of a sweatshop contract, or of a life-saver at exorbitant prices, does not, in this case, violate B's Steinerian rights. There is, however, a lingering sense that Ant's offer is impermissible, precisely because it is exploitative. If this is correct, then waiving or forfeiting a right to costless rescue does not suffice to remove the stain of exploitation from such an offer. In other words, exploitation and the absence of a Steinerian rights violation are compatible.[24]

1.5.3 Exploitation as distributive injustice

Steiner's rights-based explanation is the conceptual cousin of a distinct respect theory that fixes the exploitation baseline in terms of fairness. On the *fairness view*, exploitation obtains if and only if a transaction issues from an unfair background. I will consider two branches of this view: those referring to a *just price* and those referring to a *just distribution* of assets. The just price account, I will argue, either is misconceived, or otherwise collapses into the just distribution account.

1.5.3.1 Just price
According to the just price view, A exploits B in any transaction where A benefits:

(10) by offering B an unfair, excessively low price.

The idea of a fair price goes back to the Scholastics, and formed part of the 'Ricardian' socialists' critique of capitalism (Hodgkin 1832, Thompson 1824). Under capitalism, the Ricardian Socialists argued, workers do not get the full product of their labour performance. This is due to all manner of monopolies and market imperfections. Remove those imperfections, and workers will receive their full entitlement. The fair price for one's labour, in other words, is 'the whole product of labour' and the only such price.

A version of the just price theory has recently been revived by Wertheimer (1996), Valdman (2009), and Reiff (2013). Wertheimer suggests that the answer to the just price question turns on how close the actual price of a good is to a hypothetical fair market price. That price, Wertheimer thinks,

---

[24] I discuss the *Ant and Grasshopper* case more extensively in Chapter 3.

RESPECT THEORIES 27

can be heuristically identified with the price the good would fetch under perfect competition.[25] Recall the *Pit* case. *A* finds *B* in a pit and asks for $1 million in return for a rope, which costs $5 in a competitive market. Her offer is exploitative. Does the just price view capture the injustice of this case? I consider sufficiency first, necessity second.

Failure to pay the competitive market price is not sufficient for exploitation. For consider: *A* may be a very poor person asking for an abnormally high price from *B*, whom *A* knows to be very rich. Intuitively, there does not seem to be something exploitative about such offers. Note, for example, how counterintuitive it is to maintain that, were Senegal to erect tariff barriers to protect its domestic industries by keeping domestic prices artificially above competitive levels, it would thereby be exploiting rich Swiss tourists visiting Senegal.[26]

Nor is failure to pay the competitive price necessary for exploitation. Consider a society where women are paid to raise babies, and where women are demographically in very great abundance, while men are scarce. Women work arduous long hours, whereas men work very little, but earn high salaries, benefiting at the expense of women's labour. Those men are exploiting those women. But if there are no barriers to entry or competition in this world, such that all markets clear and all agents are price-takers, then prices are not unfair. And yet there is exploitation in this world.[27]

A distinct and more compelling version of the fairness view appeals not to a just price, but to fair distribution. The rest of this section discusses this view.

1.5.3.2 Just distribution

Advocates of the *fair distribution view* eschew talk of prices for talk of assets. So they interpret exploitation as A benefiting:

(11)   from possession of an unfairly greater share of the benefits or conditions of social cooperation than *B*.

Among the most influential defenders of (11) view are analytical Marxists, such as John Roemer and G.A. Cohen, nonmarxists, such as Richard Arneson,

---

[25] Reiff (2013) identifies that price with the good's cost of production. What I will say here applies both to the just price interpretation of Wertheimer and to Reiff's account.

[26] It does not follow that the rich cannot be exploited. I return to the question of how that happens in Chapter 3, section 3.3.2.

[27] For a wealth of similar examples (directed against the just price interpretation of Wertheimer), see Sample (2003). In section 1.6.3, I will argue that there is a more plausible, domination-based reading of Wertheimer.

28   THEORIES OF EXPLOITATION

as well as some interpreters of Rawls. In Roemer's (1996) canonical statement, exploitation complaints are, at best, morally derivative of claims about distributive justice.[28] According to Roemer, exploitation is the causal upshot of injustice in the distribution of (alienable) assets,[29] which captures the injustice of examples like *Pit* and *Two Plots*. So, for any coalition of agents A and its complement B, A exploits B only if A would be better off and B worse off, were B to withdraw with an equal share of society's (alienable) resources.

The Roemerian account is compelling. It avoids the false negatives of rights-based views and the false positives of force-based views; it also offers a cogent interpretation of structural exploitation (Roemer 1982, Zwolinski 2012) and provides a plausible general explanation for why exploitation of human by human is unjust.

Now consider the *Pit* case again. There is clearly exploitation here. But this judgement makes no reference to distributive background, or the *justice* of that background: what we have here is a person being offered bad terms, which she must accept just in virtue of a vulnerability she has. Indeed, it is part of the felicity condition for exercise of A's power over B that B, in responding to A, is alerted to that vulnerability. If exploitation judgements and judgements about just distribution are mutually irrelevant, as the *Pit* case seems to suggest, then distributive injustice cannot be a necessary condition for exploitation.[30] To make these conceptual choices more vivid, consider the following triad of claims:

(i) exploitation is unfair advantage-taking;
(ii) unfair advantage-taking entails unfair material inequality;
(iii) exploitation can arise from fair material inequality.

This triad is inconsistent: no more than two of its three claims are simultaneously assertible. So which claim is false? In light of the *Pit* case, (iii) seems compelling. (i) is taken by Cohen, Roemer, and others to be a conceptual truth, so I will grant it *arguendo*. Therefore, (ii) must be rejected. I will discuss these ideas further in Chapter 3.

I turn now to introducing the last class of exploitation theory, which is based on freedom or nondomination.

---

[28] Roemer's view is discussed extensively in Chapters 2 and 3.
[29] Assets are useful things that can be used to produce other useful things. *Alienable assets* are things like tools, machinery, factories, etc. *Inalienable assets* are things like talents, capabilities, know-how, etc.
[30] I argue this extensively in Chapter 3.

1.6 Freedom Theories

1.6.1 Exploitation as vulnerability instrumentalization

An alternative paradigm for understanding what makes exploitation unjust looks at how A and B normatively relate to each other, without immediate reference to harm, force, or distribution. Since the nature of this relationship is the main topic of this book, I will only sketch some basic contrasts.

Acts of exploitation, in general, weaponize the vulnerability of the exploitee, allowing the exploiter to take advantage. What makes the *Pit* relationship exploitative, for example, is the nature of the power relationship between A and B. The candidates for the 'exploiter' predicate are therefore not limited to feudal lords or monopolists, as in teleological theories, or rentiers and patrimonial capitalists, as in respect theories. Rather, 'exploiter' is a more pervasive feature of human civilization, one that does not presuppose harmful absence of competition or background injustice in distribution. Consider some variants of this thought.

According to the *vulnerability view*, A should not, other things equal, enrich herself by playing on B's vulnerability. A's exploitation of B is therefore interpreted as A benefiting:

(12)   by taking advantage of B's vulnerable state.

(12) shifts the emphasis from distributive (in)justice to the instrumentaliza-tion of vulnerability.[31] More precisely: A exploits B if and only if A and B are embedded in a relationship in which A instrumentalizes B's vulnerability to appropriate (the fruits of) B's labour.

To illustrate the idea, consider a garden-variety complaint against capital-ism. Capitalists use workers (extract labour time from them) to obtain a benefit (profit), by taking advantage of their vulnerability (their propertylessness). The only controversial aspect of the demonstration that capitalists exploit workers consists in showing that this use of workers is somehow degrading, demeaning, disrespectful, or inimical to their autonomy. But capitalists are constrained, on pain of survival *as* capitalists, to treat their workers merely as sources of profit, just as they treat their machinery. So if exploitation is instrumental use of others, then capitalists exploit workers, and the exploitation claim goes

---

[31] Variants of this view have been defended by Goodin (1985) and Wood (1995).

30 THEORIES OF EXPLOITATION

through without recourse to premises about distributive justice (see Wood 1995, who makes a cogent case for this conclusion).

The Achilles heel of this theory is that it is not sufficiently discriminating; it generates false positives. It seems to imply, for example, that rich surgeons or gardeners who benefit from the lamentable state of my liver, or my patio, necessarily exploit me. This is reason enough to consider a more discriminating freedom-based theory.[32] The rest of this chapter discusses variations on that more discriminating theory.

1.6.2 Exploitation as domination

A freedom-based alternative to the vulnerability view holds that what makes exploitation unjust is abuse of power. Exploitation, in other words, is to be interpreted as A benefiting:

(13)   through the domination of B.

On the *domination view*, A exploits B if A benefits from a transaction in which A dominates B: exploitation is the dividend A extracts from B's servitude.[33] If the domination view holds, then unfairness (along the lines of (10) or (11)) is neither necessary nor sufficient for exploitation. Take necessity first. Suppose A offers B a fair price for some good, which B buys. The offer is higher than B's ability to pay, or high enough to constitute abuse of power—in short, the offer, if accepted, dominates B. Then the offer is exploitative. Proposals can be fair *and* exploitative. Now take sufficiency. Suppose A offers B an unfair price for some good, which B buys. The unfair price A offers does not involve abuse of power—in short, the offer does not dominate B. Then the offer is not exploitative. The relationship between exploitation and unfairness, on the domination view, is one of mutual irrelevance.[34]

Now, one advantage of the domination view is that it is conceptually more discriminating than the vulnerability view. That is, the instrumentalization of vulnerability is a necessary but not sufficient condition for domination, which is why surgeons and gardeners do not necessarily exploit patients and patio owners, respectively. Rather, what makes or breaks the case for exploitation is

---

[32] I discuss the vulnerability view further in Chapter 3, section 3.4.

[33] Variants of this view have been defended by Levine (1988), Goodin (1988), and Vrousalis (2013, 2016, 2019a, 2021).

[34] I defend the claims of this paragraph in Chapter 3.

whether the relationship between A and B involves A treating B as her servant and, in so doing, extracts a dividend from that servitude. I will argue that such treatment obtains just when A unilaterally subjects B's purposiveness to A's own ends. A corollary is that the 'exploiter' predicate is not limited to feudal lords, harmful monopolists, rentiers, and patrimonial capitalists. The predicate now extends to all who unilaterally control alien purposivenesses, including human labour power. All capitalists are exploiters, on this view, and for that reason.

I conclude this chapter by arguing that Wertheimer's influential theory of exploitation presupposes something like the domination view.

1.6.3 Wertheimer's domination view

According to Alan Wertheimer, 'A exploits B when A takes unfair advantage of B' (Wertheimer 1999, p. 16). In discussion of the relevant fairness-making features, Wertheimer turns to the idea of 'fair market value', that is, 'the price that an informed and un-pressured seller would receive from an informed and unpressured buyer if [some good] were sold on the market' (Wertheimer 1999, p. 230). This makes his view sound like the just price account I sketched in section 1.5.3. Despite appearances to the contrary, I will show that the justification of Wertheimer's claims presupposes something like the domination account.

Philosophers have criticized the idea that competitive market prices or cost of production can furnish a 'just price' that can be used to gauge whether a given market transaction is exploitative.[35] But there is an alternative, domination-based, explanation for this *market proceduralism*. Consider the following argument:

(13)　Exploitation is enrichment through power over others.

(14)　The competitive market price is the only price that reflects absence of power over others.

So (15)　The competitive market price is the only appropriate baseline for dubbing a transaction exploitative.

Wertheimer affirms (15) because he affirms something like (14). And if that is true, then he *must* affirm a premiss like (13), which is the domination view.

---

[35] See, for example, Arneson (2016), Sample (2003), and section 1.5.3.

32 THEORIES OF EXPLOITATION

To substantiate these claims, consider the following passage:

[E]ven though a competitive market price does not reflect a deep principle of justice, it does reflect a crucial moral dimension of the relationship between the parties in the transaction. The competitive market price is a price at which neither party takes special unfair advantage of particular defects in the other party's decision-making capacity or special vulnerabilities in the other party's situation. It is a price at which the specific parties to the particular transaction do not receive greater value than they would receive if they did not encounter each other. It may or may not be a 'just price,' all things considered, but it may well be a nonexploitative price, for neither party takes unfair advantage of the other party.   (Wertheimer 1996, p. 232)

What counts as a 'special vulnerability', or as 'special unfair advantage'? Suppose B is a group of people selling themselves into slavery and A is a group of slave buyers. There is a large market for slaves, such that both the slave buyers and the slave sellers are price-takers. When markets clear, each member of A owns at least one member of B. All members of B will be exploited by some member of A. But none of the former suffers any *special* vulnerability, and no member of the latter takes special unfair advantage. Indeed, if all slaves are treated equally well, then the case can be made that they are treated fairly.[36] So the case cannot be made that A does not exploit B, competitive slave markets are compatible with exploitation, and 'special' vulnerability is unnecessary to charges of exploitation.

If not 'special vulnerability', then why not just 'vulnerability'? That is, a better Wertheimerian justification for enlisting the machinery of markets is as a heuristic for tracking down instances of unjust abuse of power.[37] On this reading, Wertheimer affirms (15) *because* he affirms something like (14).[38] But

---

[36] St. Paul famously exhorted masters to treat slaves fairly (in *Colossians* 4:1), so he must have thought that possibility conceptually coherent.

[37] Consider, again, the nature of Wertheimer's (1999) examples: corporations and consumers (chapter 2), colleges and athletes (chapter 3), professional couples and surrogate mothers (chapter 4), insurance companies and accident victims (chapter 5), psychoanalysts and patients (chapter 6). These are all cases where A has power over B. When things go well, the use of power does not betoken domination. These are cases where, in accordance with (14), transactions reflect the hypothetical competitive price. Everyone is a price-taker. When things do not go well, A's power dominates B, and that is the source of A's enrichment. These are cases where transactions do not reflect the competitive market price. On this view, competitive prices have a purely epistemological function: they are a kind of domination-barometer. When A offers B terms that exceed the competitive price, A abuses her power over B and enriches herself on that basis. When A offers terms that do not exceed that price, A does not abuse her power.

[38] In Chapter 2, I will argue that (14) is false. An anomymous referee points out that Wertheimer (2011) abandons this view.

(15) follows from (14) only in conjunction with (13). Therefore, Wertheimer affirms (13), which is a statement of the domination view.

This book further vindicates the domination view against the most promising alternatives, including the vulnerability view (12) and the distributive view (11). I now summarize the arguments of this chapter and review the gameplan for the rest of the book.

Conclusion

This chapter painted a broad-stroke picture of the conceptual landscape on exploitation. It distinguished between three main species of exploitation theory: *teleology-based*, *respect-based*, and *freedom-based* accounts. Each class of theory was organized around an exploiter-archetype. The teleogical class took its archetype from the feudal lord and monopolist and was largely limited to them. The respect class took its archetype from the rentier and the patrimonial capitalist. The freedom class, which is the main topic of this book, took its archetype from the capitalist and banker who unilaterally subsume the purposiveness of the direct producer. The chapter then addressed the implications of each theory, paving the way for the arguments that follow.

Looking ahead

In Chapter 2, I sketch an account of freedom as nonsubjection to the ends of others. I then apply it to capitalist relations of production with the help of a simple model of economic reproduction. Capital, I argue, is a kind of subsumed labour. In Chapter 3, I show that the domination account makes better sense of the *Pit* case and cognate examples, from slavery to patriarchy to capitalism. It also explains the distinctive position of exploitation complaints on the moral landscape—which the vulnerability and fairness views tend to trivialize. In Chapter 4, I show how the domination view resonates with the idea of structural domination. I defend a definition of structural domination as regulated domination: any given instance of domination is structural just when it involves a triadic relation between dominator, dominated, and regulator— a social role that contributes non-contingently to the reproduction of the domination (dominator/dominated) dyad. In Chapters 5 and 6, I discuss implications of this theory for actually existing capitalism and international

34 THEORIES OF EXPLOITATION

relations, respectively. And in Chapter 7, I discuss institutions capable of overcoming exploitation, as elaborated in the earlier chapters.

Further reading

The two most comprehensive philosophical treatments of the concept of exploitation to date are Wertheimer (1999) and Sample (2003). For an overview of the recent literature, see Wertheimer and Zwolinski (2016). I now list some important topic-specific contributions.

Teleological accounts. Buchanan (1984) defends the harm view of exploitation. Van Donselaar (2009) defends a mutual-advantage account.

Respect accounts. Sample (2003) defends the mere-means account. Steiner (1984) defends a rights-based view. Holmstrom (1977), Peffer (1990), and Reiman (1987) defend variants of the force-inclusive view. Nearly all analytical Marxists, including Cohen (1995) and Roemer (1982, 1996), in addition to nonmarxists, such as Arneson (1981, 2016a) and Valdman (2009) defend the distributive injustice view. Reiff (2013) defends the just price view.

Freedom accounts. Goodin (1985, 1987) and Wood (1995) defend variants of the vulnerability view. Snyder (2008) discusses the connection between exploitation and needs. A variant of the domination view receives important exposition in Wood (1972) and, more recently, in Wood (2014). Vrousalis (2013, 2016, 2019a, 2021) defends the domination view.

Exploitation theory has recently received interesting treatments in applied ethics. Risse and Wollner (2013, 2019) apply exploitation concepts to international trade agreements and trade justice. Wertheimer (2011) and Wenner (2012) discuss exploitation in clinical research. Mayer (2005) and Attas (2000) discuss guest workers. Zwolinski (2007) and Mayer (2007) discuss sweatshops. Shelby (2002) discusses prostitution. Brewer (1996) and De-Shalit (1998) are accessible introductions to the connections between exploitation and imperialism, on the one hand, and global justice, on the other. Greasley (2012) offers a cogent summary of the exploitation debate in the context of commercial organ donation. Structural exploitation is discussed in Zwolinski (2012) and Young (2011). On the connections between exploitation and race, see Shelby (2002) and Mills (2017). On exploitation and gender, see McKeown (2016) and Young (1990).

PART II
THEORY

2

Domination at Work

Theories of exploitation face three urgent questions. First, what makes exploitation *unjust*? Second, what is the *metric* of exploitation complaints, the yardstick for their individuation and measurement? Third, what is the *modality* of these features under different social formations, that is, what gives exploitation its historical specificity under slavery, serfdom, patriarchy, and capitalism? Liberal political philosophy, in its canonical statements in Rawls and Dworkin, couches its answer to the injustice question in terms of coercion, rights, or fairness; to the metric question in terms of (access to) welfare, goods, capabilities, or a combination thereof; and to the modality question by appeal to the mutually consensual nature of transactions which, in the case of capitalism, reflects the positions of reciprocally situated commodity owners.

This book offers better answers to these questions. In this chapter, I argue that what makes exploitation unjust is that it constitutes domination-induced unilateral service to others. In Chapter 3, I show that this form of servitude is necessarily cashed out in terms of labour time or effort and that competing accounts of exploitation fail to do justice to the servitude dimension. It follows that the concept of surplus labour is central to charges of exploitation, a centrality that does not presuppose any controversial claims about the determination of prices or a labour theory of value. And in Chapter 4, I will show that what distinguishes capitalism historically is the way it reproduces a structural dilemma between no work and dominated work.

I now summarize the argument of this chapter. According to the domination account of exploitation, the theoretical starting point is how power converts others into servitude and how that servitude, in turn, redounds as benefit. As a matter of logic, servitude presupposes dominion. So what is dominion? This chapter argues that it is subjection of purposiveness to the choices of others. Applied to work, such subjection means unilateral control over productive purposiveness: human labour capacity. I then argue that capital is a historically specific form of that subjection, namely *monetary* control over the labour capacity of others.

This chapter has eight sections. Section 2.1 introduces the Non-Servitude Proviso, an account of domination at work. Section 2.2 broaches three

Exploitation as Domination: What Makes Capitalism Unjust. Nicholas Vrousalis, Oxford University Press.
© Nicholas Vrousalis 2023. DOI: 10.1093/oso/9780192867698.003.0003

38 DOMINATION AT WORK

justifications for the Proviso: Kantian, republican, and recognitional. Section 2.3 illustrates the Proviso with the help of a simple economic model. Section 2.4 discusses the implications of the Proviso for capitalism and capitalist accumulation. Section 2.5 discusses the role of money, the crucial distinction between money as a means of exchange and money as capital, and their relationship to unilateral control over labour capacity. Section 2.6 distinguishes between different forms of domination and explores the distinction between domination at work and domination in the workplace. Section 2.7 discusses exemptions to the Proviso and contrasts it with different specifications of what makes exploitation unjust. And section 2.8 explains why exploitation is inherent to capitalism.

2.1 The Non-Servitude Proviso

The French Revolution taught us to think about equality, liberty, and solidarity as three faces of the same value: the equal independence of the individual in community with others. This book uses that general idea to develop an account of exploitation as domination. According to this account, exploitation is what happens when alien wills exercise unilateral control over your purposiveness, thereby converting you into their servant. How do you serve others *without* being their servant? Rousseau and Kant offer a promising answer: by serving institutions that support the conditions of the freedom of all, and therefore the conditions of your own freedom, you serve others without being implicated in their *ends*.[1] The Rousseau/Kant idea applies quite generally, but this book undertakes to apply it to social relations between human producers.

To take a concrete example, suppose that omelettes are the only means of consumption and that, if I am to nourish myself, I must produce an omelette. As an omelette *consumer* I have set myself an end; as an omelette *producer* I must use means to pursue and fulfill that end. Now, as long as you and others own the eggs, I can produce the omelette only by your permission. This makes my ability to set and pursue the end of omelette production— my productive purposiveness—subordinate to your unilateral will. When that subordination is expressed in extraction of unilateral labour flow from me,

---

[1] Here is Rousseau: 'How to find a form of association [...] under which each individual, while uniting himself with the others, obeys no one but himself, and remains as free as before.' (Rousseau 1968, p. 60). And here is the more specific Kant: '[B]eing one's own master [means that] if he must acquire from others in order to live, he does so only by alienating what is *his*—and hence [...] he *serves* no one other than the commonwealth.' (Kant 1996, p. 295, emphases in original). I discuss Kant's political economy of independence in Vrousalis (2022).

you exploit me. Omelette redistribution will not solve this problem, insofar as it leaves the mode of omelette *production* untouched, no matter how much it ameliorates the mode of omelette *distribution* in my favour. Egalitarian egg *pre*distribution does better, but still subordinates my omelette production to your will, insofar as it does not preclude your ownership or control of the omelette-producing cookshop. And again, when that control eventuates in unilateral labour flow, you exploit me. The rest of this chapter refines and elaborates these simple ideas.

To focus intuitions, consider:

Pit—*A* and *B* are alone in the desert. *A* finds *B* lying at the bottom of a pit. *A* offers *B* costless rescue, on condition that *B* works for *A* for $1/day for the rest of her life, or pays *A* $1 million.

A's offer is exploitative, such that, if *B* accepts it, she will be exploited. The purpose of this book is to explain why *A* treats *B* unjustly in this and similar cases, despite the fact that their agreement is uncoerced, voluntary, and mutually beneficial.[2] I will first offer an explanation for why a *Pit*-like contract exploits *B*. The idea is that the contract ropes *B*'s purposiveness into unilaterally serving *A*'s, something to which *A* is not, by right, entitled. I will then explain why asking for $1/day or for $1 million are, in principle, equivalent, as both cases entitle *A* to a share of the exercise of *B*'s productive purposiveness to which she is not, by right, entitled. Chapter 3 will extend these ideas to the sale of sexual services, gestational labour, and body parts.

2.1.1 Introducing the Non-Servitude Proviso

A central concern of the domination account of exploitation is the form of social control over the net product and, by implication, over the surplus product.[3] 'Forms' of control range from slavery, feudalism, and the patriarchy—where control over the net product is established through coercion in the labour process—to capitalism—where control over the net product is market mediated, value constituted, and noncoercive. Capitalism is unlike all

---

[2] In Chapter 3, I will argue that *A*'s offer might be forthcoming against the background of reasonable alternatives and perfect justice in distribution—*B* might, for example, have failed to purchase costless (or very cheap) insurance against falling in pits. This would not make *A*'s offer any less exploitative.

[3] The net product is total output minus nonlabour inputs; the surplus product is the net product minus labour inputs.

40 DOMINATION AT WORK

pre-capitalist economic formations, in that control over labour capacity appears like action at a distance: it never involves *direct* control over alien agency. I elaborate the possibility of domination without direct control in section 2.3. The rest of this section introduces and defends my account of servitude and domination.

A generic concern with agency is normally justified by a fundamental commitment to freedom: the independence of the individual. Individual independence, in general, consists in nonsubjection to the choices of others. Consider the *Pit* case. A's behaviour is unjust because she controls not just any contingent end that B might set and pursue, but rather B's wholesale ability to set and pursue choiceworthy ends, quite independently of her ability to work for \$1 or pay \$1 million. What matters here is that B gets roped into unilaterally serving A, thereby sacrificing something of agential significance. A, in other words, comes to unilaterally control B's purposiveness and not just her contingent purposes, including the end of costless pit exit.

Applied to work, individual independence is violated when alien wills[4] possess unilateral control over the exercise of your labour capacity in a way that subjects the conditions of your agential purposiveness to theirs. This includes *Pit*-like relations, of the form: 'My rope for your productive powers!' Unsubjected purposiveness, by contrast, is described by the:

> *Non-Servitude Proviso*—For any agents or groups engaged in mandatory mutually affecting cooperation under a division of labour, and barring any special justification that exempts them, none should possess unilateral control over the labour capacity of any other.[5]

The Non-Servitude Proviso is a transhistorical normative criterion of freedom at work. It concerns mandatory cooperation in the sense of cooperation institutionally necessary for unsubjected mutual purposiveness. The idea behind the Proviso is that, as long as production goods are scarce, mutual independence will require social labour.[6] Note that this says very little about

---

[4] These wills could be persons or organizations. This implies a distinction between personal and impersonal forms of authority. Unlike the former, the latter involves 'a body of authoritative rules picked out by a certain procedure' (Hussain 2023, p. 89).

[5] An agent is any human who can use external means to perform intentional actions. To serve another is to perform an action in that minimal sense, such that the form of service that constitutes servitude presupposes that ability. It follows that non-agents can be harmed, disrespected, or used as mere means, but cannot themselves be exploited. Naturally, this does not mean that their extreme vulnerability cannot be used by would-be-exploiters to exploit others.

[6] According to the Proviso, wilful laziness is fine, but its rightful performance under conditions of scarcity presupposes work. It follows that arguments for the 'right to be lazy', like Paul Lafargue's, only

control over the *product* of labour itself. Saying more requires a theory of justice in the transfer of goods and services, once a set of prior property rights in useful things has been established. Rather, any such set must incorporate the Proviso's concerns by ensuring that *unilateral control over things does not confer unilateral control over persons*. I now explain what this means and what it enables us to explain.

In the context of mandatory social cooperation, the Proviso establishes a presumption against unilateral control over the social labour of others, the exercise of their productive purposiveness. You possess unilateral control over my labour capacity if, in the description of our respective roles in the division of labour,[7] you possess control over the content, intensity, or duration of my labour process which I do not possess over yours. This means that there are things you can order or get me—'bind' me—to do over which I have no say, and over which you are not (legally or conventionally) obligated to consider my judgements, interests, or goals. According to the Proviso, such control over the labour capacity of others is presumptively unjust. What does 'presumptively' mean?

Consider an analogy with polygamy. One good argument against institutionalized polygamy is that it involves unilateral control of one married partner over another.[8] Polygamy is presumptively unjust in the sense that, whatever reasons might count in its favour—for example, that it is mutually consensual or beneficial—there is always a presumption against unilateral residual control over purposiveness and its conditions. Capitalist relations between consenting adults are presumptively unjust in a similar sense: they are the civil society equivalent of polygamy.

The Proviso censures this unilateralism. It establishes a *prima facie* case against unilateral control over the labour performance of others. It implies that, if A and B perform independently required cooperative work—*social labour*—then they may work (un)equal amounts of time, as long as that (in)equality does not only reflect unequal power. If the Proviso is violated, such that A unjustly possesses unilateral control over B's purposiveness,

---

get things half right. For even moderate scarcity subjects the enjoyment of a right to be lazy to the will of the industrious. So, under anything other than Star-Trek-like material abundance, rightful laziness is impossible.

[7] That is, the true description of our *de facto* powers over each other, whether legally constituted or otherwise. See Searle (1997) for an argument that all institutional relations, including power relations, entail deontic powers of some sort. Searle disagrees with Cohen (1978, chapter 4), who argues that powers are not necessarily normatively constituted. My argument is compatible with both positions.

[8] 'The person who surrenders herself gains only a part of the man who gets her completely, and therefore makes herself into a mere thing.' (Kant 1996, p. 428). Kant takes violation of the Proviso to entail the reification of persons. I discuss reification in section 2.7.

42   DOMINATION AT WORK

then *A dominates B*. Exploitation is what happens when the dominator benefits through such domination. So, on this view, exploitation is the activation of the extractive dispositions of the powerful: it is a dividend of servitude.[9]

2.1.2   Freedom and mode of production

These definitions imply a general taxonomy of different forms of unilateral control over the labour capacity of others across different *modes of production* of the net product. Slavery and feudalism, for example, involve unilateral control over labour capacity through direct coercion. The Non-Servitude Proviso is clearly violated in these cases. Patriarchy is similar, in that it involves coercive control, by men, over the (sexual) labour of women. But, unlike traditional slavery and serfdom, the patriarchy seems compatible with meaningful exit options for women. For it is conceptually possible, under the patriarchy, that individual women can exit their individual marital relationships, or even retain the socioeconomic wherewithal never to marry.[10] Yet, for as long as the role of women within the (legal) description of the family remains subordinate to the role of men, women as a whole remain subjected to the choices of men. In other words, the patriarchy violates the Non-Servitude Proviso, not because the labour of any individual woman is dominated, but rather because the labour of *women* is dominated. Similar things can be said about polygamy and prostitution.

Capitalism is akin to the patriarchy, in the sense that it is compatible with meaningful exit options for individual workers.[11] But the availability of such options—through labour rights, the welfare state, or an unconditional basic income—does not suffice to emancipate the workers from the domination of capitalists, any more than the availability of divorce suffices to emancipate women from the domination of men. The slavery and patriarchy examples show that a free, voluntary, uncoerced contract does not, in general, suffice to waive the requirements of the Proviso: one might freely contract into slavery or into an abusive marital relationship. This does not make such relationships

---

[9] I refine this account of exploitation in Chapter 3, where I also discuss effort as an alternative metric for exploitation complaints.

[10] For a defence of this idea see Pateman (1988, pp. 131–3). I discuss the relationship between patriarchy and capitalism in Chapter 4.

[11] The idea of symmetric anonymity, worker-to-capitalist, in the context of capitalist exploitation is due to Cohen (1988).

just. By the same token, a dictatorship may offer good, even lucrative, exit options to its subjects. This makes it no less dictatorial for those who stay. So it is the Proviso, or something like it, that establishes the conditions for a just contractual relationship and not the other way around.[12] I now offer three provisional justifications for the Proviso.

2.2 Justifying the Proviso

The Non-Servitude Proviso can be elaborated as follows:

(1) Domination is subjection of purposiveness to the (arbitrary) choices of others.
(2) In any system of mandatory mutually affecting cooperation under a division of labour, control over the labour capacity of others that is not independently justified constitutes domination in the sense of (1).

I will discuss three widely discussed philosophical accounts of (1): Kantian, broadly based on the idea of a moral right to independence; republican, broadly based on a conception of arbitrary power; and recognitional, broadly based on a conception of interpersonal recognition. My purpose here is not to provide a complete justification for the Proviso, but rather to steer the conversation about the injustice of exploitation in the direction of the domination theory.

The Kantian argument for the Proviso goes roughly as follows: all humans have an innate moral right to external freedom, 'independence from being constrained by another's choice... insofar as it can coexist with the freedom of every other in accordance with a universal law.' (Kant 1996, p. 393). Independence, on this view, is about being able to set and pursue ends with means that are rightfully yours. Domination, by contrast, consists in my thwarting your agential purposiveness, subjecting your ability to set and pursue ends to mine. This establishes (1), excluding the bracketed term. A Kantian may now construe (2) as follows: cooperation at work involves constraint by another's choice, insofar as one agent (or group of agents), A, unilaterally controls

---

[12] I will discuss the Proviso's implications for capitalism, and for the crucial distinction between labour and labour power, in Chapter 5.

44 DOMINATION AT WORK

the labour process of another, B, including the labour/nonlabour input mix, and has possession of B's final product.[13] Kantian independence therefore countenances the Proviso.

The republican argument has a similar structure: unfreedom consists in subjection to arbitrary power. All power over others that is not compelled to track their judgements, interests, or goals is arbitrary.[14] This establishes (1), including the bracketed term. A republican may now argue for (2), as follows: work relations involving A's unilateral control over B's labour process, including the labour/nonlabour input mix, and legal possession of B's final product, are instances of arbitrary power. Republican independence therefore countenances the Proviso.[15]

Finally, the recognition argument for the Proviso goes as follows: free recognitive agency consists in the ability to act by having your rational intentions—intentions whose contents are independently justified—taken by others as reasons. For example, B's rational intention to eat gives A a reason not to obstruct B's eating, by taking B's rational intention to eat as a reason not to obstruct that eating. When the realization of B's rational intention is at A's discretion, B is subjected to A's choices. This establishes (1), excluding the bracketed term. The recognitionist may now argue for (2), as follows: work relations involving A's control over B's labour process, including the labour/nonlabour input mix, and legal possession of B's final product, give A discretion over the realization of B's rational intentions about production—what gets produced when and how. Free recognitive agency therefore countenances the Proviso.[16]

This concludes my sketch of three separate justifications for the Non-Servitude Proviso. In practice, all three theories allow that the Proviso is satisfied if B had an equal say on all matters that subject her labour capacity to A's decisions, and vice versa.[17] The result generalizes to any sufficiently developed

---

[13] See Ripstein (2009) for a recent defence of Kant's general account of independence and Ellerman (1988) for a defence of its work-specific application that draws upon Kant's moral philosophy. Like Ellerman but unlike Ripstein, I do not think that a commitment to independence can justify private property without the Proviso or something like it. Indeed, as I argue in section 2.3, capitalist private property *contradicts* the Proviso.

[14] See, for example, Pettit (1999) and Laborde and Maynor (2008).

[15] For variations on these republican themes in connection with work, see Anderson (2015), Breen (2015), Cohen (1989), Gonzalez-Ricoy (2014), and Gould (1988).

[16] I defend both premises of the recognitionist argument in Vrousalis (2020b); see also Julius (2016).

[17] So, for example, hospital workers who perform gardening and workers who perform surgery should, in principle, have an equal say on matters of mutually affecting cooperation in the hospital. The Non-Servitude Proviso suggests that such a say should extend to the whole material division of labour, possibly beyond national borders. I discuss this conclusion in Chapter 6.

economy with a complex division of labour and concomitant labour flows.[18] I now put the Proviso to work, with the help of a simple economic model.

2.3 Reproducible Exploitation

To motivate the domination account of exploitation further, and to demostrate its general applicability, I will use a simple model of economic reproduction due to Roemer (2017). My intention is to provide an account of the central injustice of capitalism that works as an *alternative* to Roemer's, without disputing widely shared assumptions about the constitution of prices, markets, and rational agency.[19] A convincing ecumenical critique of capitalism cannot be based on idiosyncratic methodological or behavioural assumptions its defenders do not share.

The model I will consider involves a single consumption and production good, produced through a rudimentary division of labour across two sectors with different technologies, under the assumption of optimizing economic agents and instantaneous market clearing.

2.3.1 Collective ownership (I)

There are 1000 peasants who own the means of production collectively. These means amount to 500 units of seed corn. Each peasant wants to enjoy subsistence forever and, subject to that constraint, maximize her weekly leisure. Subsistence requires consumption of one unit of corn per week. There are two technologies, the *Factory Farm* and the *Forest*. The input–output relations are as follows:

---

[18] Suppose each agent in the economy represents a node in a graph. Each node either gives or receives labour (or both). The assumption here is that every consumer receives a portion of total social labour—a portion of the net product. If labour is homogenuous across producers, it is possible to calculate the *net* labour share received by each node, for any number of nodes and bilateral relations. Suppose that, in general economic equilibrium, some nodes represent net labour flow. If that flow is due to a violation of the Proviso, then it represents exploitation. For a seminal treatment of labour flow in a competitive capitalist economy under perfect competition see Roemer (1982).

I discuss the net flow assumption in Chapter 3.

[19] These assumptions may be unrealistic, but they only function to set up a baseline model. Roemer (1982, 1996) has generalized the model to economies with many agents, classes, goods, and technologies.

46 DOMINATION AT WORK

Factory Farm: $1c + 1l \rightarrow 2c$.
Forest: $3l \rightarrow 1c$.

In the *Factory Farm*, each peasant produces two units of corn, by using up one unit of seed corn and one unit of labour—say, one day a week.[20] In the *Forest*, each peasant produces one unit of corn by increasing her labour input to three days a week.

In this economy, there is a Pareto efficient and egalitarian equilibrium in which each peasant spends 1/2 a day working in the Farm, using up 1/2 a unit of seed corn, producing a total of 1000 units of corn and netting 1/2 corn each (for a total of 500 units of corn). Then each works 3/2 days in the Forest, receiving 1/2 unit of corn (for a total of 500 units). In equilibrium, each peasant works for two days. Total labour time in this economy is 2000 days and there is no exploitation.

2.3.2 Capitalist ownership (II)

Now contrast economy (I) with a capitalist economy, in which all of the seed corn is owned by ten capitalists. The remaining 99 percent own nothing but their capacity to work. Roemer argues that this economy will have a labour market, in which the only market-clearing real wage (in terms of units of corn) is 1/3. Intuitively, this is entailed by the nature of the outside option: since the Forest allows the worker to subsist outside the Farm by earning 1/3 corn per day, the demand for labour in corn would be too high above 1/3 and too low below it.[21] Note that corn is here both a measure of value and a means of exchange (of labour power). The rest of this section elaborates on the exploitation properties of economy (II).

In equilibrium the capitalists will hire 500/3 ($\approx$ 167) peasants, each working for three days per week, and netting one unit of corn each. The remaining 2470/3 ($\approx$ 823) peasants will work in the Forest for three days each, earning one unit of corn. Finally, the capitalists will appropriate 1000 units of corn. They will spend 500 to replace their capital stock and 500/3 as wages. The remaining 1000/3 ($\approx$ 333) is their total profit.[22]

---

[20] Value-theory traditionalists may replace days with hours.

[21] As will become transparent below, the existence of this outside option matters, but only insofar as it attenuates the hold of the owners of capital stock over the ability of others to set and pursue productive ends, as dictated by the Proviso.

[22] In corn units, we have: c500 (fixed capital) + c167 (variable capital) + c333 (surplus value) = c1000.

REPRODUCIBLE EXPLOITATION 47

In this economy, total labour time is 2970 days per week (990 peasants times three days each). According to the domination account of exploitation, these extra 970 days of labour expended, compared to economy (I), comprise exploitation. More precisely, each of 167 factory workers must work an extra day, for a total of three days. Since the daily wage is 1/3 corn, the worker attains subsistence only by working two out of three days gratis for the factory owner. Moreover, by dint of the ownership-induced scarcity of factory work compared to economy (I), each of the remaining 823 peasants must spend an extra day working in the forest.[23]

Generalizing from capitalist economy (II), Roemer argues that:

> Three conditions are necessary for exploitation to emerge in this model: (1) unequal ownership of the capital stock, (2) a labour market, and (3) scarcity of capital relative to the labour available for employment. All three conditions must hold for exploitation to occur. (Roemer 2017, p. 268)

Roemer shows that the existence of a labour market, condition (2), will not, of itself, generate exploitation when either (1) or (3) fail to hold. Consider, for example, a situation without collective ownership, in which every peasant owns an equal share of 1/2 corn, such that (1) does not hold. The division of labour reflects economy (I): each peasant works for 1/2 at the Farm, netting 1/2 corn. She then works in the Forest for one and a half days, producing another 1/2 corn. She therefore nets a total of one unit of corn. In this private ownership economy each attains subsistence, the capital stock is reproduced, and there is no exploitation.

A more interesting case involves some peasants hiring others, such that only (2) and (3) hold.[24] Here, both 'capitalists' and 'workers' work for a total of two days each. There is a 'profit' but no surplus labour, over and above the 2000 total days necessary for reproduction. There is therefore no exploitation.[25] In a

---

[23] In the Appendix to this chapter, I discuss the implications for this economy if material productivity were to increase by half.

[24] In the egalitarian, private ownership economy of the previous paragraph, 250 peasants work exclusively in the Farm for half a day, using up their seed corn of 125, netting 125 units of corn (1/2 each). This means they fall 125 units short of subsistence. They must therefore sell their labour power to the other peasants. That demand for labour can be met by the remaining 750 peasants, who will work exclusively in the Forest, two days each. This gets them 2/3 corn each, for a total of 500 units. Each of 750 peasants then hires a Farm peasant, who will work up the Forest peasant's 1/2 corn for the equilibrium wage of 1/3 corn. In this equilibrium, each of the 250 peasants works an extra 11/2 days, earning 1/2 corn. Added to her original Farm income of 1/2, this meets her subsistence threshold. The residual of 250 units from the net product accrues to the 750 peasants as profit (1/3 corn each).

[25] Roemer shows that this result can arise without a labour market, for example, if the 750 peasants of the previous example were to rent out their 375 units of seed corn to the 250, at the rate of 66 percent.

48 DOMINATION AT WORK

sense, there is also no *capital* in this economy, as no peasant has corn-conferred title to unilateral control over the labour performance of any other.

I now use Roemer's model to elaborate on a general corollary of the Non-Servitude Proviso, namely that any economy that violates conditions (1)–(3) is exploitative, *regardless of its origins*. In other words, there is such a thing as 'clean' capitalist accumulation and even *that* form of accumulation gives rise to injustice.

2.4 Implications for Capitalism

This section studies the purest form of capitalist accumulation imaginable: 'clean' capitalist accumulation through capitalist 'ingenuity and hard work'. I show why, by the Proviso, even this form of capitalism is unjust. The result is significant because it shows capitalist accumulation to be unjust in its purest and most idealized form. It is, moreover, relevant that critics of capitalism sometimes assume that what makes it unjust are violent enclosures, colonialism, or plunder. These are not, I will argue, *necessary* features of capitalist accumulation. To think otherwise is to suggest that clean capitalist accumulation—accumulation without these features—is not, as such, unjust. And it then follows that capitalism is not, *as such*, unjust. I proceed by considering a simple case of cleanly-generated capitalist accumulation, that is, of a clean—nonviolent, noncoercive—transition from an economy like (I) to an economy like (II).

2.4.1 Capitalist ownership (III)

This is the same setup as in collective-ownership economy (I), the only difference being that some peasants no longer want to consume one unit of corn in perpetuity. About a sixth of the total population are beginning to want more, which boosts corn demand. Ten enterpreneurial peasants conceive of a plan.

The ten begin working in the Forest for six-and-a-half days a week. Each spends half a day in the Farm, netting half a unit of corn. She then works in

---

Roemer (1982) argues that this result generalizes to economies like (II). In Chapter 6, I will show that this conclusion rides roughshod of Marx's important distinction between the capitalist *mode of exploitation* (which credit and labour markets may share) and the capitalist *mode of production* (which requires a labour market).

IMPLICATIONS FOR CAPITALISM   49

the forest for six days. Of this, she spends one and a half days working for subsistence, which produces half a unit of corn, and another four and a half days, which produces another 1½ units of corn. This surplus she saves, week in, week out. In thirty-three weeks, the ten will together own 500 corn. This will allow them to start their own private Factory Farm. Reproduction in this economy will work as in capitalist economy (II): assuming the wage is ⅓, the ten will hire the 167 non-ascetic peasants to work for three days each. Of the resulting net product, they will earn a profit of 333 units of corn (33.3 each), paying the non-ascetic peasants 167 corn as wages. Surplus labour is equal to 333 days and amounts to exploitation.[26]

What we have here is an invisible-hand process which, starting from a condition of rightful collective ownership and absolute equality (economy (I)), turns into something resembling an infinitely reproducible capitalist economy (economy (II)). No force, no violence, no colonies, no robbery.[27] What could possibly be wrong with this situation? More precisely, *how could this transition from a just initial situation, through just steps, produce an exploitative, and therefore unjust, outcome?*[28]

Consider, again, the *Pit* case. The Non-Servitude Proviso censures A's behaviour in that example, regardless of (the justice of) distributive background or the presence of reasonable alternatives for B. It does not matter, for example, whether B ended up at the bottom of the pit by failing to save resources, by eating the soil, or by failing to buy cheap insurance against soil erosion. By the Proviso, A cannot permissibly offer costless rescue in return for thousands of hours of labour—at least, barring some independent justification for doing so.[29] The same is true of capitalist economy (III): it does not matter if

[26] In economy (I), the non-ascetic peasants can each get an extra unit of corn by working the collectively owned seed corn in the Farm for an extra day, for a total of 167 days. So total labour time in this economy will be 2167 days (the 2000 days of economy (I) plus 167). But once the capital stock beyond the original 500 seed corn becomes privatized, the non-ascetic peasants can only get their 167 extra units of corn by working for another 333 days, producing 333 days of surplus labour for the capitalists.

[27] It is irrelevant that this invisible hand process may be unrealistic: critics of capitalism want to undermine the best possible arguments for capitalism, which mean granting their opponents the strongest possible version of these arguments. In the case of Marx, for example, this meant that ahistorical theoretical abstractions are methodologically acceptable (see, e.g. MECW vol. 28, p. 23ff) and that they should include the assumption of perfectly competitive and 'frictionless' markets (see, e.g. MECW vol. 35, p. 276ff).

[28] This is one of Nozick's (1974) challenges to egalitarian political thought. The most comprehensive socialist response to Nozick is Cohen (1995). Cohen's critique of Nozick is vitiated by a commitment to luck egalitarianism, which inconsistently countenances cleanly generated capitalism. I discuss Cohen's arguments in Chapter 3.

[29] One might object that A is entitled to ask for compensation equal to the opportunity cost of rescue. But talk of opportunity costs is misplaced, not just because I have assumed that A can rescue B costlessly, but also because the economic cost to A is morally irrelevant. What matters is whether, in rescuing B, A sacrifices something of comparable *moral* significance within the terms of the Proviso.

50 DOMINATION AT WORK

it is arrived at from a just original situation (such as economy (I)) through just steps (clean capitalist accumulation). The end result, capitalist economy (III), violates the Proviso. The argument for this conclusion is as follows.

2.4.2 How capital violates the Proviso

Capitalism solves the problem of labour 'difficulty'—the allocation of labour inputs across economic units with different capital intensities—by expressing the value of the exercise of labour capacity in terms of the value of its product.[30] Because the seed corn is concentrated in a few hands, so is the value of the net product. And since unilateral control over the net product confers unilateral control over labour capacity (in this case, through the labour market), the seed corn becomes something it was not in economy (I), namely unilateral *control over persons in the form of control over things.* The seed corn, in other words, becomes *capital.*

More concretely, in economy (III) ten capitalists come to control 500 units of seed corn. The non-ascetic peasants have an interest in this product and can access it by renting out their several labour powers—their ability to work— to the capitalists. So control over the value of the final product entitles the capitalists to control over the productive purposiveness of those peasants, indeed more control than any of the peasants enjoy over any of the capitalists.[31] Now each capitalist can produce her own subsistence individually and still have corn left over, corn which begets her unilateral control over the labour performance of sixteen others. This is how economy (III) violates the Proviso. Note, moreover, that this conclusion is independent of *how* economy (III) is arrived at.[32] And since the violation of the Proviso is expressed in the form of extraction of surplus labour, economy (III) is exploitative. I now explain

---

Such sacrifice on A's part is structurally impossible in *Pit*-like cases: Pfizer never risks the purposiveness risked by unvaccinated potential Covid-19 sufferers.

[30] Whether in units of commodity money, fiat money, or corn, as in Roemer's single-commodity economy.

[31] Morishima (1973) and Roemer (1982) have proven that, for any economy like (II), if the corn remuneration of any 'factor' of production is less than one, then the rate of profit in that economy must be positive and vice versa. This 'Fundamental Marxian Theorem' assumes that the real wage is determined by the value or relative scarcity of the commodity bundle it contains. See Bowles and Gintis (1981) for a defence of this interpretation and Yoshihara (2017) for a critical overview.

[32] That is, unless the ten would-be capitalists have a special justification that exempts them from equal control over the non-ascetic peasants' labour. *Pace* Roemer, the capitalists' greater patience, greater talent, even greater effort, do not suffice to grant them unilateral control over the other peasants' labour performance.

IMPLICATIONS FOR CAPITALISM   51

the significance of the distinction between exploitation and domination in the context of these stylized examples.

2.4.3 Domination without exploitation

I begin with a clarification. The Proviso does *not* say that A dominates B only if A extracts unreciprocated labour flow from B. That is, the Proviso is compatible with A and B working an equal amount of time, or no time at all. Rather, the Proviso emphasizes *power* over labour, regardless of actual labour contribution or the distribution of its fruits. This has important implications for the dispositional nature of the freedom critique of capitalism. The following example elaborates:

People's capitalism (IV)
This is the same setup as in capitalist economy (II)—the 1 percent owns all the seed corn—with two amendments. First, the ten capitalists work in the Farm for three days each, that is, as much as the other peasants. Second, the capitalists institute a system of *profit-sharing*, such that each peasant, including the capitalists, consumes an equal amount of corn.[33] In equilibrium, the capitalists earn a profit of 343 corn. This profit is then equally distributed to all, giving each peasant a final consumption of 1.3 corn. I now explain why even this economy, which features a perfectly egalitarian final distribution, runs afoul of the Non-Servitude Proviso.

In economy (IV), the total amount of labour performed is 3000 days (500 in the Farm; 2500 in the Forest). If necessary labour amounts to 2000 days, surplus labour is equal to 1000 days. But no surplus is *consumed* by the capitalists, so there is no exploitation. Roemer infers from this that labour extraction is irrelevant to complaints of economic injustice. But this inference is unacceptable.[34] For the ten capitalists directly control the working lives of 157 peasants (and indirectly of 833). Contrast a case where the capital stock is jointly owned, as in economy (I). Here the peasants could collectively decide to work an extra day each, for 3000 days in total. Such a collective decision

---

[33] An extra ten peasants must now work in the Forest, for a total of 833. Assuming the equilibrium wage remains constant at 1/3 corn, then only 157 peasants will work in the Farm, together with the ten capitalists. A total of 500 days are worked in the Farm; 30 days by the ten capitalists and 470 by the peasants. The former net 343 units of corn and the latter 157.

[34] Roemer's inference is effectively criticized in Cohen (1995, chapter 8). I discuss it further in Chapter 3.

52   DOMINATION AT WORK

would not violate the Proviso, insofar as it did not reflect unilateral control, by ten capitalists, over the working lives of any other.

So what matters, according to the Proviso, is who *controls* the net product and, by implication, the labour capacities of others. Once again, capital is monetized control over alien labour capacity. Whether that control translates into exploitation—*actual* unilateral labour flow—is secondary. So economy (IV) and its philanthrocapitalists violate the Proviso, but without exploiting.[35]

To make this argument more vivid, consider Pettit's (1999, pp. 50–55) well-known example:

> *Kindly Master*—*A* owns a slave, *B*, but never actually interferes with her. Moreover, *A* never extracts a surplus from *B*'s labour.

In this case, *A* does not exploit *B*. But that hardly matters. What matters is that *B* is enslaved, such that *A can* readily exploit *B*. Such exploitability is censured by the Non-Servitude Proviso, on the grounds of unilateral or arbitrary or misrecognitive control over *B*'s purposiveness. In other words, *A* dominates *B*, and that suffices to dub their relationship unjust, regardless of the (justice of the) distributive background that gave rise to it or the availability of alternatives. As I explained in Chapter 1, this theory dubs as exploitative a wider class of transactions than just the monopolist, the rentier, or the patrimonial capitalist (who benefits against the background of unjust distribution).

Summing up, the Proviso implies that, morally speaking, distribution is subordinate to production. That is, the Nozickian-transition economy (III) is unjust not because it is distributively unjust—it may not be, if it issues from clean capitalist accumulation. Rather, it is unjust because *it gives a small minority of ten capitalists unilateral control over the working lives of hundreds of others*. Exploitation is what happens when that control is activated in order to squeeze unilateral labour flow out of the labour capacity of those others. I now extend these ideas to garden-variety monetary transactions, by elaborating the distinction between money and capital.

---

[35] In section 2.3, I discussed Roemer's example of an egalitarian, private ownership economy with wage labour but no exploitation. In that economy, no surplus labour is *produced*; in economy (IV) no surplus labour is *consumed*. Neither economy is exploitative. But both violate the Proviso, for in both cases a coalition of agents has unilateral control over the labour of others.

2.5 The Role of Money

Having explained how capitalist exploitation might work in a simple reproducible economy, I now explain how the Non-Servitude Proviso deals with cases that do not involve vertical authoritative control over the labour capacity of others. Consider the variant of the *Pit* case in which *A* offers *B* costless rescue, on condition that *B* pays *A* $1 million. How does that offer violate the Proviso?

The answer trades on the already-established contrast between economies (I) and (II). In collective ownership economy (I), corn is both a means of consumption and a means of exchange, but the 500 units of seed corn is not *capital*, in the sense of monetized unilateral control over alien purposiveness. In capitalist economy (II), by contrast, the seed corn entitles ten capitalists to 500 days of labour, which includes 333 days of surplus labour, all performed by 167 peasants. This contrast between money *as a means of exchange*—in this case, corn—and money *as capital* characterizes any capitalist economy in which the means of production (the seed corn) are scarce and privately owned, that is, where Roemer's conditions (1) and (3) are met. I now explain the import of this distinction between money and capital.

Back to the *Pit* case. Suppose that, by working for $1/day for *A* the rest of her life, *B* will produce her basic necessities and create a surplus of $1 million (in net present value) for *A*. Suppose, further, that this is equivalent to borrowing $1 million when she finds herself in the pit and paying it to *A* up front. Insofar as rope-ownership constitutes capital in the *Pit* case, so does ownership of its money-equivalent of $1 million. In other words, ownership of ropes (or millions) gives those who own them title to the unilateral labour performance of others. It scarcely matters that *B* now owes the same labour performance to the money lender; all that matters is that her structural resourcelessness comes to entitle owners (of ropes or money) to such performance. And since, barring an independent justification, that title violates the Proviso, it is unjust.

This explains my original distinction between money as a means of exchange and money as capital. The owner of money as a means of exchange is like the owner of a theatre ticket: her ownership only entitles her to consumption of the product of the exercise of alien labour capacity—the play. The owner of money as capital—for example, the theatre owner—is a capitalist, in the sense that her ownership entitles her not only to the product of the exercise of alien labour capacity, but also to unilateral control over that capacity

54 DOMINATION AT WORK

(e.g. of the actors) itself. This, I have argued, violates the Proviso and therefore constitutes domination. One might object that B paying A \$1 million does not imply control over B's purposiveness, especially if B inherited or found that money. The objection fails, insofar as \$1 million unjustly entitles A to control over the net product, and therefore to the exercise of alien labour capacity. In other words, the purchase of the *Pit* case on our intuitions consists precisely in the amount of positional purposiveness \$1 million can muster: the value of money *just is* the amount of reified purposiveness it can muster.

These conclusions can be systematically connected to the critique of capitalist economies like (II) and (III). They are, in the sense I have just explained, *self-reproducing pit-like structures whose reproductive basis is value-constituted control over human productive power*. To see this, suppose that productive assets are scarce and privately owned. If such control over the means of production reproducibly confers unilateral control over the production and distribution of the net product,[36] then control over the means of production confers unilateral control over the labour capacity of others. So economies (II) and (III) are unjust precisely because they give a small minority of ten capitalists unilateral control over the working lives of hundreds of others. *Pace* Roemer, the distributive upshot in the means of production or consumption is secondary to this central unilateralist feature of the capitalist mode of production.

I have, so far, argued that monetary transactions under capitalism are mere appearances of the substance of capitalist production, namely unilateral control over the labour capacity of others. Capital is not mere monetary title to alien labour capacity, for it involves control one might choose not to exercise. This is the moral of the *Kindly Master* story. Unilateral control, moreover, is not tantamount to what Roemer calls domination 'at the point of production'. That is, the Proviso's normative emphasis is on work capacity, as such, and not on the workplace itself. Section 2.6 elaborates on this further implication of the Proviso: the distinction between *domination at work* and *domination in the workplace*.

---

[36] One may object to this assumption, on the grounds that my control over the net product does not automatically give me control over its distribution. But, as economy (IV) shows, it does not matter that I do not control distribution, as such. It suffices that your production- and consumption-related capacities are subject to my discretion.

2.6 Forms of Domination

This section discusses three different accounts of domination at work. Two of them have been criticized by Roemer. I will argue that, for all that Roemer's criticisms show, they do not exhaust the relevant set of possibilities.

Roemer (1982, p. 195) argues that the set of sufficient conditions for exploitation is completed by 'A being in a relation of *dominance* to B'. Roemer's dominance condition makes the exploiter's livelihood dependent on the nature of the interaction with the exploitee. In later work, Roemer explains why he came to reject his earlier emphasis on domination:

> It is necessary to distinguish two types of domination by capitalists over workers, domination in the maintenance and enforcement of private property in the means of production, and domination at the point of production (the hierarchical and autocratic structure of work). The line between the two cannot be sharply drawn, but let us superscript the two types $domination_1$ and $domination_2$, respectively... each of $domination_1$ and $domination_2$ implies exploitation, but not conversely. Hence if our interest is in domination, there is no reason to invoke exploitation theory, for the direction of entailment runs the wrong way... In certain situations, exploitation requires $domination_1$, but since we cannot know these cases by analyzing the exploitation accounts alone, there is no reason to invoke exploitation if, indeed, our interest in exploitation is only as a barometer of $domination_1$. Furthermore, our interest in $domination_1$ is essentially an interest in the inequality of ownership of the means of production, for the purpose of $domination_1$ is to enforce that ownership pattern. I maintain if it is $domination_1$ one claims an interest in, it is really inequality... in the ownership of the means of production which is the issue.
>
> (Roemer 1996, p. 73)

Given the significance of this objection to the overall integrity of the thesis defended in this book, I will study it at some length. I proceed as follows: first, I reconstruct Roemer's account of $domination_1$ and $domination_2$. I then rebut his anti-domination conclusion on the grounds that the forms of domination he discusses do not exhaust the sphere of domination *tout court*. Exploitation is simply a 'third form' of domination, equivalent to neither $domination_1$, nor $domination_2$. In the course of this rebuttal, several points of disagreement with Roemer will surface.

56 DOMINATION AT WORK

2.6.1 Point-of-production domination

Here's a reconstruction of Roemer's argument against the view that exploitation implies domination$_2$, which I will call *point-of-production domination*:

(3)   Domination$_2$ occurs only at the point of production, P.

(4)   Exploitation does not occur only within P.

So (5)   Some instances of exploitation are not instances of domination$_2$.

So (6)   Our interest in domination$_2$ cannot justify an interest in exploitation. (Roemer 1996, p. 77)

Roemer defines domination$_2$ in terms of the 'hierarchical and autocratic structure of work': (3) follows from this definition. (4) is trickier to defend. Unlike most Marxists before him, Roemer claims that A can exploit B even in the absence of labour or credit markets. Here's an illustration of that claim:

> *Friday and Robinson*—There are two producers, Friday and Robinson. Friday is poor in capital, and Robinson is rich. If they do not trade, Robinson will work eight hours and Friday will work sixteen so that each can satisfy his or her needs (assuming they're both rational, the fact that they decide to trade shows that they both benefit from trading). They only trade in final goods, and there are no labour or credit markets. In equilibrium under free trade, Friday works twelve hours, Robinson works four, and both attain subsistence.

Roemer claims there is exploitation here. Having worked for four hours, Robinson can relax for the rest of the day, while Friday toils to produce what Robinson would otherwise have produced only with an extra four hours of work:

> Robinson benefits from Friday's presence, and is able to use his wealth as leverage, through the market, to get Friday to work for him, which Friday would not have to do if he had access to his per capita share of the produced capital.   (Roemer 1996 [1985], p. 52)

I agree with Roemer's conclusion, and I also agree that it vindicates (4). It follows that exploitation does not presuppose domination$_2$ and an interest in domination$_2$ cannot justify an interest in exploitation. Note, further, that the capitalist workplace is not always oppressive in the sense of domination$_2$. The well-paid workers of high-technology firms, for example, often attest to the quality of their workplace and the meaningfulness and creativity of their work. These judgements are sometimes true; they are not censured by the Non-Servitude Proviso as blighted or ideological.[37] So, if not domination$_2$, then why not domination$_1$?

2.6.2 Property-relations domination

Is the interest in exploitation justified by appeal to domination$_1$, what I will call *property-relations domination*? No, says Roemer. His argument goes as follows:

(7)   Domination$_1$ arises from unjust property relations (i.e. distributive injustice).

(8)   Exploitation is only a 'barometer' for domination$_1$.

So (9)   We should be interested in domination$_1$, not exploitation.

(7) is true by definition. (8) says that exploitation provides an indication or prediction of domination$_1$, just as barometers indicate or predict the weather (Roemer 1996, p. 73). And since we are only interested in weather predictions because we are interested in the weather, it follows that exploitation is of no intrinsic interest, which is what (9) says. Adding the premiss:

(10)   Domination$_1$ and domination$_2$ are the only forms of domination *tout court*.

It follows that:

(11)   An interest in domination *tout court* cannot justify an interest in exploitation.

Whatever one thinks about the inference to (10), the inference to (11) seals off any appeal to domination as *explanans* of our interest in exploitation and

---

[37] Recall that what matters, according to the Proviso, is not the actual quality of the labour process, but only the fact that a few unilaterally control it. Economies like (IV) show that, much like the *Kindly Master* case, the extractive dispositions of capitalists may never be activated.

58 DOMINATION AT WORK

concludes Roemer's attack on that front. I now show why Roemer's arguments do no exhaust the conceptual field.

2.6.3 A third form of domination

My response to Roemer consists in showing that his account of domination is too narrow—that is, I refute (10). It is plausible, I think, that there are instances of domination, such that (i) they do not arise from asset injustice (i.e. are not instances of domination$_1$), and (ii) they do not take place at the point of production (i.e. are not instances of domination$_2$). Garden-variety examples of sexual domination are compelling illustrations of that possibility.[38] I now generalize the force of these examples, beginning with claim (ii).

Roemer's own *Friday and Robinson* example is purported to show that exploitation can take place in the market but outside the workplace. Why is the same not true of domination? Roemer says that Robinson 'is able to use his wealth as leverage to *get* Friday to work for him', adding that this is something 'Friday *would not have to do* if he had access to his per capita share of the produced capital' (emphases mine). It follows that Robinson unilaterally leverages Friday's vulnerability to get him to benefit Robinson (which might, as a mere upshot, also benefit Friday). According to the Non-Servitude Proviso, such treatment amounts to domination and is therefore unjust.

One reason why Roemer wants to resist this description seems to be that he takes domination to be coextensive with the absence of perfect competition:

> ... where markets for particular assets or commodities are thin ... one agent has *power over* another which he would not have in a fully developed, perfectly competitive market economy   (Roemer 1996, p. 74)

So, given that domination implies power over, it follows by *modus tollens* from the passage just quoted that 'fully developed' perfect competition excludes the possibility of domination.

Yet Roemer (and indeed Marx) thinks that *exploitation* obtains even in a perfectly competitive capitalist economy.[39] So even under 'fully developed' perfect competition, a class of people (owners of the means of production)

---

[38] I discuss such cases more extensively in Chapter 3.

[39] Which I take to be a system of generalized commodity production in which there are no externalities and in which all producers face infinitely elastic demand schedules, that is, have no *market* power.

DOMINATION, ALIENATION, REIFICATION 59

can unilaterally set others (nonowners) to work. These are exercises of power over and, indeed, instances of domination (as betrayed by Roemer's own language). Therefore the first premiss of Roemer's argument, that domination is coextensive only with the *absence* of perfect competition, is false.[40] Capitalist exploitation, in other words, is compatible with all producers being price takers and all inputs receiving their marginal products.

I now turn to (i), the view that domination always arises from asset injustice. Consider:

> *Slavery contract*—A and B are identical twins starting from exactly equal and fair bargaining positions. Each freely agrees to the following contract: on a 50/50 coin toss, the one who gets heads enslaves herself for life to the one who gets tails. B gets heads.   (see Cohen 1995, p. 47)

In this example, domination arises from conditions of full distributive justice through the voluntary, unmanipulated choices of free agents. The example shows why complaints of (Roemerian) distributive injustice are unnecessary for charges of domination.

I conclude that there are forms of domination that correspond neither to domination$_1$ (asset injustice) nor to domination$_2$ (point-of-production autocracy). If such a 'third form' of domination exists, then (10) is false and (11) fails to follow. And this is exactly the judgement sponsored by the Proviso. Its focus is not on 'the extraction of labour from the worker on the assembly line, and ... the oppressive practices that bosses use to discipline workers, to keep them working at a fast pace' (Roemer 2017, p. 274; Roemer 1996, pp. 72–9). Rather, the Proviso's focus is on the residual control over alien productive purposiveness conferred on capitalists by their control over productive assets.

2.7 Domination, Alienation, Reification

I have, so far in this chapter, explained how the domination account deals with generic forms of capitalist accumulation. I now explain how the theory appropriates traditional criticisms of the capitalist mode of production. I then

---

[40] Some philosophers claim that dominating power and market competition are mutually exclusive (see Lovett 2010, p. 79, Taylor 2016, pp. 29–65). This claim confuses *market* power with *economic*—that is, ownership-conferred—power. Perfect competition is perfectly compatible with dominating power (as Roemer himself argues in Roemer 1982, chapters 1–3). See also Rawls (1971, p. 309), who makes a similar point.

60   DOMINATION AT WORK

contrast the domination theory with other related ideas in the history of social philosophy.

As I have elaborated it, the domination theory normativizes a sentiment expressed in Brecht's *Song of the United Front*:

> And because a human is human,
> she doesn't need a boot to the face!
> She wants no slaves below her,
> and no masters above!

This stanza brilliantly expresses the Enlightenment idea that, just by dint of being human, you are entitled to having neither masters nor slaves. The Non-Servitude Proviso applies this idea to work, tying it explicitly with a theory of domination at work. The theory also provides a new glossary for old socialist concepts, such as *alienation* and *reification*. Take alienation first. On the domination theory, alienation just is the subsumption of alien purposiveness.[41] Exploitation is related to alienation in the way a disposition is related to its realization: unilateral control over labour capacity, realized as unilateral labour flow. The concept of reification, on the other hand, refers to the form alienation assumes under the capitalist mode of production: it is a *de facto* claim to alien purposiveness in the form of a relation between things—commodities and money. As I explained in section 2.4, this is the macroeconomic consequence of an asset inequality that confers control over alien labour capacity on those who control the net product.

In the interest of further elaboration of the Proviso, I now discuss some exemptions from its requirements as well as contrasts with other familiar normative theories. What counts as a 'special justification' that would exempt someone from the requirements of the Proviso? Consider a workers' cooperative (a factory, post-office, bank, hospital, school, or university), all of whose members possess roughly equal voice and exit options.[42] These workers elect managers without any reciprocal prospect that each of them would, eventually, themselves be elected manager. By this democratic decision, the democratically elected manager comes to be exempt from the requirements

---

[41] The alienation of *labour capacity* from the conditions of production under capitalism has a further, obfuscatory, function: '[A]lienation prevents the workers from perceiving the injustice of exploitation.' (Elster 1985, p. 107). The product of alienated labour under capitalism, in other words, appears to rightfully belong to the capitalist.

[42] That is, the cooperative is one person, one vote and each worker has meaningful outside options, including similar employment possibilities, should she decide to quit.

of the Proviso for the duration of her appointment.[43] So the prospective managers' obligation not to manage the labour of others is waived in virtue of the background and procedural virtues of their appointment.

If certain presumptive obligations under the Proviso are waivable, then others can be forfeited. Consider, for example, free riding on the effortful contribution of others. Under the Proviso, the industrious, non-ascetic peasants of capitalist economy (III) must retain the same degree of control over their conditions of production as their ascetic or non-industrious counterparts, such that nobody subjugates the labour capacity of others as part of a scheme of mandatory social cooperation. If the latter group is culpably lazy, or culpably free rides on the labour of the former, then they may forfeit a right to enjoying the benefits of such cooperation. To free ride in a system of mandatory cooperation is to be disposed to exploit the industrious, that is, to take advantage of their good faith and the good faith of background institutions in order to benefit at their expense. That disposition contradicts any plausible justification of the Proviso, especially if it impinges upon the structural conditions of reproduction of mutual independence. So my free riding may entitle others, at least temporarily, to sanction or exclude me from their cooperative endeavours.[44]

I now explain what the Proviso is not. First, it is not a perfectionist ideal or an account of political morality based on a certain conception of the good life.[45] One can be neutral about the nature and content of the good life and still affirm the Proviso. Indeed, this is why the Proviso entails a logically weak conception of alienation. Moreover, the Proviso does not provide a complete theory of the state or of political morality, but only a necessary part of it. The idea is that, for any system of mandatory mutually affecting cooperation between agents who must produce in order to establish their mutual independence, their system of government must include something like the Proviso. A political morality without it will be incomplete, as it will provide an inadequate justification for private property. As I argued in section 2.1, any such justification must incorporate the Proviso's concerns by ensuring that unilateral control over

---

[43] The duration and eligibility criteria for the appointment of managers would have to take into account the likelihood of creating a managerial ruling class that would, in turn, dominate the labour of nonmanager workers. I discuss this possibility in Chapter 7.

[44] The ground for exempting me is not, once again, (luck-egalitarian) distributive justice, as Arneson, Cohen, and Roemer maintain, but only the conditions of equal freedom. I discuss this issue extensively in Chapter 3.

[45] The Proviso is compatible with, but does not entail, perfectionist grounds for individual and collective self-emancipation (e.g. human flourishing, self-realization, etc.). These are all ways of spelling out the nature of human (productive) purposiveness but not what makes for its unjust subjection. That requires a further normative premiss, which is what the Proviso is all about.

62   DOMINATION AT WORK

things does not confer unilateral control over persons. The *Communist Manifesto* provides one of the clearest statements of this idea:

> Communism deprives no man of the power to appropriate the products of society; all that it does is to deprive him of the power to subjugate the labour of others by means of such appropriations.   (MECW 6, p. 500)[46]

As I will show in Chapter 5, Marx envisages the rightful liberation of the labour of the majority from the unjust control of a small minority, albeit at a high level of productive interdependence: independence and the division of labour go hand in hand.[47] Marx's view, I will argue, is an extension of the Rousseau/Kant distinction between service and servitude mooted in section 2.1.

A final contrast is worth mentioning. Any complete political morality has to reckon with work and *de facto* unilateral control over the productive purposiveness of others. But the converse does not hold: the Proviso does not exhaust political morality. That is, any given transaction that violates the Proviso is presumptively unjust. But this *pro tanto* reason may be defeated or overriden by other reasons that form part of justice.[48] I now conclude this chapter by considering why capital—monetized unilateral control over alien labour capacity—is intrinsically exploitative.

2.8 The Presence and Relevance of Exploitation Under Capitalism

The Non-Servitude Proviso evinces a distinction between the justification of a mode of production and the justification of the (historically specific) institutions that comprise it. The slaveholding mode of production, for

---

[46] Or: '[P]roperty turns out to be the right, on the part of the capitalist, to appropriate the unpaid labour of others or its product, and to be the impossibility, on the part of the labourer, of appropriating his own product.' (MECW 35 [*Capital*], pp. 583ff). For similar statements from the *Grundrisse*, see (MECW 29, pp. 462–64). I discuss Marx's historical elaboration of the Proviso in Chapter 5.

[47] Marx regrets capitalist forms of control over the labour process, but—unlike the Romantic anti-capitalists of his day, like William Morris—claims that the capitalist mode of production alone offers a path to the emancipation of the worker from the domination of capital under a richer, more complete repertoire of human needs and wherewithal to flourish. Marx thus accepts the 'historical justification' of the capitalist mode of production, with its promise of higher productivity, higher worker socialization, developed human needs and capacities, and developed human powers, as a prelude to collective self-emancipation. Why would that emancipation be worth having? The answer, for Marx, is individualistic and domination-based: it is grounded on something like the Non-Servitude Proviso.

[48] For example, if capitalist economy (II) improves everyone's overall welfare compared to collective ownership (I), then it may be all-things-considered better. But similar things may be true of polygamy, to take only one example.

THE PRESENCE AND RELEVANCE OF EXPLOITATION   63

instance, is unjust everywhere and everywhen. Indeed, the Proviso implies a stronger claim: *if humans are enslaved, then they are unjustly treated.* The italicized claim is true, even if there are no humans—even if humanity never exists, such that the antecedent of the conditional is false, the conditional itself remains true. This evaluation, moreover, is independent of the evaluation of any given institutional arrangement realizing the slaveholding mode of production, which may depend on the presence of feasible and comparable alternatives to slavery.

Some social scientists conflate these two evaluative exercises. They claim that social criticism is a necessarily comparative exercise. That is, in order to understand what is intrinsically unjust about capitalist economic structure, we must ask not only whether a putatively unjust feature is necessarily present in it; we must also show that this feature is not necessarily present in other (feasible) social systems, such as socialism. Failure in the comparative exercise is tantamount to failure in critique itself. The mooted claim is demonstrably false: critique is not necessarily comparative. Being locked in a cage for no good reason is unjust, even if there exists no (feasible) state involving cagelessness. And some injustices may be irremediable, inevitable, or even necessary. But there is a more sophisticated version of this comparativist belief. The rest of this section considers and rebuts that version, with a view to explaining why capitalism is intrinsically exploitative.

Van Parijs (1983) argues that, the more we insist on a conception of exploitation that is intrinsic to capitalism but not to socialism, the less ethically relevant that conception is. And conversely, the more ethically relevant the conception is, the less likely it is to be intrinsic to capitalism but not to socialism. So even if my account of exploitation is sound, it will not strongly juxtapose capitalism and socialism. I will illustrate this trade-off between *presence* (in capitalism but not socialism) and *relevance* with the help of two examples.

Consider, first, unequal flow of labour time (e.g. capitalist economies (II) and (III)). Van Parijs agrees with Roemer that unequal exchange of labour is necessarily present in capitalism but not in socialism (e.g. economy (I)). Under socialism, the means of production are administered by workers and, on a good day, are enlisted to reward work in proportion to, say, effortful contribution. More generally, they are never mobilized to reward mere ownership. So exploitation as title to (the fruits of) alien labour performance is necessarily present in capitalism and not socialism. But who cares? The young, old, sick, and disabled will not produce much. They will therefore tend to be net beneficiaries in terms of income, wealth, and labour time. But the sheer fact of unequal labour flow between them and the working

64 DOMINATION AT WORK

majority, seems not to be unjust. 'Exploitation' seems to be *present*, but morally irrelevant.

Second illustration: take any conception of exploitation that seems morally relevant, for example, one defined in terms of an unjust distribution of resources (see Chapter 1, section 1.5.3). Van Parijs claims that there is nothing intrinsic to capitalism making it distributively unjust, and nothing intrinsic to socialism making it distributively just. The cleanly generated capitalism of economy (III), he argues, vindicates this suspicion. So exploitation as distributive injustice is morally *relevant*, but not necessarily present under capitalism or absent under socialism. There is, once again, a presence-relevance trade-off.

I now show how the domination account of exploitation establishes both presence and relevance. Throughout this chapter, I have argued that exploitation involves title to unilateral labour flow. And since that unilateralism follows from the fundamental institution of capitalism—unequal control over scarce productive assets—this establishes presence under capitalism. What about relevance? This book defends the view that exploitation is unjust because it involves domination. Exploitation is a dividend of servitude, cashed out in surplus labour. Under capitalism, such service *literally* assumes the form of currency—labour has a monetary expression, which is what enables money to convert humans into its servants or, better, into *the servants of those who are sufficiently moneyed*. So capital just is pecuniary title to unilateral control over alien labour capacity.

So, if it is admitted that domination and servitude are a legitimate dimension of moral concern and that capitalism builds that relation into the conditions of market exchange, then both of Van Parijs' conditions (relevance, presence under capitalism but not under socialism) are satisfied. Hence exploitation as subsumed labour performance constitutes a counterexample to the presence-relevance trade-off and capitalism is a form of servitude—it is a cage; one from which we can and should escape.

Chapters 3 and 4 further examine the nature and core injustice of our imprisonment in that cage.

Conclusion

This chapter explained how power converts others into servitude and how that servitude, in turn, redounds as benefit. I began by arguing that domination is subjection to the choices of others. Applied to work, subjection

THE PRESENCE AND RELEVANCE OF EXPLOITATION   65

to the choices of others is unilateral control over their labour capacity. So exploitation consists in extraction of unilateral labour flow on the basis of subsumed purposiveness. It is therefore a violation of the requirements of rightful individual freedom. This account of freedom is based on the Non-Servitude Proviso, which received three justifications: Kantian, republican, and recognitional. I then explained implications of the Proviso for capitalism and capitalist accumulation with the help of a simple economic model. In Chapter 3 I will further refine the Proviso and discuss its implications for generic human vulnerability, needs, rights to the body, and gestational labour.

Appendix: Productivity growth

What would happen in the transition from joint-ownership economy (I) to capitalist economy (II) if productivity were to increase by 50 percent? Consider economy (I). Suppose the invention of a new technology increases the material productivity of the factory by half ($1c + 1l \rightarrow 3c$). Then the peasants would achieve reproduction by working there exclusively, for half a day each. They work for a total of 500 days, enough to produce 1500 units of corn, of which 500 replaces the original seed corn. The higher productivity allows them to expend only a fourth of total labour compared to Roemer's original economy.

Now consider economy (II). With constant wages, the peasants will perform as much labour as in (II): 167 will work at the Farm for three days, receiving one unit of corn as wages, while 823 will work in the Forest for another three days, receiving one unit of corn each. The main difference is that the capitalists will now appropriate a total of 1500 corn. Of this, they will spend 500 to replace the existing seed corn, 167 as wages, and keep the remaining 833 ($\approx 2500/3$) as profit. So when productivity increases by a half, surplus labour almost triples. The total labour performed in this economy is 2970 days (as in (II)). But the labour necessary for the workers' subsistence is only 500 days. So total surplus labour here is 2470 days. Each peasant must work six times longer (three days/week, as opposed to $1/2$ days), for the same consumption, in order to feed ten capitalists.[49]

---

[49] An anonymous referee points out that there is alternative equilibrium in this economy: the capitalists offer a wage of 990/500, earning one unit of corn as profit, and each peasant works for 500/990 days. Even in this equilibrium, and by dint of capital's control over the conditions of production, each of 990 peasants must work one percent longer to feed ten capitalists.

3

How Exploiters Dominate

This chapter further develops and defends the idea that exploitation is a form of domination, self-enrichment through the domination of others. In a slogan, exploitation is a dividend of servitude—a benefit the powerful extract by treating the vulnerable as their servants. I will refine this idea, defend it against criticism, and argue that it is superior to competing contemporary accounts of exploitation. More precisely, I will argue that exploitation is cashed out in terms of labour time or effort. This renewed emphasis on labour can, I argue, unify ideas about generic vulnerability and the relevance of human needs, as well as concerns about markets in human organs and gestational labour. It also restores the centrality of labour to an account of exploitation without presupposing any controversial claims about the determination of prices or values in the economy.

The chapter has five sections. Section 3.1 discusses the metric, or currency, of exploitation complaints, focusing on seminal work by John Roemer. Section 3.2 discusses the metaphysics and phenomenology of the domination account. Section 3.3 situates a variety of putative exploitation complaints squarely within the domination account and discusses their implications. Sections 3.4 and 3.5 show that the domination account is superior to two competing contemporary liberal accounts, one based on vulnerability (due to Allen Wood) and one based on fairness (due to Richard Arneson, G.A. Cohen, and John Roemer).

3.1 Metrics of Exploitation

Exploitation theory is largely concerned with the control and distribution of the surplus from positive-sum transactions. As I explained in Chapter 1, such transactions are particularly interesting when mutually consensual and beneficial. This section applies the account of domination canvassed in Chapter 2 to that set of transactions. Consider a variant of a previous example:

Exploitation as Domination: What Makes Capitalism Unjust. Nicholas Vrousalis, Oxford University Press.
© Nicholas Vrousalis 2023. DOI: 10.1093/oso/9780192867698.003.0004

METRICS OF EXPLOITATION   67

Pit—*A*, *B* and *C* are alone in the desert. *A* and *C* find *B* lying at the bottom of a pit. *A* proposes to extract *B*, on condition that *B* works for *A* for a wage of $2/day for the rest of *B*'s life. *C* also proposes to extract *B*, on condition that *B* works for *C* for $1/day for the rest of *B*'s life. *B* accepts *A*'s offer.

The *Pit* case involves a proto–labour–market relation, similar to the one illustrated by the peasant economy of Chapter 2.[1] Now, accepting *C*'s offer of $1/day or *A*'s offer of $2/day is a significant improvement over *B*'s pre-proposal situation of $0/day. In addition, all have the assurance that, were *B* to reject one offer, she could still get out by accepting the other.

The motivating intuition is that *Pit* involves exploitation; the question is why. The answer I offer in this book is that it matters, from the point of view of freedom, who serves whom and why. I now show that, for all the criticisms levelled against the idea of surplus labour, it remains conceptually indispensable to understanding why *A* exploits *B* in *Pit*-like cases.

3.1.1 Unequal exchange of labour

That humans are disposed to serve each other is a feature of social cooperation and a fact about their social nature. This book asks what distinguishes such mutual service from servitude. In Chapter 2, I argued that the distinguishing feature is domination, as contrasted with individual independence: nonsubjection to the choices of others. Applied to work relations, such independence is violated when others possess unilateral control over your labour capacity in a way that subjects your agential purposiveness to theirs. I also argued that the idea of unsubjected productive purposiveness is supported by the:

Non-Servitude Proviso—For any agents or groups engaged in mandatory mutually affecting cooperation under a division of labour, and barring any special justification that exempts them, none should possess unilateral control over the labour capacity of any other.

The Proviso establishes a presumption against unilateral control over the labour capacities of others. The question is how to think about that total

---

[1] Once again, the agents here could be persons, groups, or classes.

68 HOW EXPLOITERS DOMINATE

stock of labour capacities and the labour flow that constitutes their collective exercise. One of Marxism's enduring legacies to exploitation theory is a set of definitions based on the *unequal exchange of labour*. Unequal exchange offers a specifically labour-based interpretation of what it means to take advantage of another. On this interpretation, A exploits B *only if B* unilaterally serves A, or, equivalently, A extracts unreciprocated labour flow from B.[2] When the extent of that unreciprocated labour flow corresponds to the difference between B's net product and her subsistence bundle, A exploits by extracting B's whole surplus.

This surplus-labour metric of exploitation has some attractive features. Suppose A owns two slaves, B and C. B is very productive: she produces a surplus S over and above what she needs for subsistence. A appropriates $S. C$, on the other hand, is not very productive: she produces just enough to survive. A does not appropriate any surplus from C, and hence does not benefit at C's expense. It is plausible that A exploits B, but not C. The surplus labour definition resonates with this intuition.[3] The definition is also versatile enough to allow that the labour contribution variable is defined as a proportion of total labour expended to produce the net product. So one can use the idea of surplus labour to construct a general equilibrium theory of exploitation, that is, a structural account of the distribution of labour flow in the economy, as well as its forms of reproduction.[4]

A further advantage of the surplus labour definition is that it can be straightforwardly related to the notion of effort. Instead of representing a share of labour time, labour contribution might represent the amount of effort expended, or the amount of effort discounted by the amount one *can* expend. Call the discounted form of effort *relative effort*.[5] Absolute and relative effort

---

[2] Unreciprocated labour flow is a generalization of the Marxian idea of the extraction of surplus labour. The *locus classicus* here is Roemer (1982). Roemer showed that, under certain assumptions about original endowments and preferences, total labour time in the economy will decompose into a group of agents who optimize by consuming *more* labour than they give in production (presumptive exploiters) and a group of agents who optimize by consuming *less* labour than they give (presumptive exploitees). See Chapter 2 for a stylized example, which makes no assumptions about the determination of prices.

[3] Note that the definition is uncontaminated by assumptions about the determination of the value or price of *individual* commodities: it neither entails nor presupposes such a theory. It is therefore orthogonal to the *Ricardian* labour theory of value, which Roemer (1982) and Cohen (1979) mistakenly attribute to Marx.

[4] If the product of labour, in the economy as a whole, has a monetary expression, as it does under capitalism, and if capitalism presupposes a separation between propertied capitalists and propertyless workers, then it can be shown that the surplus labour definition satisfies certain attractive axioms, such as the 'new interpretation' of the labour theory of value. See Foley (1982) and Dumenil (1984) for the new interpretation, and Veneziani and Yoshihara (2018) for the proofs.

[5] On relative effort, see Roemer and Trannoy (2016).

METRICS OF EXPLOITATION   69

are, broadly speaking, measures of how intensely an agent endeavours to serve herself and others. Surplus labour might then be defined as (absolute or relative) effort in excess of what one needs for subsistence.

These variants on the surplus labour idea are all interpretations of what it means for B to unilaterally serve A, reflecting the distinction between *serving another and being the servant of another*. Unilateral flow of labour or effort, on this view, is necessary for exploitation. It is not, however, sufficient. If one social group *freely* optimizes by gifting whatever goods it creates through its collective efforts and with its several labour powers to another group, then, intuitively, the resulting unilateral transfer is not exploitative. This conclusion is supported by the Non-Servitude Proviso: unreciprocated or unilateral service, in and of itself, does not constitute exploitation. On the view defended in this book, unilateral labour flow or effort constitutes exploitation if and only if it issues from domination. In other words, it is A's *domination* of B that converts B's unilateral service to A into servitude.

Roemer (1985, 1996) disputes this conclusion: he claims that unequal labour flow is neither necessary nor sufficient for exploitation. Since I agree with Roemer about sufficiency, this section only considers his argument against necessity. My broader aim throughout is to vindicate the idea of exploitation as domination-induced unilateral labour flow.

3.1.2 Roemer on unequal exchange

According to Roemer, unilateral flow of labour or effort is not necessary for exploitation because asset-rich people—presumptive exploiters—may give more labour or effort to asset-poor people—presumptive exploitees—than they receive from them. Consider:

> *Domestic Servant—A* is rich and B is poor. A hires B as her domestic servant for the rest of B's life. But their preferences over work and leisure jointly imply that, in equilibrium, labour flows from A to B. That is, B will receive more labour than she gives and A will receive less.

By the definition of domination defended in this book, A dominates B in *Domestic Servant*. By the surplus labour condition, however, it is B who extracts a surplus from A's labour. So A does *not* exploit B. Roemer thinks this conclusion is mistaken: A *does* exploit B. And, if this is true, then the surplus labour definition must be false and socialists should not be interested

70 HOW EXPLOITERS DOMINATE

in exploitation as unilateral labour flow. They should focus, instead, on distribution and property relations. In this vein, Roemer proposes an alternative definition of capitalist exploitation, which goes as follows. For any coalition of agents A and its complement B, A exploits B if and only if:

> (i) were B to withdraw from the society, endowed with its per capita share of society's alienable property (that is, produced and nonproduced goods), and with its own labour and skills, then B would be better off (in terms of income and leisure) than it is at the present allocation;
>
> (ii) were A to withdraw under the same conditions, then A would be worse off (in terms of income and leisure) than it is at present;
>
> (iii) were B to withdraw from society with its own endowments (not its per capita share), then A would be worse off than at present.
>
> (Roemer 1996, p. 40)

Roemer calls this the *property relations definition*. The definition entails that labour flow is irrelevant to charges of exploitation: whether labour flows from A to B or vice versa, as long as (i)–(iii) are satisfied, it is A who exploits B.

Roemer's conclusion contradicts my normative emphasis on exploitation as domination-induced unilateral labour flow. I now argue that his argument for the definition, and hence for the irrelevance of labour flow, is invalid. It is precisely because of the nature of the *flow* that we should be interested in the transactions that interest Roemer. More precisely, Roemer's examples are insensitive to the kind of dominating power wealth confers upon the wealthy, and the kind of vulnerability wealthlessness confers upon the wealthless. The rest of this section elaborates.

3.1.3 Why surplus labour is indispensable

Consider the *Pit* case again. Suppose there is an inegalitarian distribution of ropes, such that A has a rope, which B lacks; the distribution of ropes confers power on A. That power, in conjunction with A's disposition to use it, ensures that B will find it costly to leave the pit, that is, do what she has reason to do independently of A's power. So when A's offer gets accepted, A's rope-conferred unilateral power ropes B's purposiveness into A's. It is, I think, the nature of this power, not the background predistribution which *confers* it, that makes the relationship between A and B unjust.

METRICS OF EXPLOITATION   71

To focus intuitions further, consider a cognate example due to Cohen (1995, chapter 8). There is unequal gun ownership, such that the highwayman, A, owns a gun, but the rambler, B, does not. Cohen writes: 'Highway robbery is unjust because it is a transfer of money *for the wrong reason* (to wit, in this case, the victim's fear that the highwayman will kill him).' (Cohen 1995, p. 206). But then the objectionable feature of robbery is, once again, the nature of the normative landscape that gun inequality creates—including the fact that it allows A to unilaterally subject B to her ends.[6] This makes B's action dominated.

Of course, sometimes unequal gun ownership does not lead to robbery. There is, as a consequence, no unequal exchange of labour and so no surplus extraction. In these cases, there is no exploitation. It does not follow, however, that the relationship between A and B is unobjectionable. For A has, by the Non-Servitude Proviso, presumptively unjust unilateral control over B's purposiveness. It follows that A dominates B, even if A's extractive *disposition* is unrealized. The conclusion carries over to cases like *Domestic Servant*. That is, although there is no exploitation in these cases (because surplus labour flows in the wrong direction), the injustice—A's domination of B—survives.

In response to this set of objections, Roemer (1996, chapter 5) softens his opposition to unequal exchange of labour or effort. He considers the following example, due to Erik Wright:

Rich and Poor—Consider the case of two agents, Rich and Poor, who are initially endowed with 3 and 1 units of capital, respectively. This distribution is unfair: suppose that the fair distribution is egalitarian. Rich wants to consume prodigiously, while Poor only wants to subsist and write poetry. Rich works up all his capital stock, but wants to consume even more than what is thereby produced, and so Poor hires Rich to work up Poor's capital stock, paying Rich a wage and keeping enough of the product to enable him to subsist... I previously wrote that Rich did exploit Poor in this example, but I now do not think so. Therefore I would substitute, for clause [(iii)], the following: *[A] gains by virtue of the labor of [B]*.

(Roemer 1996, p. 106, emphasis added)

---

[6] For discussion of Cohen's own vacillations on the significance of labour flow for exploitation, see Vrousalis (2015, chapter 4).

72 HOW EXPLOITERS DOMINATE

Since Rich would be worse off if Poor withdrew with her *actual* share, and given that Rich would be worse off if Poor withdrew with her *per capita* share, Roemer's property relations definition implies that Rich exploits Poor. But this is counterintuitive, Roemer concedes: the counterfactuals in his definition do not tell us enough about the nature of the relationship between Rich and Poor to pick it out as exploitative.[7] So Rich does not exploit Poor. Roemer emends the definition accordingly. But now the question arises: *why* is it that, on Roemer's emended definition, the exploiter, A, must gain by virtue of B's labour? What is so special about gain from another's labour?[8]

The answer, I submit, must have something to do with relations of dominion and servitude: *who serves whom and why*. By reintroducing labour into his definition, Roemer smuggles something like a domination account into his conception of exploitation. It is significant, in this connection, that an early version of the property relations definition (Roemer 1982, p. 195) replaces term (iii), the 'withdrawal with one's own share' condition, with: 'A being in a relation of *dominance* to B'. If I am right, Roemer's conception of exploitation has come full circle, from 'dominance' (Roemer 1982), to maldistribution (Roemer 1985), back to domination (Roemer 1996).

There is therefore strong justification for thinking about exploitation in terms of surplus labour. The domination account does not strictly presuppose the surplus labour condition, but that condition does support my original motivating distinction, entailed by the concept of exploitation, between serving others and servitude to others. In what follows, I will assume that exploitation complaints are cashed out in terms of labour time or effort. More precisely: A exploits B only when A receives unilateral service from B, in accordance with some variant of the surplus labour condition. So unilateral labour flow is a necessary, though insufficient, condition for exploitation. I now explain how domination completes the set of sufficient conditions.

3.2 Vulnerability and Domination

In Chapter 2, I provided three arguments for the Non-Servitude Proviso: Kantian, republican, and recognitional. On all of these theories, there exists a class of injustices that consists in A subsuming B's purposiveness to her own, thereby converting B into her servant. Exploitation is a subset of this

---

[7] The case can even be made that Poor exploits Rich. I discuss this possibility in the Appendix.
[8] In section 3.2.3, I ask whether there is something special about labour *tout court*.

VULNERABILITY AND DOMINATION   73

set of injustices; it is the realization of an *extractive dominating power* of the powerful, one that, I have argued, must be cashed out in terms of unilateral flow of labour or effort. Exploitation, by implication, is the dividend A extracts from B's servitude. This section elaborates on exploitation's connections with vulnerability, on the one hand, and with domination, on the other.

3.2.1 The place of vulnerability

Exploitation generically entails the weaponization of vulnerability, the using and playing on another's weakness. But what is vulnerability? Vulnerability is sometimes conceived as a two-place relation between a person (including the person's well-being) and an object: for example, B is vulnerable when B stands under a boulder, such that the boulder is likely to fall, harming B. What I will call *social vulnerability*, on the other hand, is a three-place relation. Social vulnerability involves at least two agents, A, B, and a thing. Here A has her finger on a button, which controls the boulder, or the first aid kit; A possesses the wherewithal to remove B from harm's way, or to ameliorate any harm that befalls B.

These relational properties—vulnerability to, and dependence on—are irreducibly social forms of powerlessness: they imply that some agent has a measure of control over the vulnerable party's means and the realization of her ends. Any complete theory of exploitation must, in principle, be able to construct a macro-composite index incorporating these diverse dimensions of disempowerment into a single metric of social vulnerability.

But what is the relationship between social vulnerability and social power? On my understanding of that relationship, vulnerability is to power what defeat is to victory. Call this the *equivalence claim*.[9] Equivalence explains the sense in which B is vulnerable, and A powerful, in the *Pit* case. Equivalence also allows all manner of structural relationship between the powerful and the vulnerable. For example, the victory of one army may be constituted by the defeat of many, just as the defeat of one army may be constituted by the victory of many. By the same token, the power of individual or group A may be constituted by the

---

[9] The equivalence claim can be thought of as the non-normative parallel of the Hohfeldian relation between liability and power. According to Hohfeld (1919), if A possesses a normative power, then A can change B's first-order Hohfeldian incidents (B's claims, permissions, and so on). Conversely, if B possesses a liability, then A can change B's first-order incidents. Normative liabilities and normative powers are logically equivalent.

74 HOW EXPLOITERS DOMINATE

vulnerability of many Bs, and the vulnerability of B may be constituted by the power of many As.[10]

Now, the instrumentalization of vulnerability is necessary but not sufficient for exploitation. What completes the set of sufficient conditions is a specific form of instrumentalization, that is, A's unilateral control over B's purposiveness. The rest of this section elaborates on the direction of explanation in these notions.

3.2.2 The priority of domination

If to exploit is to benefit through the domination of others, then exploitation is a form of domination. More precisely, the order of explanation goes as follows:

(a) A exploits B.
So
(b) B does not merely serve A, but is also A's servant.
So
(c) A dominates B.

I have argued throughout for the entailment from (a) to (b). This section and section 3.3 make a final positive case for this inference. Sections 3.4 and 3.5, in turn, rebut two alternative popular explanations, both of which contradict the inference from (a) to (b).

Exploiters, I have argued, necessarily treat weakness as an opportunity for self-advancement, whether they know it or not. In terms of the phenomenology of this treatment, A, the exploiter, arrogates to herself a kind of superior status: whether by action or omission, she treats her own ends as superior to B's, while steering B towards treating her own ends as subordinate. Consider the *Pit* case again: A's offer seems to degrade B's ends, ranking them as less urgent than A's. At the same time, B's ends are taken as a parametric feature of A's situation to be played on, indeed weaponized, for A's benefit. B, on the other hand, can only improve her own lot by accepting that ranking, indeed by seeing herself as someone whose ends lack priority. When B takes A's *Pit* offer as a reason to serve A, B responds to A's power and not to some independent justification. And since this power-induced transaction involves

---

[10] These conceptual configurations are all consistent with what may be called *structural* vulnerability, which I discuss in Chapter 4.

unilateral control over B's purposiveness, the Non-Servitude Proviso dubs it unjust.

There is another way to state this. In *Pit*, A's proposal effectively says to B: 'You are weak, I am strong. Take my power (to press your labour power into my service) as your reason (to serve me).' When the ploy succeeds—that is, when the proposal is credible and has illocutionary force—both A and B come to treat B as smaller than she is, to wit, as someone who takes her mere parametric features as a reason to serve A. B is treated as smaller than she is, in the sense that she cannot do what she has reason to do (work, sleep, write poetry) without responding to B's power. Instead, B's normative identity is reduced to responding to A's unilateral control over those mere features and abilities of B's that A finds useful. When A uses her power to get B to act in this way, she treats B as a servant.

The foregoing is an argument for the explanatory priority of domination. A question immediately arises about the moral relevance of labour, or productive purposiveness as such. There is an ancient Marxist belief, dating back at least to Plato's *Republic*, according to which labour—the intentional exertion of mind and muscle to affect worldly outcomes—is, in some sense, special. This specialness inverts the order of explanation from (a) to (c), such that the domination of human by human is derivative of or metaphysically subordinate to exploitation. On this view, to exploit someone's whole person is to treat that purposiveness *as* her mere features, that is, to treat her as less than *she* is. So, for example, to exploit a woman sexually is to treat her as if she were her genitals; to exploit a manual worker is to treat her as if she were her body; to exploit a mental worker is to treat her as if she were her brain; and so on. Call this the *exploitation-first view*.

On the exploitation-first view, exploiters necessarily treat exploitees as fragments, not of their own body, but of their own person.[11] A person is thereby reduced to the hands and legs and brain and genitals that serve her master and control over which enables such servitude. Domination, on this view, is exploitation *minus* the domination-induced benefit to the exploiter: domination just is exploit*ability*, that is, vulnerability to unilateral surplus labour extraction. This view is extensionally equivalent to the domination view; it merely reverses the direction of explanation from (c) to (a). Both views, moreover, affirm the lemma that to be someone's servant is to have your labour subsumed by them. So, even if the exploitation-first view is sound, the main questions raised in this chapter remain. I now discuss some important implications of these two views.

---

[11] Contrast Marx's famous discussion of Menenius Agrippa in Marx (1976, p. 481).

76 HOW EXPLOITERS DOMINATE

3.3 Masters, Billionaires, Offers, Kidneys, Surrogacy

3.3.1 Master and servant

Can the dominated exploit the undominated? Wood (1995) argues that instances of pilfering, looting, and small-scale manipulative extraction show that servants can exploit masters.[12] But servants do not, by definition, dominate masters. Therefore exploitation does not entail domination. It follows that the domination account defended in this book is false. More precisely:

(α) If A exploits B, then A dominates B.
(β) Only masters can dominate servants.
(γ) Servants can exploit their masters.

Claim (α) is the domination account; claim (γ) is Wood. Claims (α)–(γ) are not jointly assertible. Crucially, if one affirms (β) and (γ), then it follows that (α) is false. For if there are exploiters who are not masters, such that they do not dominate, then the domination account fails. In defence of (α), I will argue that (γ) is false. I note, in passing, that it is possible to construe pilfering, looting, and manipulative extraction by servants merely as forms of *resistance*. This is one conceptual strand in James Scott's (1987) magisterial account of peasant resistance, which seems to imply that servants cannot exploit their masters. Rather, pilfering and looting merely attenuate the exploitation of servants *by* masters, giving the former a modicum of control over their own lives. This line of argument is promising, but I will not pursue it further. Instead, I will show that (γ) should be rejected for another reason, having to do with the contextual nature of power ascriptions.

In general, the ascription of a domination relationship is time and context sensitive, where context includes information about the resource distribution and background structure. Suppose Goliath possesses mastery over David in contexts C_1 and C_2, whereas David only possesses mastery over Goliath in context C_3. What enables David to destroy Goliath, if he does so, is not his powerlessness, but his (contextually circumscribed) mastery over Goliath.

If this description of the David and Goliath case is sound, then it is conceptually possible that B possesses *local* mastery over A, such that A is B's local servant. A possesses *global* mastery over B if A possesses a sufficient amount

---

[12] See his subtle discussion of Doyle Lonnegan, the main gangster antagonist in the movie *The Sting*.

MASTERS, BILLIONAIRES, OFFERS, KIDNEYS, SURROGACY 77

of local mastery, that is, possesses dominating power over B in a sufficiently large set of (contextually indexed) contexts. Wood's examples of exploitative looting, pilfering and manipulation must therefore be construed as instances of local power, indeed of *local mastery*. As pilferer, you have temporarily, however fleetingly, inverted the social order of master–servant. Now note that, on the domination view, exploiters are, necessarily, local masters. If this is true, then it follows that (γ) is false and (α) are (β) compossible: master-exploiting servants possess *local* mastery over their *globally* servant-dominating masters. Mastery and servitude, I conclude, are less rigid designators than Wood's argument allows.

This conclusion highlights an important dimension in the choice of axiomatic framework. Suppose A locally exploits B by extracting five hours of dominated surplus labour (e.g. in the workplace), while B does the same to A (e.g. in the family). Is total exploitation in this example zero? Or it is double (ten hours)? On an *additive model*, any given exploitative transaction between the same agents must be added to the total. On a *subtractive model*, it can make up for a prior exploitation by the other party. Scott's account of peasant resistance, for example, seems to presuppose something like the subtractive model. Although I believe that the additive model is intuitively more compelling, I leave this choice of axiomatic framework open for the rest of the book.

I now elaborate on the exact scope of the 'offices' of mastery and servitude I have just described.

3.3.2 Exploiting billionaires

Can billionaires be exploited? The *Pit* case, and examples like it, seem to imply that exploitation is possible only if the exploitee is in dire need, lacks reasonable or acceptable alternatives, or is in circumstances of deprivation or duress.[13] These putative presuppositions are all false. Consider:

> *Lawn Mower*—Zuckerberg knows a secret of Gates' that Gates does not want known. Zuckerberg has no moral obligation not to reveal it, despite the harm it will inflict on Gates, and no moral obligation to reveal it. Zuckerberg asks

---

[13] Variants on this idea have been defended by Sample (2003) and Snyder (2008), among many others.

78 HOW EXPLOITERS DOMINATE

Gates to mow his lawn for the year, in return for nonrevelation of the secret. Gates grudgingly agrees.

In *Lawn Mower*, Zuckerberg does not threaten Gates with something independently impermissible—he is permitted to reveal the harmful information. But he does *do* something impermissible, namely exploit Gates. This judgement goes through independently of Gates' basic needs or functionings. That is, *whatever* the threshold for satisfaction of basic needs and reasonable alternatives, Gates meets it, even by his own reckoning, both before and after the sensitive information is revealed.[14] So, if Zuckerberg exploits Gates, then complaints of exploitation go through independently of claims about basic needs and reasonable alternatives. It suffices that Zuckerberg has unilateral control over Gates's effort function—power enough to get Gates to perform some drudgery, such as mowing Zuckerberg's massive lawn for a year—and that such control is not independently justified. Gates performs domination-induced unilateral service for Zuckerberg; he is exploited.

Of course, needs matter. But that is the mattering of moral *weight*, not the mattering of moral *ground*. That is, Zuckerberg's exploitation of Gates is much less morally urgent than Foxconn's exploitation of Shenzhen workers; there are very weighty reasons to try to attenuate the latter before the former. This does not, however, affect the ground of the complaint, which is, in both cases, the conversion of Gates and the Shenzhen workers into someone's servant. And, as I explained in section 3.3.1, the locality or globality of domination ascriptions may also affect their weight.

I now further elaborate on the possibility and nature of exploitative offers.

3.3.3 Lucrative offers

According to the domination account of exploitation, it is not only true that billionaires can exploit billionaires; it is equally true that lucrative offers can be exploitative. Consider:

Lecherous Offer—*A* is a lecherous billionaire; *B* earns the median wage. *A* says to *B*: 'If you sleep with me, I'll give you $1 million. *B* accepts the offer.

---

[14] Is Gates vulnerable to Zuckerberg? On my view, he is both vulnerable in the sense of being under Zuckerberg's power and vulnerable to exploitation. Contrast Valdman (2009) and Liberto (2014), who defend a narrower account of vulnerability.

MASTERS, BILLIONAIRES, OFFERS, KIDNEYS, SURROGACY   79

According to the Non-Servitude Proviso, *Lecherous Offer* is an instance of domination. Does *A* exploit *B*? It depends. The theoretical reason for this ambivalence is that, normally, the *labour content* of $1 million is higher than the labour content of sexual intercourse. This means that, in *Lecherous Offer*, labour may be flowing the wrong way—from *A* to *B*, rather than vice versa. The rest of this section elaborates.

Suppose that the domination account is true, such that exploitation is domination-induced unilateral labour flow. Suppose, further, that *Lecherous Offer* involves domination, in the sense I have already mentioned. If *A* is to exploit *B*, then the amount of labour given by *B* must be greater than the total labour given by *A*. Suppose the labour content of sexual intercourse is eight hours. In the contemporary United States, the labour content of $1 million in 2018 prices is about 14,000 hours.[15] In other words, if the $1 million represents A's labour, and if A's labour is average labour, then *Lecherous Offer* involves A giving 14,000 hours and getting eight. Labour flows the wrong way, from rich to poor, in which case *A* seems not to be exploiting *B*.[16]

Three remarks are relevant here. First, *Lecherous Offer* is an extreme case of a very widely observed phenomenon that generally *does* involve exploitation, namely sex work. Sex workers provide sex in return for a market-determined price. In general, these prices will be lower than $1 million—otherwise demand would be negligible—and tend to reflect a labour content lower than the median or average wage. This implies that sexual labour will, in general, tend to flow from poor to rich—sex worker to client. The domination account *does* dub these cases as exploitative. Second, in the case of *Lecherous Offer*, it matters whether these 14,000 hours—and the $1 million, which is its monetary expression—were accumulated by *A* through his own labour, or through the labour of others. The intuition that *A* exploits *B* may ride on the idea that these 14,000 hours are not *his* to give. If, for example, these hours are the fruit of prior exploitation, then *A* may yet be exploiting *B*. Third, whatever the source of these hours, *A* dominates *B*, even if he does not exploit her.

Now, these methodologically individualistic quibbles may be socially irrelevant to judgements of exploitation, because they ignore *structure*. That is, in order to ascertain whether *A* is an exploiter and *B* an exploitee, we need to know how much labour each contributes and receives as a proportion of

---

[15] The monetary expression of a unit of average labour is given by the ratio between net national product and total hours worked to produce it. My assumption in making the labour-content calculation is that the monetary expression of labour stands at about $70/hour. On the very idea of the monetary expression of labour, see Foley (1982) and Dumenil (1984).

[16] *Lecherous Offer* might therefore be relevantly analogous to the *Domestic Servant* case of section 3.1.2.

80 HOW EXPLOITERS DOMINATE

total social labour, what power relation explains their share, and how their claim to that share is reproduced. So, although it is conceivable that *A* does not exploit *B* in *Lecherous Offer*, there is no conceivable capitalist society in which that eventuality is realized. For, as a matter of structural necessity, capitalism confronts workers with a dilemma: choose between no work—unemployment—and dominated work. Sex workers, like most workers under capitalism, grasp the second horn of this dilemma.[17]

I now explain how these ideas extend to organ markets and reproductive labour.

3.3.4 Kidneys and surrogacy

Are markets in human organs exploitative? Given its emphasis on production, it might seem that the domination account of exploitation excludes, or at least misunderstands, a class of presumptively exploitative transactions, namely exploitation through the sale of blood and human organs. This class of transactions includes the *Pit* case, with the only difference that *A* demands, say, *B*'s kidney, in return for costless rescue. How does the domination account deal with these kinds of cases?

Selling your kidneys, or your blood, can be an instance of exploitation. These transactions not only fall under the generic definition of exploitation offered in this book—self-enrichment through the domination of others; they also involve labour extraction. For the reproduction of our blood and kidneys requires *labour*. To think otherwise is to misunderstand the invariably effortful, often arduous, and sometimes painful, relationship to our own bodies and the bodies of others. A healthy kidney takes time and care to produce and maintain, effort exerted by the kidney owner and by others who contribute directly to its reproduction.[18] Consider:

> *Kibney*—*B* owns a household pet, Kibney. *B* has spent years caring for Kibney, keeping her alive and healthy. Unbeknownst to *B*, a healthy Kibney can be used as a perfect kidney transplant. *A* subsequently finds *B* in a pit. She offers *B* costless rescue in return for Kibney. *B* takes the offer.

---

[17] I discuss the moral bind of capitalist reproduction in Chapter 4. Wollner (2018) offers a relevant defence of structural exploitation and its modal implications.

[18] It is relevant that those others are usually women. The care required for social reproduction is overwhelmingly undertaken by women—mothers, nurses, nannies, and so on. So when the kidney owner is exploited by giving a kidney, her exploiter may, in addition, be benefiting from the structural injustice of a gendered division of labour.

AGAINST THE VULNERABILITY VIEW 81

In *Kibney*, *A* is exploiting *B*, in the sense of coming to control an unjust share of social labour—in this case *B*'s pet-caring reproductive labour. More precisely, the example suggests that, if *A*'s position of power comes to unilaterally entitle her to *B*'s pet-caring labour, then *A* dominates *B*. And if that labour flow is realized, as it is in *Kibney*, then *A* also exploits *B*. The analogy extends, I think, to self-caring labour in relation to any part of one's body.[19]

Now consider contract pregnancy. This involves unilateral alien control over a woman's reproductive capacity. Since that capacity is assimilable to productive purposiveness, as I have defined it, it comes under the purview of the Non-Servitude Proviso; contract pregnancy thereby violates it. And since the domination of the surrogate mother involves unilateral labour flow, in the form of her gestational care for the embryo, surrogate motherhood is exploitative. There is, finally, a conditional version of this argument: if contract pregnancy is exploitative, then so is organ donation for money. Humans are, in a relevant sense, 'pregnant' with their own organs.

These are only some ways of preserving the emphasis on unilateral labour flow in the light of influential presumptive counterexamples, which conclude my exposition on the domination account of exploitation. This account does not stand or fall with the idea of labour extraction. But it does lose intuitive appeal without it, since the master distinction between service and servitude becomes more difficult to draw. I now offer further refinements, by contrasting the domination theory with, and defending it against, influential competing theories of exploitation.

3.4 Against the Vulnerability View

One competing account of the unjust features of *Pit* is the *vulnerability view*. On this view, *A* exploits *B* if and only if *A* treats *B*'s vulnerabilities as opportunities to advance her own interests (Wood 1995, p. 136). *A*'s *Pit* offer, for example, qualifies as treating *B*'s vulnerabilities as opportunities to advance her own interests. Therefore, *A* exploits *B*. Richard Arneson maintains that the vulnerability view expresses sentiments that are 'too high-minded' (Arneson 2016a, p. 10). He asks us to imagine:

---

[19] This conclusion does not presuppose that organ transplants, transfusions, and the like are costly to donors or recipients. Even if Kibney can painlessly enter the recipient's body and work 'out of the box' as a perfect kidney transplant, the exercise of unilateral control over Kibney's reproduction is still exploitative.

82 HOW EXPLOITERS DOMINATE

> *Cancer Treatment*—I live in an isolated rural region, in a region in which health care insurance is unavailable. There is only one qualified surgeon in the territory. After a routine check-up she informs me that I have a cancer that will swiftly kill me unless surgery is done. Only she can do the surgery. I'd be willing to give everything I own in exchange for the needed surgery, but the actual price she charges is modest, better than fair. This is business as usual for the surgeon. She makes her living by striking bargains like this with people in conditions like mine. She makes a good living.
>
> (Arneson 2016a, p. 10)

Arneson maintains that there is nothing exploitative about the surgeon's behaviour in this example. Yet she *does* take advantage of the patient's vulnerability, or treats it as an opportunity to advance her own interests. The vulnerability view thus generates false positives. Richard Miller has recently argued, along similar lines:

> Allen Wood . . . has claimed that capitalist exploitation is, prima facie, wrong because it derives from workers' weakness or vulnerability and all benefits derived from another's weakness or vulnerability are, prima facie, wrong. But the latter description of the tainting feature leads to the absurd conclusion that oncologists and personal trainers are engaged, *prima facie*, in a morally shady enterprise.   (Miller 2017, p. 23)

I now argue that the domination view does not take the surgeon or the personal trainer to be exploiting, for it is not a variant of the vulnerability view.

The first thing to note is that the original *Pit* case and the *Cancer treatment* case are importantly distinct, as the latter involves stipulation of a 'modest, better than fair price' (Arneson 2016a, p. 10).[20] How is this fair price determined? On Arneson's view, exploitation necessarily violates a fairness baseline, the distributive outcome that maximizes some responsibility-constrained prioritarian value function. Call this the *fairness view*—I will discuss its plausibility later. For the moment, it suffices that the domination view, much like the fairness view, can discriminate between *Cancer treatment* and *Pit*. For *Cancer treatment* does not imply that A, the surgeon, dominates B, the patient. Let me explain.

In Chapter 2, I argued that a necessary condition for domination is that A subordinates B's purposiveness to her own, thereby treating B as a servant. One

---

[20] I note, in passing, that 'modest' entails nonzero price, a position that is not argued for by Arneson.

elaboration of this condition is the Non-Servitude Proviso. Its implications are suggestive of how the domination view and the vulnerability view part ways: the Proviso is not clearly satisfied in Arneson's and Miller's examples. Why think, for example, that Arneson's surgeon subordinates the patient's purposiveness? To ascertain that, we need more information about background structure and about the form of the surgeon's control over the patient's actions. So the domination view does not, on the face of it, generate the kinds of false positives that Arneson attributes to the vulnerability view. By implication, the former is generically more discriminating than the latter.

Arneson also charges the domination view with overgenerating exploitation complaints in another class of cases. For example:

> Comeupance—For a time my wife is unemployed, and her bargaining position when it comes to family interactions is weak. I successfully demand that we watch a steady diet of horror movies and grade B action films. The tables are suddenly turned. She now has a good job and I have no steady income. She now drives a hard bargain when the question arises, what movies to see. We end up watching a stream of romantic comedies, which she likes far more than I do.   (Arneson 2016a, p. 11)

In response to this example, Arneson claims that 'the transaction as described contributes toward an overall just outcome (more just than would occur if the transaction did not occur) and does so in a way that is not procedurally unfair or wrongful' (Arneson 2016a, p. 15). It therefore does not involve exploitation. *Pace* Arneson, I think that two of these three judgements—namely, that *Comeupance* is procedurally innocuous and that it is not exploitative—are questionable. Suppose that A prefers horror and B prefers comedy. They arrive at the following arrangement: B will be A's slave on Mondays and A will be B's slave on Tuesdays. Monday slavery implies that both watch horror—satisfying A's preference—and Tuesday slavery implies that both watch comedy—satisfying B's preference.

This trading-place slavery is surely objectionable, procedurally and otherwise. It is also exploitative.[21] So *Comeupance* and trading-place slavery seem to share an unjust feature, namely mutually beneficial reciprocal domination.[22] On the domination view, therefore, both cases involve exploitation.

---

[21] See Chapter 3, section 3.3.1.
[22] One important difference between the two examples is that *Comeupance* originally involves patriarchy—the structural domination of women. This feature could be assumed away if both agents in Arneson's example were male.

84 HOW EXPLOITERS DOMINATE

Arneson has a rejoinder. He offers a 'reciprocity' version of the same example, in which A and B take turns, alternating between horror and comedy. He maintains that B's power over A 'ensures this fair result occurs'. When this happens, '[s]he brings about a just outcome by a not unfair means.' (Arneson 2016a, p. 19). Thus, although B possesses power over A, and B benefits from that power, B does not exploit A.

Arneson's amendment is too underdetermined to yield his conclusion. For surely it matters whether B gets A to watch comedy through credible threats of enslavement, beating, or death, *even if* A can credibly threaten similar sanctions should B not watch horror. In other words, when the rotation occurs in such a way that A and B dominate each other, the outcome—whether fair or unfair—is tainted. That outcome is more like trading-place slavery and less like a kingdom of ends: it is a reciprocity of servitude, not freedom. On the domination view, to exploit is to benefit through such servitude. Arneson's examples, as presented, seem compatible with exploitation, in that sense.

3.5 Against the Fairness View

I now turn the tables against Arneson, Cohen, and Roemer. I do this by vindicating the domination view against the fairness view. On the fairness view, A exploits B if and only if A takes unfair advantage of B, where the unfairness baseline is decided by background distribution. I will adhere to one influential formulation of this view, due to Arneson, and raise two objections: one from *lenience* and one from *trivialization*. According to the lenience objection, the fairness view is too lenient on predatory, but prudent, proposers. According to the trivialization objection, the fairness view trivializes the concept of exploitation, making it a mere upshot of distributive injustice. If successful, these objections, in conjunction with the positive account defended in this book, suffice to shift the burden of proof on the nature and grounds of exploitation.

3.5.1 The lenience objection

Like Cohen and Roemer, Arneson subscribes to a luck egalitarian definition of the fairness baseline, according to which we 'maximize a function of human well-being that gives priority to improving the well-being of those who are badly off and of those who, if badly off, are not substantially responsible

AGAINST THE FAIRNESS VIEW   85

for their condition in virtue of their prior conduct' (Arneson 2000, p. 340). Equality in the relevant metric is desirable if and only if it is responsibility-constrained. The rest of this section explains why this account is inadequate. Consider:

> *Ant and Grasshopper*–Ant works hard all summer and has ample provisions for the winter. Grasshopper lazes about and in January has an empty cupboard. Without interaction, Grasshopper will end up with welfare level two, which amounts to dire misery, and Ant with three, bare sufficiency, and in this scenario Ant is comparatively more deserving; the gap between the welfare level Ant has and what he deserves is far greater for him than is the comparable gap for Grasshopper. Ant proposes to sell some provisions to Grasshopper at a very high price. Grasshopper accepts the deal, though he would prefer to pay less and get more. With this deal in place, Grasshopper ends up with welfare level three and Ant with twelve. Even after this transaction, Ant's welfare level is less than he deserves, by comparison with the situation of Grasshopper.   (Arneson 2016a, p. 11)

Arneson claims that 'there is nothing *prima facie* wrongful' in what the Ant does when she charges for (costless) provisions at a very high price.[23] He thinks this conclusion follows from the unfairness view. *Pace* Arneson, this valid argument shows why the fairness view is false. More precisely, if the *Pit* case involves exploitation, then so does *Ant and Grasshopper*. Suppose, for example, that by failing to accumulate provisions, Grasshopper finds herself incapable of fighting soil erosion. This lands her at the bottom of a pit. Ant walks up to her to offer a sweatshop contract for the rest of Grasshopper's life, when she could have offered costless shelter. The possibilities, in the relevant metric, are:

(Ant, Grasshopper)

   (i): do nothing: (10, 0);
  (ii): sweatshop: (11, 1);
 (iii): shelter: (10, 2).

Now, it is plausible to think that Ant has an obligation to help Grasshopper. But one need not have a view on *that* to believe that (ii) is morally worse than (iii). That is, *if* Ant decides to help (decides to do something other than (i))

---

[23] Note that exploitation does not presuppose monopoly power or the absence of competition: the 'very high price' might reflect the perfectly competitive cost price of such provisions.

86 HOW EXPLOITERS DOMINATE

then she must not opt for (ii), in part *because* doing so constitutes exploitation. I take the widely shared intuition expressed in this consequent as evidence that the domination account is plausible. But now note that, if (ii) involves exploitation, then distributive injustice furnishes no necessary condition for it. For, according to Arneson, all of (i), (ii), (iii) are equally acceptable at the bar of distributive justice.[24]

Arneson—along with Cohen and Roemer—has nothing to oppose to such a cleanly generated sweatshop contract on exploitation grounds, and this is an embarrassment to his claims to offering an egalitarian theory of exploitation. He can, of course, reply that a cleanly generated sweatshop faces exploitation-independent objections. But this is beside the point: Chapter 2 showed that cleanly generated capitalism is interesting precisely because of *the pit-like nature it shares with its unclean cousins*. Some pits, like some capitalisms, are cleanly generated. Yet both are exploitative. This result generalizes, I believe, to *any* theory of exploitation that posits some defensible account of distributive injustice as a necessary condition for exploitation.[25]

According to the domination view, by contrast, Ant's behaviour in *Ant and Grasshopper* is no different from *A's Pit* behavior: both prey on the weak for self-enrichment, when both have the (costless) option of helping without so preying. Both thereby muster their power to convert others into their servants and, in so doing, exploit them.[26]

Arneson rejects this conclusion. He believes that the fairness view will not always take 'excessive' offers to be exploitative, independently of the historical sequence of events that led to them. Luck egalitarianism is, after all, a historical entitlement theory of justice (see Cohen 2011, Chapter 6). But then his view lets some forms of predatory behavior, such as Ant's, completely off the hook.

---

[24] (ii) is, after all, an upshot of Grasshopper's own choices or faults. One can construct examples where the demands of distributive justice are not only unnecessary for, but also *contradict* (what are, intuitively) claims of exploitation.

[25] Take another prominent example: Rawlsian leximin. Leximin does indeed dub (iii) as the most just distribution of widgets, and therefore seems to give the intuitive answer. But the result is misleading. Suppose the shelter outcome turns out to provide no substantial improvement in Grasshopper's condition, as follows:

(Ant, Grasshopper)
  (i) do nothing: (10, 0);
  (ii) sweatshop: (11, 1);
(iii) shelter: (10, 1).

In this case, leximin dubs (ii) as the most just distribution, and therefore produces the same counterintuitive result (and so does maximin, which recommends choosing between (ii) and (iii) on a coin toss). Exploitation and distributive injustice again part ways.

[26] This does not mean that Grasshopper's behaviour is morally permissible. It is impermissible on non-exploitation grounds and may be impermissible on exploitation grounds. See Ferguson (2016) and Chapter 7 for a critique of unconditional basic income along these lines.

AGAINST THE FAIRNESS VIEW   87

This is the *obverse* of Anderson's (1999) famous complaint that luck egalitarianism is too harsh on vulnerable, but imprudent, proposal recipients. That is, whether or not Anderson is right, *luck egalitarianism is too lenient on predatory, but prudent, proposers*. In treating such proposers too leniently, the fairness view generates false negatives.[27]

Dworkin (2000) offers a similar objection. He maintains that our choices should reflect the costs they impose on others. Applied to cases like *Ant and Grasshopper* this idea sounds compelling. But its general application as a theory of justice overreaches, because the justice of any given instance of burden-shifting depends on a prior entitlement to impose such costs. If you really like omelettes, and I buy the last few eggs, thereby depriving you of means to omelette production, I cannot be expected to bear the cost to you of that purchase. Things are different if I deprive you of the ability to nourish yourself or to set and pursue ends, independently of the specific end of omelette consumption. It follows that domination—the subsumption of your purposiveness—is prior to the concern for burden-shifting or opportunity costs. And conversely, if my setting and pursuing ends requires eggs, and if eggs are very scarce, then the requirements of my agency require that I pay a high price, so high that the egg owner comes to hold my agency hostage. Once again, my entitlements and my cost-reflecting choices part ways.[28]

There are, of course, weaker specifications of the Dworkinian position. One of them is the idea that it is bad, because unfair, if some are worse off than others through no fault of their own. This thought carries no presumption that pit-ridden people can permissibly be denied rescue, or even that they themselves can permissibly fail to buy cheap insurance against rescue. But, unless we are told how these normative constraints are justified, they seem like mere adjuncts to the luck egalitarian theory. The Non-Servitude Proviso's emphasis on mutual independence can justify these normative constraints, so it is potentially complementary to a weak specification of the Dworkinian position. It is therefore possible that, although unfairness and exploitation are distinct injustices, they may have complementary explanatory roles.

---

[27] Arneson's attempt to soften the harshness of luck egalitarianism by appeal to a desert-based, as opposed to a choice-based, specification of luck egalitarianism, or by acceding to a pluralist understanding of its well-being requirements (2016a p. 11), is moot in cases like *Ant and Grasshopper*. For Grasshopper is not merely imprudent; she is completely undeserving (absolutely or comparatively, pluralistically or monistically). And yet exploiting her still seems wrongful.

[28] This neither entails nor presupposes a commitment to subsidizing 'expensive tastes', as Cohen (2011) would have it. The whole debate between Cohen and Dworkin set out from a false moral generalization.

88 HOW EXPLOITERS DOMINATE

I conclude this chapter by raising a further objection against strong versions of the fairness account, especially those defended by Arneson, Cohen, and Roemer.

3.5.2 The trivialization objection

There is another, more general, problem with the Arneson, Cohen, and Roemer unfairness view, namely that it trivializes the concept of exploitation. Consider:

> *Free Riders*—Farmers take turns standing sentry at night, or are asked to pay a fair share of the costs of maintaining the sentry scheme, which provides safety for all neighborhood residents as a kind of public good. For residents of the neighborhood, if anyone gains sentry scheme safety, all residents must gain some of this good... Some residents decline to pay their fair share of the costs of maintaining the scheme. They do this in order to free ride; they understand that others will continue to supply the good even if they decline to contribute. This is unfair taking of advantage, I would say, and exploitive. But the free riders are not plausibly viewed as possessing social power over the other cooperators.   (Arneson 2016b, p. 6)

According to Arneson, the non-cooperators exploit, but do not possess power over the cooperators. The former *a fortiori* do not dominate the latter. Therefore, Arneson maintains, exploitation does not presuppose domination.

Unlike Arneson, I believe that the non-cooperators only exploit if the explanation for the cooperators' cooperation can be traced back to the power of the non-cooperators. Recall that the Non-Servitude Proviso is about independently mandatory cooperation (e.g. for mutual protection). If a group of non-cooperators can shirk its duties at the expense of the cooperators, such that the former subjects the latter to its unilateral choice, then the former exploits and thereby dominates the latter. The Proviso censures the office of the non-cooperators, just as it censures the office of those standing above pits in the expectation that others will fall into them, thereby providing a source of enrichment. In all of these cases, the non-cooperators have some degree of unilateral control over the cooperators' purposiveness. So if the non-cooperators in *Free riders* extract sentry services through such power and not through mere luck, then they engage in acts of exploitation.

AGAINST THE FAIRNESS VIEW   89

It does not follow, however, that *all* unfair free riding counts as exploitation. If the non-cooperators benefit through no control over the cooperators' conditions of agency, then they merely benefit unfairly. Consider a parallel case where *A* wants to get to the other side of river. She trips and falls into *B*'s boat. *A* free rides on *B*'s rowing effort, which helps her get to the other side of the river. It is plausible that *A* takes advantage—perhaps even *unfair* advantage—of *B*. On the domination view, however, she does not exploit.[29] Only subjection-grounded advantage-taking constitutes exploitation, on that view.[30]

On the fairness view, by contrast, 'unfair treatment' and 'exploitation' are used interchangeably. What is the extra purchase of saying that *A exploits B*, on this view? Arneson's answer is 'not much': 'I come empty pockets when asked, what moral principle or standard determines what makes voluntary exchange fair or unfair, exploitative or nonexploitative.' (Arneson 2016a, p. 28). Perhaps, on Arneson's view, exploitation terms serve to *categorize* fairness terms. It is unclear how they do even that. But suppose that Arneson is right about the concept of exploitation, whose contours are defined by the fairness view. I claim that there is a concept distinct from Arneson's, call it *explomination*, whose contours are defined by the domination view, and which takes cases like *Pit* and *Ant and Grasshopper* as paradigmatic of unjust advantage-taking. If I am right about these instances, then explomination captures features of unjust advantage-taking that are surplus to exploitation: explomination is explanatorily superior to exploitation in that respect. We should think of cases like *Pit*, *Ant and Grasshopper*, and *Comeupance* in terms of explomination, not exploitation.

There is, I conclude, a fundamental disagreement between advocates of the fairness view and advocates of the domination view as to the bigger picture: the latter takes exploitation claims to be about relations of dominion and servitude. The former takes them to be about unfairness and maldistribution. On the one hand, the fairness view gives the wrong verdict on cases like *Ant and Grasshopper* and *Pit*. If the lenience objection is sound, then the fairness view generates false negatives. On the other hand, the fairness view is unable to account for the distinctive features of naked instances of unfair treatment— such as the boat case—and cases involving abuse of power—such as *Free riders*.

---

[29] Depending on the details, the case can be made that *A* has power over *B* even in the boat case: an invisibility cloak, for example, would certainly confer power on *A*, so as to make *B* exploitable in the way required by the domination view.

[30] Recall that exploitation is only *a* reason against an exploitative transaction. Unfairness and exploitation are distinct injustices.

90 HOW EXPLOITERS DOMINATE

If the trivialization objection is sound, then the canonical liberal view deprives exploitation claims of any distinctive moral bite. It should be rejected for these reasons.

Conclusion

This chapter has argued that exploitation is a form of domination, namely self-enrichment through the domination of others. According to the domination account, such self-enrichment involves the power-induced extraction of unilateral service from others. I have argued that this account of exploitation is distinct from competing theories of exploitation; that it captures intuitions about predatory behaviour and about the special explanatory function of exploitation complaints surplus to these theories, and that it is superior to these theories for these reasons. More specifically, the domination account provides a novel way of thinking about generic vulnerability, as well as about sex and organ markets, reproductive labour, and lucrative offers on the basis of claims of unilateral control over alien labour. Chapter 4 discusses the structural nature of these complaints, when they are structural.

Appendix: Rich and poor

Section 3.1.3 mooted Roemer's *Rich and Poor* example. The example is important, because it implies that labour flow is indispensable to any account of exploitation. Yet the example seems to involve domination-induced unilateral labour flow, *on the part of Poor*. Are we to infer that Poor exploits Rich, in Roemer's example? I think we should. Here's why.

In Roemer's setup, Rich and Poor's respective endowments of 3 and 1 are not proportional to the power each of them has over the other. Indeed, in *Rich and Poor*, Poor has more power over Rich than vice versa. And if Poor can rope Rich into unilaterally serving Poor, then Poor exploits Rich. This is a palatable conclusion because Roemer's world is not our world. In our world, total wealth is normally proportional to power over others. This has to do with the specific form that wealth assumes here.

More precisely, our world is well-described, as a first pass, by this sentence: 'The wealth of those societies, in which the capitalist mode of production reigns, presents itself as an "immense heap of commodities."' (Marx 1976, p. 125). If this is true, if wealth in its totality is power-conferring, and if enough social relations are commodified, then social wealth will confer power on those who possess enough commodities. That power, *capital*, is monetary title to unilaterally command the labour performance of others in the economy as a whole.[31] So either *Rich and Poor* does not represent a capitalist society—in which case Roemer's endowments are *not* capital—or Rich is not really rich and Poor is not really poor, in the relevant sense.

---

[31] This is one of the great discoveries of Marx's critique of political economy, which I discuss in Chapter 5.

4

Structural Domination in the Market

This book argues that exploitation is a form of domination: it is the realization of the extractive powers of the powerful. If this is true, then structural exploitation is simply the realization of the *structurally conferred* extractive power of the powerful. More precisely, structural exploitation is a relational property that includes more than the interagential dyad between exploiter and exploitee. That surplus quality of specifically *structural* exploitation, I now argue, recalls questions about agency and structure, as well as theories of class and state.

This chapter develops these ideas. It argues for the cogency of the concept of structural domination and for its application to capitalist economic structure. The chapter develops and defends a triadic account of structural domination, according to which structural domination (e.g. patriarchy, white supremacy, capitalism) is a three-place relation between dominator(s), dominated, and regulator(s)—the constitutive domination dyad plus those social roles non-contingently upholding it. The chapter elaborates on the relationship between structure and agency from the perspective of both oppressor and oppressed and discusses the deduction of the concept of the capitalist state from the concept of capitalism. On the basis of these definitions, it shows that structural domination under capitalism presupposes collective power but not joint agency or shared intentions on the part of the dominators.

The chapter has two parts. The first, conceptual, part argues that structural domination is a triadic relation. The second, normative, part applies this idea to capitalist economic structure. More precisely, section 4.1 discusses the grounds of domination and introduces the triadic account of structural domination. Sections 4.2 and 4.3 use that account to offer a definition of structural domination. Section 4.4 argues that the capital relation, the relation between capital and labour, is one of domination. Section 4.5 explains under what conditions that domination becomes structural. It does this by arguing that the concept of capitalism entails the concept of the state. Section 4.6 introduces the agential account of the state and discusses its connections with collective agency. Section 4.7 distinguishes between two forms of structural exploitation: vertical and horizontal. Section 4.8 discusses the girth of the capitalist cage across space and time.

Exploitation as Domination: What Makes Capitalism Unjust. Nicholas Vrousalis, Oxford University Press.
© Nicholas Vrousalis 2023. DOI: 10.1093/oso/9780192867698.003.0005

4.1 The Structure of Structural Domination

The account of structural domination provided in this chapter is meant to be compatible with different theories of what makes domination unjust: Kantian, republican, and recognitional.[1] These grounds pertain to *individual freedom*: the independence of the individual. Individual independence, in general, consists in nonsubjection of purposiveness to the choices of others. Applied to work relations, such independence is violated when others possess unilateral control over your productive purposiveness—your labour capacity. This chapter studies the structural dimension of these complaints, when they are structural.

I begin by studying the logic of structural domination. Cages, cathedrals, molecules, and propositions have structures. To say that a cathedral has a structure is to say that there is a relation between its parts—wall, buttress, nave, and tower. The constituents of this structure constitute the cathedral, not its structure. It follows that cathedral structure can survive even if all its constituent parts are replaced: Notre-Dame Cathedral's structure would survive even if all its walls and buttresses were simultaneously replaced. The same is true of other social structures. Consider prisons. Wholesale replacement of all of a prison's constituents—its staff, cells, bricks, or mortar—need not affect its structure. The question is what constitutes that structure.

4.1.1 Structural power relations in general

This section argues that a complete description of specifically *structural* power relations involves a triadic relationship between those who possess power, those who are subject to power, and certain third parties—role-occupants or norm-internalizers—whom I will call *regulators*. To focus intuitions, consider:

Promise Relation—Promisor promises Promisee to give her a copy of *Crime and Punishment*.

Promises are institutional facts[2] that confer on Promisee a power over Promisor—in this case, the deontic power to demand or waive compliance with Promisor's antecendently undertaken obligation. Call this the *constitutive*

---

[1] For a juxtaposition between these three views, see Chapter 2.
[2] On institutional facts see Rawls (1955) and Searle (1964).

94   STRUCTURAL DOMINATION IN THE MARKET

power dyad. The institution of promising defines, in addition to offices (such as the promisor/promisee dyad), moves (under what conditions the utterance 'I promise' counts as a promise), penalties for noncompliance, and so on.[3]

Now contrast:

Promise Structure—Promisor promises Promisee to give her a copy of *Crime and Punishment.* Regulator is a bystander disposed to reward Promisor's compliance with her obligation and to penalize noncompliance.

Regulator's addition to the example completes the structure (or practice)[4] of promising: regulators define offices and legitimate moves, in addition to instituting and enforcing payoffs corresponding to these moves. Regulators thereby *impart structure* to the promise relation by stabilizing existing offices and by providing assurance of compliance to their officeholders—a function that requires independence from these offices.[5] That is, even when the regulators are existing officeholders, their actions as regulators do not exemplify their offices, as such: Promisor, for example, is not *promising* when she takes steps to ensure that she can fulfill existing promises or perform new promises in the future. In her regulative role, Promisor may be enforcing, applying or interpreting the content of an existing promise, as long as others grant her independent title to do so.

This idea generalizes: a complete description of any structural power relation involves a three-place relation[6] between the officeholders of the constitutive power dyad plus the regulators (in this case: Promisor, Promisee, Regulator). In other words:

(1)   Structural power relations are triadic relations.

In terms of our original cathedral analogy, regulators relate to the constitutive power dyad in the way cathedral roofs relate to cathedral walls: without the roof, the walls are unstable and, in a sense, structurally incomplete. To put the architectural analogy in old-fashioned sociological terms, bases need

---

[3] As I explained in Chapter 2, these need not be legal obligations. A surgeon is someone widely recognized as being able to successfully perform surgery and who will, in appropriate conditions, do so. The institution of surgery confers offices and deontic powers on both surgeon and patient, whether legal or merely conventional.

[4] I use 'practice' and 'structure' interchangeably, as does Rawls (1955).

[5] Ripstein (2009, chapter 6) argues that the normativity, determinacy, and enforcement of private rights requires some form of public power. My account of structure is complementary to Ripstein's.

[6] Strictly speaking: a $n + 1$-place relation, where n is the number of places in the power relation.

THE STRUCTURE OF STRUCTURAL DOMINATION 95

superstructures.[7] I now explain how structural power is related to structural domination, by arguing for:

(2)   Structural domination is a structural power relation.

Roughly speaking, the idea behind (2) is that if the dominator's power is structural, then the vehicle of that power is a third-party role which may, but need not, be occupied by the dominator herself.

4.1.2   Structural domination in general

To motivate the contrast between interagential and structural features, consider:

> *Interagential Domination*—Man finds Woman in a pit. Man can get Woman out at little cost or difficulty, but demands an extortionate price to do so. Man would have done the same to a man and a man could just as easily have found himself in the pit.

The account of domination defended in this book holds that an agent dominates another just when he unilaterally, arbitrarily or misrecognitively subjects her choices to his own ends. Suppose that *Interagential domination* is objectionable in that sense, such that Man dominates Woman.[8] Even so, given that he would have done the same to a man, and that a man could just as easily have found himself in the pit, Man does not dominate *as* man; Man's domination of Woman is merely interagential. Contrast:

> *Structural Domination*—Regulator pushes women, and only women, into pits. Regulator pushes Woman into a pit. This enables Man to demand an extortionate price from Woman in return for extracting her from the pit.

In this example, Regulator confers structure to the domination relation, in exactly the same way that Regulator confers structure to the promise relation. More precisely, Regulator makes the domination structural *and* gives it its discriminating character (in this case, as a form of sexism). Moreover, if power

---

[7] See Cohen (1978, p. 231) for an influential defence of this claim. In section 4.4, I discuss the relevant sense of 'need' and reject Cohen's specification of it as too weak.

[8] Types ('man', 'woman') are, I assume, extensionally individuated.

and vulnerability are extensionally equivalent, as I argued in Chapter 3, then Man's structural power entails Woman's structural vulnerability further and vice versa.

Some philosophers think that all power has this triadic character. Wartenberg (1988), for example, suggests that *all* power relations involve regulators—he calls them 'peripheral social others'. It follows that all power is triadic. But Wartenberg's premiss is untenable: in the two-person world where Adam extorts Eve, we should think that Adam dominates Eve, and that's the end of it. Some domination is merely dyadic and therefore not structural.[9] I now elaborate on the position of the regulators in structural power relations.

In the examples used so far, the regulators help constitute the constitutive power dyad while remaining somehow external to it. External in what sense? Consider the relationship between cathedral wall and roof. Cathedral walls have powers, including the power to support each other. What confers that power on each wall, let us suppose, is the cathedral's roof. But what *confers* a power is not identical[10] with that power or with its possessor; to think otherwise is to commit the vehicle fallacy. So roofs can co-constitute the power of walls (e.g. the power to support other walls), while lacking that power themselves; roofs *regulate* the constitutive power relation between walls. I claim that all instances of structural domination have the same triadic structure: they involve *pit-like dyads constituted by third-party entities—the regulators—who complete the triad*. Figure 4.1 illustrates this point schematically.

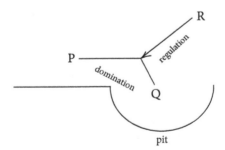

Figure 4.1 Regulated domination

---

[9] Wartenberg uses the teacher–student relationship as an illustration of the putatively general point that *all* power is structural: 'A student's well-being is affected by the grade in the first place only through the mediation of human being situated outside of the classroom, who use the grade as a sign that results in their administreting "harm" to the student' (Wartenberg 1988, p. 322). This argument confuses individual instances of the practice of student grading, which may involve 'harm', with the general practice of student grading and evaluation. 'Harm' is not part of the constitutive conditions of grading and neither is the 'harmful' disposition of third parties. Otherwise we couldn't meaningfully speak of 'harmless', 'justified', or 'good' evaluation practices and powers. Gädeke (2020) defends Wartenberg's position.

[10] That is, conceptually distinct and extensionally nonequivalent.

THE STRUCTURE OF STRUCTURAL DOMINATION   97

One virtue of this account of structural power is that it does not confuse power, its possessors, its vehicles, and its effects. Structures, from prisons to universities, are vehicles of power, but cannot themselves possess power. It follows that structures cannot dominate anyone. Moreover, the possessors of power, from prison guards to professors, need not themselves confer power on the offices they possess. Power, its possessors, and its vehicles are distinct co-constitutive features. Finally, the effects of power—for example, on subjectivity—bear no necessary connection to its constitution, which is why they are peripheral to the study of domination.[11] I provisionally conclude that structural domination is a triadic relation. To summarize the conceptual part of the argument so far:

(1)   Structural power relations are triadic relations.

(2)   Structural domination is a structural power relation.

So (3)   Structural domination is a triadic relation.

Claim (1) is the theory of structural power sketched above. Claim (2) is part of the definition of structural domination. If this argument for (3) is sound, then structural domination just is a relationship between dominator P, dominated Q, and regulator R. Now, it is worth noting that P and Q might themselves be regulators, although not in their roles as dominator/dominated. So, for example, when the playground bully exhorts her friends to bully vulnerable others, or sharpens the stick she will use to perform her bullying, she is not *bullying*; rather, she is making (future) bullying possible. In so doing, she acts as regulator, not *as* bully. Structure, it bears repeating, allows agents to occupy multiple offices, other than the offices of dominator/dominated. I now elaborate on some implications of this view.

It follows from my account of structural domination that the existence of the office of regulator constrains dominators to act in certain ways, at least if their acts are to constitute the domination of others. Roofs regulate, and, in so doing, *constrain* what walls can do. By the same token, Regulator constrains what both Man and Woman can do in *Structural Domination*. These constraints, however, are not necessarily unfreedom-conferring. That is, it is false that dominators like Man are unfree *qua* dominators. Instead, the existence of Regulator is what enables Man to systematically dominate Woman, that is,

[11]   Much of the contemporary debate on 'biopolitics' fails to register these distinctions. See Searle (2009, p. 152).

98 STRUCTURAL DOMINATION IN THE MARKET

makes Man structurally powerful and Woman structurally vulnerable.[12] So certain structural constraints are merely enabling, as opposed to unfreedom-conferring. To think otherwise is to confuse domination's conditions of possibility (i.e. the existence of regulators) with its *subject* (i.e. the dominator). This conflation between the subject and ground of domination can be theoretically consequential. For example, it pervades Vaclav Havel's otherwise illuminating discussion of the 'post-totalitarian system'. Let me explain.

Havel (1985) shows that the individual greengrocer who ostentatiously signals her commitment to the Party line in her grocery does not do it because she is committed to the ideal. Rather, she does it out of fear of being accused of disloyalty *by symmetrically situated others*. Havel brilliantly demonstrates that this equilibrium is upheld through a 'dictatorship of the ritual'. But it does not follow, as he suggests, that this is a dictatorship without dictators.[13] That is, despite the Party officialdom's inability to directly apply and enforce sanctions for disloyalty, the dictatorship of the ritual confers on that officialdom a reputation of power over others. And since the 'reputation of power is power',[14] the Havelian rituals confer power on Party officialdom. The officialdom, in other words, draws its power from the ritualistic behaviour of nonofficials such as the greengrocer. In my terms: some nonofficials are regulators of the official/nonofficial power dyad, and their existence is the *ground* of official power. But officialdom is still the *subject* of that power. Similar strictures apply to structural domination in the case of gender, race, and class, as I will argue below.

Drawing on the set of claims defended in this section, I now offer a definition of structural domination.

4.2 Structuration = Regulation

The triadic account of structural domination implies the following definition of structural domination:

Regulated Domination—A given instance of domination is structural just when it involves a triadic relationship between powerful agent(s) P, disem-

---

[12] That prison guards or slaveowners are structurally constrained to do what constitutes the domination of prisoners or slaves does not make prison guards and slaveowners unfree. It is precisely due to regulator-constituted constraints that the dominators are free and the dominated are unfree. See Frye (1983) for an extensive argument to that effect.

[13] See Basu (1986) for a rigorous defence of Havel's inference.

[14] Hobbes (1994, p. 70).

STRUCTURATION = REGULATION 99

powered agent(s) Q, and regulator(s) R, such that (i) P dominates Q and (ii) R regulates that domination.

On this view, structural domination is *regulated*, that is, domination co-constituted by agents or roles external to the constitutive power dyad. Call this the *regulation condition*.[15] The regulation condition does not, by itself, tell us what domination does to the dominated. By way of illustration, consider common-stock instances of the patriarchy: the wife-abusing husband, the lecherous male boss, the pornographer who stigmatizes women. What makes these instances of structural *domination*?

A possibility that suggests itself is that women under the patriarchy are faced with a dilemma between performing an independently valuable activity *by the leave of men* and not performing it at all. Patriarchal norms, for example, make women unfree by making them either abstain from familial relations altogether or participate on men's terms.[16] Similarly, when pornographic norms restrict access to empowering sexual possibilities for women, women have to choose between nonsex and sex in conformity with the model of male fantasy. Call this the *double-bind condition*.[17] Both regulation and double-bind are central to the arguments that follow. I now consider some provisional implications of these definitions.

Regulated Domination is a modal definition of structural domination, in two senses. In the first place, it implies that structural domination is not just about the actual choices of structurally dominated agents or groups, but also about their *subjunctive* choices. That is, according to this definition, Q is dominated even in the nearby possible world in which she abstains from any interaction with P: the unmarried woman in a patriarchal society and the celibate woman in the pornography-saturated society are both dominated. In the second place, the definition explains a modal feature of structurally dominated choice, namely the clustering of subaltern optimizing behaviour

---

[15] The most philosophically advanced critics of structural domination are feminists. For some recent and relevant examples, see Cudd (2006), Einspahr (2010), Haslanger (2010), MacKinnon (1989), Marin (2018) and Young (2011).

[16] I discuss the double anonymity of patriarchies that allow exit options in Chapter 2, section 2.1.

[17] If the regulation and double-bind conditions hold, then patriarchy may be the collective power of women, lost to men, *as* men. The double-bind condition explains how unsubjected purposiveness is removed from women's choice sets; the regulation condition explains how, through the intervention of the regulators, that restriction attains its pro-men determinate directionality. *Regulated Domination* therefore implies that patriarchy is the systematic disempowerment of women with respect to their ability to self-direct their free purposiveness. Under the cover of legal and informal norms, devised, upheld, and enforced by the regulators, women's powers are placed at the disposal of—are alienated to—men 'in a male way' (MacKinnon 1983, p. 645). Once again, women's powers are lost to men, *as* men.

100 STRUCTURAL DOMINATION IN THE MARKET

around the disjunction of abstinence from social interaction and domination. The thicker the bars, the thicker the clustering, and the fewer the opportunities for the undominated option of free, mutually-affirming activity.

To conclude this section: I have offered a triadic definition of domination and suggested that this definition fares well in many of the cases that exercise liberals, republicans, and feminists. I now ask what counts as a regulator in the definition of structural domination.

4.3 Defining the Regulation Function

A regulator is any agent or role-occupant contributing appropriately to the creation, reproduction, or perpetuation of the constitutive power dyad.[18] The question is what counts as 'appropriately'. I consider three possible specifications of the regulation function: causal, expressive, and moralized.

(a) *Causal regulation*: R is a regulator just when R contributes causally to P's domination of Q.

(b) *Expressive regulation*: R is a regulator just when R contributes expressively to P's domination of Q.

(c) *Moralized regulation*: R is a regulator just when R is morally responsible for P's domination of Q, or for preventing or attenuating that domination.

Specification (a) is too weak. Suppose I trip over a wire, causing the leader of the feminist revolution to fall on a bus, causing her to die, causing the patriarchy to survive. I have causally contributed to the reproduction or perpetuation of the patriarchy. But my tripping is only an expression of maladroitness, not of the patriarchy: I am no regulator. So (a) is false.[19]

On specification (b), my behaviour must somehow *express* the constitutive power dyad, indeed expressively uphold it. In other words, to count as a regulator, I must, in principle, be able to interpret my action as a move imbued

---

[18] I prefer 'regulators' over 'structural constraints', because 'regulators' do not merely *constrain*: they may confer intelligibility, meaning, and stability to human action. The emphasis on constraints tends to construe the grounds of domination excessively narrowly.

[19] The same applies to causally robust, even *functional*, explanations of my tripping over the wire: *pace* Cohen (1978), functional explanations are too weak to buttress the regulation function. Garden variety functionalisms, by implication, are unlikely to make much sense of structural domination.

with salient institutional meaning,[20] even if I am not morally responsible for its (possibly oppression-perpetuating) consequences.

Specification (c) is stronger, because it requires moral responsibility. On specification (c), if I succeed in dissociating myself morally from domination, or bear no responsibilities towards its remedy, then I am not a regulator. The feminist husband under patriarchy and the republican prince under monarchy, for example, are not regulators. At least this follows if collective responsibility is individually decomposable.

Of these three specifications, I shall exclude (a) and remain non-committal between (b) and (c). The usefulness of the regulation function consists in this: if P dominates Q and if that relation satisfies (an appropriate specification) of the regulation function, then that domination is structural. Knowing this can help us better understand the nature of the domination, as well as ways of resisting it. For example, it would seem that a Havelian 'dictatorship of the ritual'-type theory only requires a (b)-type regulation function. Some socialists and nearly all liberals, on the other hand, assume (c)-type regulation functions. I will return to this in section 4.5.

To summarize the argument so far: a domination relation between humans counts as structural just when it is triadic, that is, involves a (set of) regulator(s) who express, are responsible for, or fail to remedy the dyadic domination relation. This concludes my discussion of the logic of structural domination. I now turn to the normative part of the argument, which applies *Regulated Domination* to capitalist economic structure.

4.4 How Capitalists Dominate

This section builds on Chapters 2 and 3 to explain how capital dominates labour under capitalism. 'Capitalism', it bears repeating, designates the structure discussed in Chapter 2: unequal private ownership of scarce productive assets, along with a labour or credit market conferring access to these means. I begin by discussing the nature of the abstract relation between capital and labour. In section 4.5, I explain how the addition of the state imparts structure to that relation, that is, makes capitalist domination a form of structural domination.

---

[20] This does not mean that I must intend its effects. It might simply mean that the effect is discursively available to me as an explanation of my action after its performance. This availability may require what Haslanger (2012) calls a 'cultural schema'.

102   STRUCTURAL DOMINATION IN THE MARKET

Consider:

Interagential Capitalist Domination—Capital has money, Labour does not. Labour needs means of consumption, which she cannot obtain without money. So Labour places her labour power at Capital's disposal, in return for money. Capital appropriates the product of Labour's labour, sells it for money, returns half the money to Labour, and pockets the other half as profit.

This interagential relation involves monetized unilateral control over alien purposiveness. On this description, capital is not fundamentally a property or class relation, although it presupposes both private property and class division.[21] So private property can co-constitute the capital relation without being identical with or reducible to that relation.[22] Rather, the capital relation is, fundamentally, a form of *reification*: the relation confers upon Capital unilateral control over Labour's labour power in the form of a relation between the things that each of Capital and Labour own. This control, in turn, enables Capital to exploit Labour. So it is reification that makes the capital relation conceptually and historically distinctive.[23]

I now explain why *Interagential capitalist domination* involves domination. The general idea was explained in Chapter 2 and goes as follows. Suppose that omelettes are the only means of consumption and that, if Labour is to nourish herself, she must produce an omelette. As long as Capital owns the eggs, Labour can produce the omelette only by Capital's permission. This makes Labour's ability to set and pursue the end of omelette production—her productive purposiveness—subordinate to Capital's unilateral will. When that subordination is expressed in extraction of unilateral labour flow, moreover, Capital exploits Labour.[24]

---

[21] Recall that roofs can co-constitute a power relation—say, of wall over wall—without being identical with or reducible to that power relation, since the vehicle of a power relation is not identical or reducible to that relation.

[22] Despite what generations of Marxists, from Lenin to Roemer, have held: see, for example, Sweezy (1942), Cohen (1978) and Roemer (1982), among many others who assimilate the capital relation into a property or class relation.

[23] That is, conceptually distinct from patriarchy or white supremacy and historically distinct from other forms of class division. I offer a more precise definition of reification in Chapter 2.

[24] It bears noting that Capital dominates Labour, even if Labour performs meaningful work and even if Capital is a decent employer. Meaningful work does not guarantee nonsubjected work and vice versa. In respect of the first false entailment, from meaningful work to unalienated labour, consider the case of the slave performing interesting and socially useful work. The possibility is conceptually coherent. But her labour is subject to the will of the master. In respect of the second false entailment, from nonsubjection to meaningful work, consider the work of poor peasants under eternal primitive communism. Suppose that they must push rocks all day, because rock-pushing is available and useful. Suppose, further, that it is near-impossible, psychologically, to enjoy such work, or to find meaning in

This generic description suggests a double bind of capital similar to that of the patriarchy. Just as women under the patriarchy must choose between being excluded from familial or sexual relations and participating on terms set out unilaterally by men as a whole, so workers under capitalism must choose between being excluded from work altogether and working at the unilateral discretion of the capitalists as a whole. This makes capitalism, patriarchy, and white supremacy structurally homologous: all three restrict the choice sets of the subaltern to a dilemma between social abstinence and domination. The worker under capitalism, the woman under patriarchy, and the nonwhite person under white supremacy are all dominated in that sense.

I now explain how the abstract relation in *Interagential Capitalist Domination* becomes structural. The missing third relatum, I argue, is the capitalist state.

4.5 Capitalism Entails the State

This section explains the transition from the logical abstraction of the capital relation to capitalism, that is, to capitalist economic structure. Consider:

Structural Capitalist Domination—Capital owns the cookshop. He gives propertyless Labour a cooking job. In labour-market equilibrium, Labour places her labour capacity at Capital's disposal, in return for money. Capital appropriates Labour's labour, sells its product for money, returns half the money to Labour *in the form of a wage*, and pockets the other half as profit.

Unlike the *Interagential* case, the *Structural* case posits the existence of a labour market, which presupposes the existence of wage labour, which presupposes that Capital owns Labour's conditions of production. This move from the dyadic *Interagential* case to the triadic *Structural* case confers structure on the dyadic relation between Capital and Labour. Who regulates that relation when it is structural?

The answer can only be the *capitalist state*, the only coercive enforcer of Capital's private property in scarce productive assets satisfying a non-causal characterization of the regulation function. Consider cookshops. Modernity lends expression to the private ownership of cookshops through the institution

---

it. This shared labour performance is still unsubjected. So the relationship between nonsubjected and meaningful work is one of mutual irrelevance.

104 STRUCTURAL DOMINATION IN THE MARKET

of property law.[25] Property law, in turn, requires a legal system, which, in turn, requires a state. So capitalist structure presupposes the capitalist state as its regulator-in-chief.[26] The capitalist state claims exclusive title to interpret, apply, and enforce private property on the part of all its subjects. It does this by interpreting, applying, and enforcing, among other things: (i) Capital's control over Labour's conditions of production, (ii) Labour's control over her own labour power, and (iii) the exercise of these control rights through the institution of contract. This incidence of control rights, in turn, confers on Capital power over Labour's productive purposiveness, in two ways: Capital comes to control access to consumption goods and to the means used to produce them. So the structural triad (dominator, dominated, regulator) takes the form (capitalist, worker, state).[27]

The concept of capitalism, I conclude, presupposes the concept of the state. More precisely, the application of my definition of structural domination, *Regulated Domination*, to capitalism yields something like the concept of the capitalist state:

(4)   The capitalist state completes the triad of capitalist structural domination by regulating the capital relation—the domination of labour by capital.

It follows that Kant (1996, p. 409; 6:256) and Nozick (1974, part I) are right to deduce an idea of the state from the very idea of private property, in conjunction with certain generalizations about the nature of right.[28] But both signally and consequentially fail to note that such a state is compatible with the monetized mastery of the propertied over the propertyless and, conversely, with the monetized servitude of the propertyless to the propertied. Marx and

[25] When Marx disparaged the writing of socialist 'recipes ... for the cookshops of the future' (Marx 1976, p. 99), he was unaware of contemporary intellectual property law, which turns even socialist recipes, such as this book, into sources of profit.
[26] Why couldn't capitalists regulate the constitutive power dyad by themselves (e.g. through private police and armies)? There are good explanations for why they would necessarily fail in that task (see Elster 1985, Nozick 1974, Ripstein 2009). Bases need superstructures, and that need is built into the logic of private property.
[27] Naturally, the capitalist state regulates the constitutive power dyad in more ways than just protecting private property. It may foster competition, manage the national debt, maintain ideological 'civil society' institutions, provide basic public goods, and so on. Moreover, the state is not the only regulator of capital's constitutive power dyad. The dominant party to the dyad, the capitalists, is another source of regulation. For example, capitalists are normally engaged in a competitive struggle to maximize profit, which means they are structurally constrained to penalize the noncompliance of other capitalists with the profit-maximizing norm—that is, to drive them out of business. Competition, along with private property, are constitutive moments of capitalist structure.
[28] Kant's exposition is not, of course, about capitalism, whereas Nozick's is an explicit attempt to defend its purest expression.

Engels do not so fail, when they note that 'Communism deprives no man of the power to appropriate the products of society; all that it does is to deprive him of the power to subjugate the labour of others by means of such appropriations.' (MECW 6, p. 500).

I now summarize the arguments of the preceding sections. I have argued for a triadic definition of structural domination and for its application to capitalist social relations. The abstract capital relation, I have argued, consists in monetized unilateral control over alien labour capacity. Since such control violates the Non-Servitude Proviso, it is an instance of domination. And this domination of Labour by Capital is structural when it is regulated by the capitalist state, the only coercive enforcer of property rights expressively and morally implicated in the reproduction of that dyad.

I now discuss the implications of this account of structural domination for the nature of the agency of capitalists and the state, as well as for the modes of exploitation that obtain under capitalist economic structure. The overarching idea is that the regulation account of structural domination can make sense of capitalist domination without hypostatizing Capital and Labour as supra-individual entities,[29] while keeping power distinct from its possessors, vehicles, or contingent effects.

4.6 Capital's Agentlessness

Does capital constitute shared or collective agency? This section argues that it does not. If I am right, this is a boon for the regulation account of structural exploitation, which explains how an agentless process can be structural. More precisely, capitalist structure, on my view, is *collectively power-conferring but agentless*. It is, in that respect, like the structure of a prison whose guards lack collective or shared agency. In passing, I will also explain how this account of capitalist domination may be compatible with an account of the *state* as a collective agent.[30]

I begin by explaining capital's agentlessness. On a widely held view, due to Bratman (2014) and Gilbert (1996), shared agency requires *shared intentions*, that is, P's and Q's intentions *that P and Q* perform an act, each by doing her part in that performance. These shared intentions must, moreover, 'mesh', in

---

[29] The most famous such theory is due to Lukács (1923).
[30] What I say also applies, I think, to patriarchy and white supremacy.

106 STRUCTURAL DOMINATION IN THE MARKET

the sense that the content of P's participatory intention must cohere with Q's. I now show that capitalist structure requires nothing of the sort.

To focus intuitions, consider:

> *Catallaxy Prison*—Catallaxy prison has 990 prisoners and 10 guards. Some guards are former prisoners: they achieve guardhood by squeezing through the (few available) cell loopholes. The size of these loopholes is subject to capacity constraints, including the rate of growth of the prison, and guard rule over the prison itself. The proportion of guards in the total population ends up hovering at around 1 percent for the whole duration of the prison's long existence, through nobody's plan or intentional design.

In *Catallaxy Prison*,[31] prisoners squeeze into guardhood from the prison population, subject to capacity constraints and guard rule over prisoners. By assumption, there is a feasible prisonless alternative, in which all 1000 people are free, but where there are no longer guards and prisoners, such that the former are worse off and the latter better off. The guards therefore have an interest in maintaining prison structure. But it does not follow that they have shared and meshing intentions of the Bratman/Gilbert variety, that they optimize by forming them, or even that they optimize by accepting some collective decision procedure as theirs (Hindriks 2018).[32]

More generally, the reproduction of domination in *Catallaxy Prison* only requires that: (i) individual prison guards are motivated by self-interest, (ii) what serves the guards' collective self-interest serves their individual self-interest,[33] and (iii) the guards are individually capable and willing to enforce their collective self-interest. Claim (iii) is subject to a free-rider objection: how do individual guards ensure that other guards enforce discipline? The exact answer is irrelevant to our purposes. Perhaps, acting as regulators of

---

[31] Friedrich Hayek uses the term 'catallaxy' to name a state of realization of spontaneous market order. The term seems more appropriate to a warship ('HMS Catallaxy') or a prison ('HMP Catallaxy'). As it turns out, all three senses have the same referent.

[32] Consider prison guards P_1 and P_2. P_1 knows that it is in P_2's interest not to let too many prisoners through the loophole; the same is true of P_2. By the structural assumption, moreover, all guards are symmetrically disposed. But, if this is true, then neither P_1 nor P_2 need have any intention that they enforce discipline or control the loophole *together*; it is consistent with their collective exercise of power that they lack shared intentions of the Bratman/Gilbert variety. P_1, for example, violates no requirement of rationality if she gets on with enforcing discipline, all the while expecting—falsely, as it turns out—that P_2 will fail to do her part.

[33] Whether they realize it or not. Note that the individual guard's realization that her individual self-interest is in the collective interest of guards, indeed her *motivation* by collective self-interest, does not entail Bratman/Gilbert-type intentions. For P_1's subplans may not mesh with P_2's; P_1 may even consider them incompatible with P_2's.

CAPITAL'S AGENTLESSNESS   107

the prisoner relation, the guards monitor each other's performance, punish defection, and reward cooperation. It does not follow that they have shared intentions or, more strongly, meshing shared intentions. So the collective power of prison guards does not presuppose shared agency on their part. If the collective power of capitalists is similar, then capitalism is collectively power-conferring but agentless.[34]

There is, however, a way that capitalism might *indirectly* presuppose agency. Consider the following argument:

(5)   Capitalism presupposes the capitalist state.

(6)   The state is a collective agent.

So (7)   Capitalism presupposes collective agency.

If (6) is true, then the regulator of the capital relation is a collective agent. It follows that capitalism is a triadic relation between two agentless classes of agents (capital and labour)[35] and a collective agent who regulates the dyad. I have no quarrell with (7). But I now argue that the soundness of the argument just rehearsed does not impugn the agentlessness of capitalism *as such*. This can be glimpsed by the following variant of *Catallaxy Prison*:

Prison Warden—This is the same setup as in *Catallaxy Prison*. The only difference is that the guards and prisoners jointly elect a warden. The warden is elected from the whole population of prisoners and guards through universal suffrage. Her mandate is to promote the quality of life of both guards and prisoners, subject to capacity constraints. Thanks to a long-lasting overlapping consensus between guards and prisoners, the proportion of guards in the total population ends up hovering at around 1 percent for the whole duration of the prison's long existence, through nobody's plan or intentional design.

In *Prison Warden*, the conditions for shared agency are satisfied (see Pettit and Schweikard 2006, Lawford-Smith and Collins 2017): the warden's election

---

[34] We could go further: the collective power of capitalists is the alienated collective power of workers, that is, the collective power of workers, lost to capitalists, *as* capitalists. If this is correct, then capitalist power is an expression of the joint several powers of workers, separated from them as an alien power in the form of money. What would it mean for workers to reappropriate that power as an expression of *their* individual powers? If the argument of this book is sound, then that would mean organizing production as an expression of omnilaterally authorized public power.

[35] More precisely: two classes of agents that are not *necessarily* agents themselves.

108   STRUCTURAL DOMINATION IN THE MARKET

is a joint action by the population of guards and prisoners. The case can then be made that the warden's electors constitute a collective, or group agent.[36] But the existence and reproduction of prison structure *itself* are not (the upshot of) shared agency; nor do they presuppose any such agency. In other words, it is entirely consistent with *Prison Warden* that guards and prisoners lack any intention to reproduce prison structure and that each lacks any intention to do her part in that reproduction. So, once again, *the collective power of the guards does not entail shared agency on their part*. Similar things may be true of the prison inmates.

Liberal capitalism is like *Prison Warden*, in that it allows forms of (possibly democratic) shared agency *subject to* capitalist domination. More importantly, *Prison Warden* captures a distinctive feature of that domination: much like the power of the separately optimizing prison guards, capitalist power can reproduce itself spontaneously, without shared and meshing intentions on the part of capitalists. Perhaps for that reason, capitalist power can—by dint of periodic elections, welfare provision, trade unionism, codetermination, and other palliatives—systematically conceal its nature as a form of domination.[37] The theory of structural domination defended in this chapter makes sense of this idea, without hypostatizing class agency and without conflating domination with the dominators (prison guards, capitalists), with the vehicles of domination (prison structure, capitalist structure), or with its effects.

I now explain how these structural relations facilitate exploitation. If capitalist domination is structurally conferred unilateral power over labour capacity and if that power eventuates in surplus extraction—unilateral labour transfer—then it constitutes structural exploitation. Structural exploitation is exploitation that obtains by dint of a structural power relation: one's social position of structural power and another's of structural vulnerability. The rest of this chapter discusses modes of structural exploitation under capitalism and their implications for exploitation across space and time.

---

[36] List and Pettit (2011, pp. 37–41) discuss the logical problems this raises.

[37] Why don't the prisoners just elect an abolitionist warden? Many plausible explanations have been offered. Some say that a majority of electors must be in the grip of 'false consciousness', such that it does not see the bars; others say that the majority sees the bars, but not the whole cage; yet others say that it sees the cage, but believes that it is better off inside. Some of these beliefs will count as false consciousness if they issue from, say, brainwashing or propaganda. A more interesting suggestion is that these beliefs are justified, indeed true. Przeworski (1985) argues that breaking the capitalist cage may be very costly in the short run—so costly that workers are individually *and* collectively better off encaged. So the main explanation for why we are stuck in the capitalist cage may not be that we are silly or ideologically blighted. Rather, capitalism makes escape prohibitively costly for us all.

4.7 Modes of Capitalist Exploitation

I will illustrate two modes of structural capitalist exploitation, that is, two ways in which capitalist economic structure engenders the exploitation of the direct producer: *vertical exploitation*, which concerns authority relations within economic units and *horizontal exploitation*, which concerns market relations across economic units.

4.7.1 The vertical case

Consider:

> *Vertical*—Capital owns the cookshops of the future. She hires Labour who, in equilibrium, will work a total of sixteen hours. The monetary expression of total labour time is unity, such that the net product is worth $16. Capital appropriates and sells this net product; she consumes $8 (equivalent to eight hours of labour) and pays Labour $8 as wages (equivalent to eight hours of labour).[38]

In this example, Labour is alienated from scarce productive assets, which are controlled by, indeed 'personified' in, Capital. This allows Capital to appropriate a surplus product, such that, in equilibrium, Labour comes to consume eight hours less labour than she produces, while Capital consumes eight hours more. So, by dint of her power over Labour, Capital extracts unilateral service from Labour in the form of profit. By the Non-Servitude Proviso, Capital dominates Labour. *Vertical* is therefore an instance of vertical capitalist exploitation, a kind of hired servitude.

Now, in most capitalist economies, vertical exploitation will not involve only capitalists and workers: 'where management and ownership of firms come apart, those who direct the action of the exploited are not necessarily those who benefit' (Wollner 2018, p. 12). A typical rebuttal to this suggestion says that management and ownership, *taken together*, constitute the capitalist, such that Capital exploits as one collective agent.[39] But this is too quick: capitalists and

---

[38] I assume that individual labour times reflect average labour input. These equivalences, I have insisted throughout this book, do not presuppose the Ricardian labour theory of value. The only assumption is that total net output is the monetary expression of a certain amount of total labour, which is what the 'monetary expression of labour time' means. See Foley (1982) and Dumenil (1984).

[39] Szigeti and Malmqvist (2019) discuss necessary and sufficient condition for joint exploitative agency.

110 STRUCTURAL DOMINATION IN THE MARKET

managers do not always act jointly, not least because their objective functions differ—the principal-agent problem shows its balding head.

The right way to think about these cases need not, I think, appeal to joint action or shared agency. Rather, exploitation occurs in these cases 'because a pattern of action...emerges through coordination between agents, who even though they do not constitute a group agent, succeed in exploiting, for example by performing various parts in some overall pattern, such that the exploitee suffers the exploitation-specific wrong of (a) wrongfully having her action directed by others, (b) in a way that also violates distributive norms' (Wollner 2018, p. 12). On this picture, capitalist and manager spontaneously and independently act in such a way that leads to the exploitation of Labour; moreover, *their respective claims to control over alien purposiveness reflect that fact*. It does not follow that they are, as a result, engaged in joint action; they are, in that respect, like the separately optimizing prison guards.

This concludes my discussion of vertical exploitation. I now consider a more exotic set of cases.

4.7.2 The horizontal case

Consider a variant of John Roemer's *Friday and Robinson* example (Roemer 1996, p. 52):

> *Horizontal*—There are two cooperatives, Robinson Inc. and Friday Inc., trading only in final goods. Each firm has five employees and is operated democratically. Robinson Inc. is capital-rich, Friday Inc. is capital-poor. The economy-wide net product is worth $80 and the monetary expression of labour time is unity. In equilibrium, each member of the Robinson Inc. coop works four hours and receives eight hours of labour time (expressed in her individual income of $8), while each member of the Friday Inc. coop works twelve hours and consumes eight hours (expressed in her individual income of $8).

Despite the absence of capitalists and bosses in *Horizontal*, there is still unilateral labour flow. Table 4.1 summarizes the contrasts between the two examples (the top two rows summarize *Vertical*, the bottom two *Horizontal*).

Does the *Horizontal* case involve exploitation? I think it does, at least if Robinson Inc.'s market success fails to reflect innovation, effort, and talent—productive efficiency, more generally—as opposed to mere wealth inequality.

Table 4.1 Vertical and horizontal exploitation

	Works	Consumes	Net earnings
Capital	0 hours	8 hours	$8
Labour	16 hours	8 hours	$8
Worker (Robinson Inc.)	4 hours	8 hours	$8
Worker (Friday Inc.)	12 hours	8 hours	$8

For then the transfer of labour from Friday Inc. to Robinson Inc. violates the Non-Servitude Proviso, since it cannot even draw the exemption of superior efficiency. The unilateral labour transfers of Table 4.1, in other words, reflect nothing but unilateral control over alien purposiveness. So the *Horizontal* case is an instance of horizontal exploitation, a kind of *un*hired, market-induced, servitude.

I conclude this chapter by explaining how these modes of structural exploitation extend through space and time.

4.8 The Cage's Girth

This section extends the preceding discussion to the spatial and temporal parts of the capitalist cage. It argues that, although exploitation can extend across distance in space—across states and nations—it does not extend across non-overlapping generations in time. I begin with distance in time.

4.8.1 Across time

Can you exploit posterity? The temporal parts of the capitalist cage get reproduced, generation after generation, through the process of capital accumulation canvassed in Chapter 2. By that model, it would seem that, in contributing to the reproduction of a cage that will imprison them, earlier generations necessarily dominate future generations. This suggestion is only half true. It is true in the sense that those who contribute to the construction and reproduction of the cage—adding a bar here and there, adding a brick here and there, ensuring compliance here and there—either dominate future generations or are complicit in that domination. But not *all* members of earlier generations so contribute. So not all of them dominate or are complicit in such domination. Does this mean that generations *cannot* exploit each other?

112 STRUCTURAL DOMINATION IN THE MARKET

The question is uninteresting if its scope is restricted to overlapping cases: across overlapping generations, the young can certainly exploit the old and vice versa.[40] Things become more interesting in cases of non-overlapping generations. Suppose there are n generations, $G_1, G_2, \ldots, G_n$, such that each generation only overlaps with the one succeeding it (G_1 overlaps with G_2 but not with G_3, and so on). Can G_1 exploit G_3? On the account of exploitation defended in this book, G_1 can neither exploit nor be exploited by G_3.

Consider, first, whether G_1 exploits G_3. For this to happen, it would have to be the case that G_1 ropes G_3 into unilaterally serving G_1. Now, G_1 undoubtedly has power over G_3: assuming that G_3 *will* exist, G_1 controls the identity, the number and the quality of life of G_3's members.[41] Indeed, this is why G_1 can dominate G_3, or even posterity in general. But G_1 cannot extract unilateral labour flow from G_3—G_1 cannot have G_3 unilaterally serve G_1—because G_1 is not around when G_3 is around and vice versa. *Labour and effortful contribution do not flow backwards in time.* So G_1 cannot exploit G_3.

Now consider whether G_1 can be exploited by G_3. G_3 can benefit from unequal labour or effort exchange with G_1, in the sense that G_3 can consume (the fruits of) G_1's labour. But G_3 cannot have any power over G_1 or its members. As a matter of metaphysical necessity, G_3 lacks power over the past, including over G_1's members. So G_3 cannot exploit G_1.

I provisionally conclude that, if exploitation is enrichment through unilateral or arbitrary control over alien purposiveness, then non-overlapping generations cannot exploit each other. Chris Bertram questions this conclusion. He argues that G_1 can exploit, and be exploited by, G_3. Bertram defines exploitation as follows:

> Where people are linked together in co-operation either as contributors to that co-operation or as beneficiaries to it, and where those people are able to make a contribution requiring effort, there is exploitation if and when the distribution of rewards from that co-operation fails to be roughly proportional to the distribution of effortful contribution.
>
> (Bertram 2007, p. 76)

Using this definition, Bertram imagines a temporally extended system of cooperation, in which there is a 'customary expectation on each generation

---

[40] The question of exploitation in the context of pension systems is interesting but largely unexplored. See Gosseries (2009) for some interesting suggestions.

[41] For a discussion of same and different number choices in population ethics, see Parfit (1981).

THE CAGE'S GIRTH   113

to do its part, an expectation which typically involves handing on the core assets of the scheme intact... from one generation to the next' (Bertram 2010, p. 82). It now follows that G_1 can exploit G_3 and, more interestingly, that G_1 can be exploited by G_3. A profligate generation G_3, for example, exploits G_1 when it fails to meet the customary expectation, either by consuming more or by contributing less than it should.

My disagreement is with Bertram's definition of exploitation. I do not think that the 'ability-to-contribute' principle, elaborated in the Bertram quotation, furnishes a sufficient condition for exploitation. If it did, then Ant would not be exploiting a pit-ridden Grasshopper when she asks for $1 million in return for costless winter shelter—assuming that $1 million is the level of effortful contribution Grasshopper is *expected* to provide.[42] There is proportionality of effortful contribution here, but Ant still exploits Grasshopper. More generally, the ability-to-contribute principle is not sufficiently discriminating: it seems to generate false negatives in a wide range of cases. The way to make the Bertram principle sufficiently discriminating consists in connecting effortful contribution to an account of the subjection of those providing it.[43]

4.8.2 Across space

Contemporary capitalist social relations are not only temporally but also globally extended. In Chapter 6, I discuss the relationship between capital and the state in the context of the debate on global justice. I will argue that, if exploitation is a form of domination, and if states can exploit states, then states can dominate states. That form of domination constitutes imperialism, such that a comprehensive understanding of global capitalist exploitation requires a theory of imperialism.

Does this mean that capitalist globalization does worse, in terms of domination, than its predecessors? How are we to think of the remarkable increase in average living standards in China and India over the past thirty years, for example? In both countries, the penetration of capitalist social relations into the economy has lifted millions out of poverty, reduced mortality rates,

---

[42] I discuss the *Ant and Grasshopper* case in Chapter 3.
[43] Nonexploitation, on this view, requires proportionality to effortful contribution untainted by unilateral control or arbitrary power. This is the domination account defended in this book.

114   STRUCTURAL DOMINATION IN THE MARKET

and increased literacy.[44] In Chapter 6, I will show that these questions are moot: they fail to recognize that servitude is compatible with significant improvement in most dimensions of quality of life. That is, critics of encagement need not deny—indeed, must affirm—that finding yourself locked in a capitalist cage is a significant improvement over being shackled to a feudal wall. China and India are now undergoing this shackles-to-cage transition.[45] Their economies resemble, in these respects, Europe's transition to capitalism. Chapter 5 draws upon the historical debate on the origins of capitalism to shed light on the forms and fate of capitalist exploitation.

Conclusion

This chapter has argued for the cogency of the idea of structural domination and for application of that idea to capitalist economic structure. Capitalism, I have argued, is a cage—much like patriarchy and white supremacy. The chapter defended these claims by offering a triadic account of structural domination, according to which structural domination is a three-place relation between dominator, dominated, and regulator—any role-holders that regulate the constitutive domination dyad. On the basis of this account, I argued that the concept of capitalism entails the concent of the state, whether conceived as a collective agent or not. The chapter concluded by discussing the cage's spatial and temporal girth. The rest of this book applies these ideas to theories of the origin of capitalism, to international relations, and to theories of property-owning democracy, market socialism, and worker control.

---

[44] In the case of China, the number of people in absolute poverty has been reduced by about 94 percent over the past thirty years, while adult literacy has increased from 65 percent to 98 percent in the same period (China Bureau of National Statistics 2015). In India, the reduction in absolute poverty has been even more dramatic, reducing the number of people in absolute poverty from 55 percent of the population to 21 percent. The literacy rate has also increased from about 40 percent of the adult population to 69 percent (World Bank 2011).
[45] On India, see Banaji (2010) and Bardhan (1999). On China, see Brenner and Isett (2002) and Pomeranz (2000).

PART III
APPLICATIONS

5

Capitalist Exploitation: Its Forms, Origin, and Fate

Exploitation, in general, is a dividend of servitude: domination-induced title to alien surplus labour. In Chapter 2, I explained that this generic definition of exploitation takes a specific form under capitalism. Unlike slavery, serfdom, and patriarchy, capitalists can claim title to surplus labour through contractual relations between things, that is, through mutually consensual and uncoerced market transactions. In Chapter 3, I explained why exploitation cashes out its title to alien purposiveness in terms of surplus labour. And in Chapter 4 I explained what makes this title to alien purposiveness structural when it is structural.

This chapter studies the modality questions: how exploitation becomes possible under capitalism and what historically specific forms it takes. Some of the most sophisticated answers to these two questions—of origin and form, respectively—have been provided by Karl Marx in volumes I and III of *Capital* and by contemporary elaborations of these ideas in historical sociology. In what follows, I study Marx's answers, by drawing upon the debate on the origins of capitalism. I then show how that debate can shed light on post-capitalist democratic futures.

The chapter is structured as follows. Section 5.1 presents the problem of how capital, as monetary title to alien labour capacity, performs and generalizes its historically specific form of exploitation. Section 5.2 sets out the conceptual landscape and offers some definitions. Section 5.3 discusses what Marx calls the 'antediluvian forms' of capital. Section 5.4 argues that wage-labour is not a necessary condition for capitalist relations of production and defends an alternative definition based on the idea of subsumed labour. Section 5.5 broaches and defends a related but distinctive form of subsumption that unites Marx's writings on cooperatives. Section 5.6 uses the distinction to offer a critique of market socialism. Section 5.7 discusses some implications of the subsumption definition for the connection between capital and class.

Exploitation as Domination: What Makes Capitalism Unjust. Nicholas Vrousalis, Oxford University Press.
© Nicholas Vrousalis 2023. DOI: 10.1093/oso/9780192867698.003.0006

5.1 The Problem of Subsumed Labour

It is widely held that capitalist social relations are uniquely coextensive with some set of property relations. There are capitalists, who own all of the means of production, and there are workers, who own none. This is the way capitalism was defined in the reproduction model of Chapter 2 and elaborated as structural in Chapter 4. This chapter weakens the definition of capitalist social relations, in terms of what Marx calls the 'subsumption of labour by capital'. This definition aligns the individuation of capitalist social relations with *the ways in which capitalists dominate workers*. Capitalism, I argue, takes the generic exploitation relation—the extraction of unilateral service through power over others—and builds it into the conditions of equilibrium market exchange. Nearly every monetary transaction then comes to involve *capital*, title to unilateral control over alien labour capacity.

This process of capital's appropriation of the conditions of labour, from generalized usury, to manufacturing, to mechanized industry, implicates the material mode of production in a progressively more intense exploitation and therefore domination of the worker. In what follows, I further argue that Marx's ubiquitous use of the terms 'subordination' (*Unterordnung*), 'subsumption' (*Subsumtion*), and 'domination' (*Herrschaft*) of labour by capital represents this process of embodiment of the exploitation relation into the production process. Marx's terminology, in other words, represents modes of worker *unfreedom*. I begin by introducing some basic terms.

5.2 Definitions

Chapter 2 presented a rough-and-ready model of economic reproduction that contrasted collective and capitalist property relations. This section makes the assumptions behind that model more precise. It then defends a weaker interpretation of these assumptions, one that makes capital a form of subsumed labour. I begin by rehearsing a traditional account of capitalist social relations—'relations of production'—and of their relationship to the capitalist 'mode of production'. I then offer tentative definitions of the concepts of subsumption and exploitation.

5.2.1 Capitalist relations of production

According to a traditional definition, capitalist relations of production are 'relations of effective power over persons and productive forces, not relations

Table 5.1 Relations of production

	Labour power	Means of production
Slave	None	None
Serf	Some	Some
Proletarian	All	None
Associated producer	All	All

of legal ownership' (Cohen 1978, p. 63). An effective power, according to Cohen, is a non-normative ability to effect outcomes.[1] This characterization of the relations of production permits a taxonomy of capitalist relations of production in terms of the subordinate producer's control over her labour power and means of production, as follows.

Suppose the pair (r, s) represents the direct producer's degree of control over her own labour power (r) and over means of production (s), where r and s take their values from the set $\{All, Some, None\}$. That the producer controls All of her labour power, for example, means that she enjoys a formal right of self-ownership and is therefore not liable to extra-economic coercion (see Table 5.1). According to the traditional view, the $\{All, None\}$ set of powers is both sufficient and *necessary* for capitalist relations of production: there are propertyless workers who sell their labour power to propertyful capitalists, which is what allows the latter to exploit the former. This view was already discussed in Chapter 2.

The traditional view faces well-known objections. Take, for example, antebellum slavery in the American South. In that context, '[a] producer could be coerced into working for a wage and producing surplus value' (Cohen 1978, p. 83, referring to Marx 1976, p. 925). So there are forms of antebellum slavery that involve slaves performing wage-labour without full control over their labour power—these slaves only possess a $\{Some, None\}$ set of powers. This is a presumptive counterexample to the traditional view.[2]

Consider, further, merchant and usury capital, the forms dubbed 'antediluvian' by Marx (1976, p. 266, 1981, p. 728). Under putting-out,[3] for example, the merchant makes a profit by providing raw material to the peasant, buying the final product below its market value. Putting-out is an instance of $\{All, Some\}$ relations of production, since the peasant must own some of the conditions

---

[1] In Chapter 2, section 2.1 I disputed this definition of an effective power. I preserve it here *arguendo*.
[2] For a wealth of similar counterexamples, see Banaji (2010).
[3] See Ogilvie (2008) for an introduction to the English 'domestic industry' of the 18th century.

120 CAPITALIST EXPLOITATION: ITS FORMS, ORIGIN, AND FATE

of production.[4] If putting-out betokens a capitalist relation of production—as I will argue—then it constitutes another counterexample to the traditional view.

In light of these difficulties, this chapter defends a definition of capitalist relations of production in terms of subsumed labour. In other words, a social relation is a capitalist relation of production if and only if it involves monetary title to unilateral effective control over labour power—the subsumption of labour to capital. This definition makes the capital relation compatible with any combination of the $\{r, s\}$ variables in the production relations set. Capitalist relations of production are then constituted by that subset of reproducible economic relations in which the extraction of surplus labour is subjected to the maximization of exchange value—what Marx calls the 'law of value'. The connections between these concepts will, I hope, become more transparent in the discussion that follows. I now define the concept of the mode of production and the idea of subsumed labour.

5.2.2 The capitalist mode of production

Marx's discussion of labour subsumption occurs against the background of a distinction between the *relations* and the *mode* of production. Marx uses the term 'mode of production' in at least two senses, one narrow and one broad. In the narrow sense, the mode of production refers to the kind of technology employed in production, including the technical division of labour. The narrow sense therefore excludes power and domination relations. The broader sense of the mode of production, on the other hand, includes facts about the purpose of production and the form of social labour.

In this chapter, I shall refer to the mode of production exclusively in the narrow, or material, sense. Marx often relegates claims about the power of capital over labour to what he calls the mode of 'subsumption' or 'subordination' of labour.[5] Those represent capitalist relations of production, even if they do not feature the capitalist material mode of production.

Marx's mature works, I will argue, underwrite at least *four* modes of subsumption: hybrid, formal, real and abstract. Hybrid subsumption, on the one hand, represents the way capital dominates workers under usury,

---

[4] The peasant must, however, lack comprehensive non-market access to the means of subsistence, which is what explains recourse to the merchant in the first place. I discuss this in section 5.3.

[5] Marx uses the terms *Subsumtion* and *Unterordnung* interchangeably. Skillman (2022) has argued that capitalist subsumption is a form of subordination of labour to capital, such that subordination extends to all pre-capitalist modes of production depicted in Table 5.1.

putting-out, and the domestic system. It is, in that sense, a 'transitional form' from feudalism to capitalism. Formal and real subsumption are explicitly discussed by Marx in *Capital*, volume I, and the *Results of the Immediate Process of Production*; they represent industrial capital. Finally, abstract subsumption refers to the ways capital dominates workers under the cooperative factory. It is, in this sense, a transitional form from capitalism to socialism. I will offer a complete characterization of these modes of subsumption later. I now complete the set of definitions.

5.2.3 Exploitation and subsumption

This book argues that A exploits B if and only if A extracts domination-induced unilateral service from B, in the form of surplus labour. A necessary condition for specifically *capitalist* exploitation is that surplus labour assumes the value-form, that is, the claim to unilateral control over labour is *monetized*. What enables capitalist exploitation, in other words, is the value-constituted domination of human productive purposiveness. This characterization of capitalism implies that capitalist relations of production extend beyond wage-labour, such that the traditional characterization of capitalist exploitation is too strong. Section 5.3 elaborates.

5.3 Capital Without Wage-Labour

Many students of the origin of capitalism affirm the following two theses:

(1) Capitalist relations of production presuppose wage-labour, that is, the existence of a labour market.[6]
(2) Wage-labour presupposes capitalist relations of production.

The conjunction of these two claims means that capitalist relations of production and wage-labour are extensionally equivalent. I now show that the best understanding of pre- and post-capitalist economic formations contradicts (1). Capital, as monetary control over alien labour capacity,

---

[6] A 'wage-labourer', or proletarian, is any producer who, not owning any means of production, is 'free in the double sense that as a free individual he can dispose of his labour power as his own commodity, and that... he has no other commodity for sale, i.e. he is... free of all the objects needed for the realization of his labour power' (Marx 1976, pp. 272–3). See Mandel (1974) and Cohen (1978) for refinements of this definition.

122   CAPITALIST EXPLOITATION: ITS FORMS, ORIGIN, AND FATE

extends beyond wage-labour. For the purposes of this book, I have no quarrel with (2).

5.3.1 An invalid inference

Consider a famous passage from Marx's *Grundrisse*:

> The concept of capital implies that the objective conditions of labour ... acquire a personality as against labour, or, what amounts to the same thing, they are established as the property of a personality other than the worker's. The concept of capital implies the capitalist.   (Marx 1973, p. 512)

Cohen glosses this passage as 'a compressed statement of thesis [(1)]' (Cohen 1978, p. 184, n. 2). The idea here is that, since capital implies the 'personifica- tion' of the conditions of labour in the capitalist, the existence of the capitalist implies the existence of the wage-labourer. Cohen's inference is invalid: the objective conditions of labour can acquire a 'personality as against labour' if capitalists merely hire them out to workers (e.g. through lending), as opposed to hiring workers in to use them. Whether capital hires labour or labour hires capital, it is still the 'objective conditions of labour' that dominate workers.[7]

The same invalid inference, from Marx's assertions about the alienated form of social relations to the existence of wage-labour, pervades the works of Sweezy (1942), Mandel (1974), Fine and Saad-Filho (2004), Harvey (2010) and Callinicos (2014), among many others.[8]

5.3.2 Usurers, merchants, and surplus value

I now argue that Marx actually denies (1); in Section 5.4, I will show that he is right to do so. In chapter 36 of volume III of *Capital*, Marx distinguishes between two forms of usury: lending money to 'extravagant magnates' for the

---

[7] For a formal treatment of this claim, see the isomorphism theorem in Roemer (1982, pp. 89–95). It is also discussed in Chapter 2, section 2.3 and Chapter 4, section 4.7.

[8] It is, of course, impossible that *no* capitalists hire wage-labour, such that all capital is usury or finance capital. Marx points out that this would lead to a 'tremendous fall in the rate of interest' (Marx 1981, p. 501), which would, in turn, force some finance capital into industry. But then some finance capitalists are capitalists proper. In other words, one cannot *deduce* the existence of wage-labour from the alienated conditions of labour. See Screpanti (2018) for a recent attempt to defend the deduction and its rebuttal in Vrousalis (2020a).

CAPITAL WITHOUT WAGE-LABOUR   123

consumption of luxuries and lending to 'small producers who possess their own conditions of labour' (Marx 1981, p. 729). The latter form of usurer's interest, he suggests, represents surplus value. Marx then distinguishes usury (or interest-bearing) capital under the pre-capitalist mode from the form it assumes under the capitalist mode of production (Marx 1981, p. 730). In a famous passage, he argues that:

> Usurer's capital, in this form where it actually appropriates all the surplus labour of the direct producer, without altering the mode of production; where the producers' ownership or possession of their conditions of labour ... is an essential precondition; where capital therefore does not directly sub-ordinate labour, and thus does not confront it as industrial capital—this usurer's capital impoverishes the mode of production, cripples the produc-tive forces ... and simultaneously perpetuates these lamentable conditions in which the social productivity of labour is not developed ... as it is in capitalist production.   (Marx 1981, pp. 730–1)

If this argument is sound, then several things follow. First, capitalist rela-tions of production predate the capitalist *mode* of production (in the narrow sense). Second, those direct producers subsumed under usury capital are subject to {*All, Some*} relations of production, not {*All, None*}. They differ, in that respect, from the industrial proletarian. Third, it is false that usury capital does not subordinate labour: Marx asserts that it merely fails to '*directly* subordinate labour' (my emphasis). Indeed, he later adds that '[u]surer's capital has capital's mode of exploitation without its mode of production' (Marx 1981, p. 732). In Section 5.4, I show that this 'indirect' subordination of labour by usury capital is tantamount to capitalist domination of the producer *as such*, only outside the factory. In the terms of Chapter 2, usury is domination at work, but not in the workplace.

So according to Marx, usury capital, insofar as it appropriates *newly* created value, is a capitalist relation of production. It therefore entails a relationship of dominating power geared towards the *production* of surplus value, not its mere redistribution.[9] Similar considerations apply to merchant capital: putting-out, for instance, sometimes consists in extracting newly created value.[10]

---

[9] Marx's discussion of the Indian usurer is relevant here. He writes that the usurer 'extorts ... surplus value' by charging interest to the peasant (Marx 1976, p. 1023). But then usury capital does not have a *merely* redistributive function; it is productive of surplus value and therefore constitutes a capitalist relation of production. This point is also made by Banaji, who argues that 'the price [Indian peasants receive from usury capitalists] is no longer a pure category of exchange, but a relation of production' (Banaji 1975, p. 1891). I discuss Banaji in section 5.4.2.

[10] This point has been made by Georges Lefebvre (1952), among many others.

124 CAPITALIST EXPLOITATION: ITS FORMS, ORIGIN, AND FATE

Now consider the following triad of claims:

(1) Capitalist relations of production presuppose wage-labour.

(3) Merchant and usury capital constitute capitalist relations of production.

(4) Merchant and usury capital do not presuppose wage labour.

This triad is inconsistent; no more than two of its claims are simultaneously assertible.[11] The upshot is that capital subsumes labour in a variety of ways, wage-labour being only one of them. Section 5.4 discusses capitalist subsumption before wage-labour.

5.4 Capital Before Wage-Labour

This section draws upon three important recent contributions in economic sociology to show that (1), the idea that capitalist production relations presuppose wage-labour, is false.[12] It discusses Gilbert Skillman's taxonomy of the Marxian categories of subsumption, Jairus Banaji's treatment of Indian agriculture, and Robert Brenner and Ellen Wood's account of dependence in agrarian capitalism. All of these accounts entail the falsehood of (1). We should think about capital not in terms of wage-labour, but instead in terms of monetized title to alien labour capacity.

5.4.1 Skillman on subsumption

This section makes a first case against (1), the wage-labour presupposition, by looking at industrial capital and its immediate ancestors. In his analysis of capitalist production, Marx asserts an important distinction between manufacturing and mechanized industry, discussed with consummate brilliance in chapters 14 and 15 of *Capital*, volume I. The distinction is between the *formal* and *real subsumption* of labour by capital. Under the former, sometimes identified with manufacturing, the technical basis of the mode of production has not yet 'become adequately realized—it [has] not become indispensable,

---

[11] Many students of Marx read part I of volume I of *Capital* as an attempt to deduce (1). In volume III, however, Marx asserts the conjunction of (3)–(4). Section 5.4 makes the case for keeping the conjunction. If that case is sound, then (1) must be false.

[12] This is in keeping with the reproduction model of Chapter 2, where capitalist exploitation was defined as unilateral surplus extraction and contrasted with collective ownership.

CAPITAL BEFORE WAGE-LABOUR 125

and that also means technologically indispensable' to 'producing for the sake of production' (Marx 1976, pp. 1037–38). According to Marx:

> from the standpoint of the purely formal relation—the general form of capitalist production, which is common both to its less developed stage and to its more developed stage—the means of production ... do not appear subsumed to the labourer, but the labourer appears subsumed to them.
>
> (Marx 1969, p. 390)

The 'less developed' stage of 'capitalist production' is formal subsumption; the 'more developed' real subsumption. To these different modes of subsumption there correspond different forms of surplus value (what Marx calls 'absolute' and 'relative' surplus value) and different degrees of worker independence. Crucially, however, both formal and real subsumption presuppose a complete separation of the worker from the means of production. That is, they are characterized by $\{All, None\}$ relations of production, the set of property relations uniquely coextensive with wage-labour. The necessary complement to this separation between labour and the conditions of labour is that dark archetype of modernity, the factory.[13]

The taxonomy presented so far is incomplete. For, as the discussion in chapter 36 of volume III shows, Marx manifestly believes that capitalist *relations* of production precede the factory. Indeed, it is incoherent to think that capitalist relations of production can 'transform' or 'penetrate' a mode of production in the narrow sense without predating its putatively transformed successor. Marx writes, moreover, that the 'reproduction of the handicraft system on the basis of machinery only forms a transition to the factory system' (Marx 1976, p. 589) and refers to the 'medley of transitional forms' from handicrafts to manufacturing, (Marx 1976, p. 602). He adds:

> It will be sufficient if we merely refer to certain hybrid forms [Zwitterformen], in which although surplus labour is not extorted by direct compulsion from the producer, the producer has not yet become formally subordinate to capital. In these forms, capital has not yet acquired a direct control over the labour process. (Marx 1976, p. 645)[14]

---

[13] Murray (2004) makes a cogent case for the view that Marx's modes of subsumption are not historical, but systematizing categories. He then argues that mechanized industry and manufacturing are both forms of real, not merely formal, subsumption. The latter claim contradicts my cut between formal and real subsumption. But Murray's cut, even if sound, has no bearing on the truth of (1), or on the nature of the transitional forms flanking formal and real subsumption.

[14] The hybrid forms are also discussed under the name 'transitional forms' [Uebergangsformen] in Marx's 1861–3 manuscripts. See Marx and Engels (1994, pp. 117–121).

126 CAPITALIST EXPLOITATION: ITS FORMS, ORIGIN, AND FATE

Table 5.2 Skillman's taxonomy

	Capital circuit	Mode of subsumption
Usurer	$M - \{M - C \to P \to C' - M'\} - M'$	Hybrid
Merchant	$M - C - \{C \to P \to C'\} - C' - M'$	Hybrid
Manufacturer	$M - C \to \{P\} \to C' - M'$	Formal
Industrialist	$M - C \to P \to C' - M'$	Real

It follows that 'transitional' and 'hybrid' forms represent 'indirect' modes of subsumption of labour to *capital*. That is, they constitute capitalist relations of production merely transitional to the capitalist *mode* of production, in the narrow sense. Skillman (2007, 2022) offers a helpful taxonomy of these hybrid forms. He uses Marx's expanded schema of the capital circuit: $M - C \dots P \dots C' - M'$, where $\dots P \dots$ represents the production of new value, with two modifications. The first modification uses arrows to represent the transformation of value-adding inputs into outputs, such that Marx's schema now appears as $M - C \to P \to C' - M'$. The second modification uses brackets to characterize the portion of the labour process that remains in the control of the worker. Skillman's schema is depicted in Table 5.2.

The first row represents usury capital: the usurer advances money capital M to the direct producer, who uses it to buy commodities worth C. The producer then adds value, turning C to C', which she sells for M'. She then uses the proceeds to pay interest to the usurer. Crucially, the producer retains some degree of control over her product, over the labour process, and over the process of circulation. A typical complement to this autonomy is the producer's possession of certain means of production, tools, and so on, some of which may be used as collateral for the loan. The second row represents merchant capital: the merchant uses money capital to purchase raw materials worth C. The merchant then gives these raw materials to the producer, who valorizes C to C', which is then appropriated by the merchant and sold for M'. This is, for example, how the capitalist dominates the producer under putting-out.[15] Skillman (2007) calls the subsumption obtaining under merchant capital *primitive subsumption*. I here follow Marx in calling it hybrid subsumption.[16]

The third and fourth row represent formal and real subsumption, respectively. Under formal subsumption, the worker retains a modicum of autonomy

---

[15] On putting-out, see Marglin (1975) and, more recently, Ogilvie (2008).

[16] Skillman (2007) does not include usury capital under hybrid subsumption because it does not involve direct control over the producer's surplus. But since usury does involve the subsumption of labour under the circuit of capital, and since it is, like merchant capital, an extra-factory phenomenon, I will assume that hybrid subsumption also applies to usury.

CAPITAL BEFORE WAGE-LABOUR   127

because the labour process has not been completely objectified: the manufacturing worker is still 'a fragment of his own body' (Marx 1976, p. 482), but not yet a mere 'living appendage' of the machine (Marx 1976, p. 548). This modicum of autonomy is represented in the third row by the worker's control over the labour process, which is completely foresaken under mechanized industry. The move downwards along this table, from usury to industry, schematically represents the thinning out of producer autonomy, together with the corresponding extension of capital's domination of the producer. So Skillman's elegant taxonomy *vindicates the developmental continuity between hybrid, formal, and real subsumption as capitalist relations of production*. It thereby vindicates (3), the view that merchant and usury capital constitute capitalist relations of production. This is, in a sense, the progressive materialization of surplus-labour extraction in the conditions of production, the necessary complement to capitalism's insatiable appetite for accumulation.

I have, so far, defended claim (3), the idea that merchant and usury capital can constitute capitalist relations of production. I turn now to (4), which says that one can have subsumption of labour to capital without wage-labour, indeed without a labour market. Suppose that (4) is false. That is, suppose that putting-out requires a labour market. Here the merchant optimizes by hiring a proletarian. This reduces monitoring, waste, and pilfering costs, assuming that the cost of monitoring effort is not excessively high. But then putting-out itself is unprofitable; labour markets imply the euthanasia of the putter-out. And this contradicts the anti-(4) assumption that being a putter-out is profitable when wage-labour is available.[17]

This simple argument shows why labour markets presuppose an $\{All, None\}$ set of relations of production, which renders them *incompatible* with putting-out. As Skillman points out, the historical survival of antediluvian forms of subsumption largely depended on producers' nonmarket access to nonlabour collateral, mainly land. The gradual erosion of that collateral led to the eventual demise of hybrid subsumption and ushered in the era of the factory (see Marx 1981, pp. 730–1). So hybrid subsumption does not entail wage-labour. Therefore (4) holds. Given the truth of (3), it follows that (1), the wage-labour presupposition, is false.

---

[17] Amitava Dutt points out (in private communication) that the putative inverse relationship between profitability and worker autonomy may no longer hold, indeed may never have held. There are theoretical reasons to think this, based on incomplete contracts, efficiency wages, and so on. Moreover, the inverse relationship fails to explain the persistence of subcontracting and horizontal hierarchies, among other things. A comprehensive response would, I assume, study the conditions for the emergence of hierarchies in specific industries, along the lines suggested by Rajan and Zingales (2001). All I can do here is refer to the evidence adduced by Marglin (1975), Skillman (2007), and Ogilvie (2008), as to the relative cost-effectiveness of wage labour in Marx's time.

128 CAPITALIST EXPLOITATION: ITS FORMS, ORIGIN, AND FATE

I now further illustrate the falsehood of (1) with the help of examples from Indian economic development.

5.4.2 Banaji on subsumption

Like Skillman, Jairus Banaji has recently argued that antediluvian capital constitutes capitalist relations of production. Banaji offers numerous penetrating historical studies of these relations, from early Byzantium to contemporary India. Banaji's studies vindicate (3). In his discussion of the relationship between big, middle, and proletarianized peasantry in the mid-19th-century Deccan districts of India, Banaji writes:

> the extortion of surplus-labour as surplus-value, is *not* sufficient to constitute [formal] subordination. Thus, a monied capitalist (for example, a merchant, moneylender) may dominate the small producer on a *capitalist* basis, he may, in other words, extort surplus-value from him, without standing out as the 'immediate owner of the process of production' ... Clearly, such a system, a 'preformal' subordination of labour to capital, would tend to lead in the majority of cases to the system of formal subordination ... there might be historical situations where in the absence of a specifically capitalist mode of production on the national scale, capitalist relations of exploitation may nonetheless be widespread and dominant.   (Banaji 2010, pp. 281–2)

Banaji's 'pre-formal subordination' is equivalent to Skillman's 'primitive' subsumption, both of which are equivalent to what Marx calls hybrid subsumption.[18] It follows that Banaji affirms (3): merchant and usury capital sometimes constitute capitalist relations of production.[19]

But, unlike Skillman, Banaji balks at (4), the idea that merchant and usury capital do not involve wage-labour, preferring variations on (1) instead. So, in

---

[18] Rakesh Bhandari is therefore mistaken when he claims that 'Banaji counts as formal subsumption usurious or mercantile appropriation of surplus-value from atomised peasants and craftsmen' (Bhandari 2008, p. 87). Banaji explicitly distinguishes between *pre*-formal and formal subsumption, associating usury and merchant capital with the former.

[19] It also follows from the passage just cited that, unlike what some of his critics have maintained (e.g. Post 2013), Banaji's argument does not contradict the Brenner thesis. According to Brenner (1976), the capitalist mode of production first arose in England because the nature of class relations in 17th-century England was both necessary and sufficient for that mode. But now note that this thesis is perfectly compatible with Banaji's claim that capitalist *relations* of production predate the capitalist *mode* of production. Indeed, Brenner himself admits as much in his discussion of transitional forms (Brenner 1977, p. 52, n. 43). I discuss Brenner and Post further in section 5.4.3.

CAPITAL BEFORE WAGE-LABOUR   129

response to the charge that antediluvian forms of capital do not involve wage-labour, Banaji replies that they entail 'disguised wage-labour'. He writes, for example:

> instead of seeing wage-labour as *one* form of exploitation among many, alongside sharecropping, labour tenancy, and various kinds of bonded labour...these 'forms' may reflect the subsumption of labour into capital in ways where the 'sale' of labour power for wages is mediated and possibly disguised   (Banaji 2010, p. 145)

This attempt to defend (1) is incoherent.[20] For if usury and merchant capital entail wage-labour, disguised or not, then they (trivially) presuppose industrial production. The point of distinguishing sharply between hybrid and formal subsumption, however, is to show how, in the manner of Skillman, *the factory constitutes a turning point in the economic articulation of modernity.* The factory presupposes an all $\{All, None\}$ set of production relations, that is, the 'complete expropriation' of the producer. This is not the predicament of the producer under putting-out or usury, *as Banaji's own studies show.* In other words, if 'pre-formal' subsumption entails 'disguised' wage-labour, then Banaji's distinction between formal and preformal subsumption—indeed, the whole edifice of distinctions between a 'dependent middle peasantry' and a 'semi-wage-labour peasantry' (Banaji 2010, pp. 317–323)—collapses.[21] Banaji should, in all consistency, embrace (4) and reject (1). Capitalist relations of production do not presuppose labour markets or commodified labour power.

I conclude this historical excursus by considering the influential idea of market dependence. That idea also undermines the wage-labour presupposition (1) and further supports the definition of capital as subsumed labour.

5.4.3 Brenner and Wood on subsumption

This section considers an influential account of the transition from the pre-capitalist to the capitalist mode of production. This account posits the

---

[20] It is also inconsistent with Marx's writings on the topic. See, for example, Marx (1981, p. 730), where the 'wage-slave' and the 'debt-slave' are explicitly contrasted.

[21] As Banaji himself shows, Lenin's attack against the Narodniks (on the capitalist nature of Russian agriculture) only makes sense on the assumption that capitalist relations of production do not presuppose a labour market (Banaji 2010, pp. 50–1); that is, only if (4) holds. In his debate with the Narodniks, Lenin had to reject (1).

130 CAPITALIST EXPLOITATION: ITS FORMS, ORIGIN, AND FATE

extraction of surplus labour in the value form as a necessary but not sufficient condition for the subsumption of labour by capital. On this view, what completes the set of sufficient conditions is the existence of a specific form of relationship between markets and the direct producers. This view also contradicts (1).

Robert Brenner has argued that capitalist relations of production presuppose market dependence on the part of both capitalists and producers. It is, moreover, the asymmetric nature of that dependence that explains the rise of English agrarian capitalism. Market dependence is Brenner's main explanation for the secular growth of agricultural productivity in early modern England, largely accounting for its early industrialization (Brenner 1976, 1977). E.M. Wood elaborates:

> Economic units could be market-dependent—that is, separated from non-market access to the means of their self-reproduction—without being completely propertyless and even without employing propertyless wage labourers. (Wood 2002, p. 51)

Since, according to Brenner and Wood, these forms of market dependence constitute capitalist relations of production, the Brenner and Wood account contradicts the orthodox definition of capitalist social relations. Indeed, it entails the falsehood of (1). But what exactly *is* 'market dependence'? Here is a standard formulation, due to Charles Post:

> If the continued possession of land and tools for non-producers and access to consumer goods for direct producers ... does not depend upon successful market competition, then the law of value does not operate and the unique dynamics of capitalism (specialization, technical innovation and accumulation) do not pertain.[22]

By 'law of value' Post means the imperative to produce commodities at 'socially necessary labour time'—roughly cost of production—thereby maximizing exchange value.[23] There are three different, and progressively narrower, senses of market-dependence in Post's definition: (a) The broadest sense refers to lack of non-market access to the means of subsistence and production.

---

[22] Personal communication, 29/3/16. Post (2011, pp. 23–4) similarly defines capitalist social relations in terms of 'enforced dependence' and 'subordination ... to the law of value'.
[23] These commodities need not include labour power. To assume this is tantamount to the same *petitio principii* discussed in section 5.3.1.

CAPITAL BEFORE WAGE-LABOUR 131

(b) A narrower sense refers to subjection to market competition and the law of value. (c) A yet narrower sense refers to subjection to market competition that leads to 'specialization, technical innovation, accumulation' that is also potentially labour-saving.[24]

For our purposes, (b) offers the best specification of market dependence. On the one hand, (a) is too broad: on this definition, the monopsonistic feudal lord, or Marx's 'extravagant magnate', who lacks nonmarket access to grain, is market-dependent. (c), on the other hand, is too narrow. For on this definition, the pre-1905 agriculture of Russia (Lenin's agrarian *capitalism*), the Deccan capitalism of Banaji, the decadent industries of 'actually existing socialism', and many other instances of—presumptively capital-positing—backwardness betoken non-capitalist relations of production. Market dependence is therefore best defined in terms of subjection to the law of value, not the possible effects of that law.

In light of these amendments, capitalist relations of production can now be defined in terms of (i) the production of surplus labour, (ii) subjected to the imperative of cost minimization, (iii) *unilaterally extracted by exploiters in the value form*. Capital, I have argued throughout this book, just is monetized control over alien surplus labour. This has important implications. It implies, for example, that all forms of petty commodity production—self-employment, family farms, agricultural cooperatives, etc.—that are both exploited by others and subjected to the imperatives of profit maximization involve subsumption of labour to capital. Therefore, the petty commodity production of 17th-century middle English peasants (Byres 2006) or of 19th-century American family farms (Post 2011), insofar as they are exploited (by banks, merchants, and other capitalists), betoken capitalist relations of production. And now it follows, again, that capitalist relations of production do not presuppose a labour market; capital-subsumed self-employment, for instance, is not a kind of wage-labour.

So capitalist exploitation is broader than wage labour: (1) is false and domination at work is broader than domination in the workplace. I now argue that some forms of market socialism represent yet another, distinctive, form of capitalist exploitation. This supports the definition of capital as subsumed labour used throughout this book.

---

[24] Similar vacillation about the exact nature of dependence across (a)–(c) pervades Wood (1999) and Wood (2002).

132   CAPITALIST EXPLOITATION: ITS FORMS, ORIGIN, AND FATE

5.5 Capital After Wage-Labour

This section studies capitalism's fate. It argues that there is another (transitional) mode of subsumption, one that Marx left almost completely unexplored, save for some suggestive remarks in volume III of *Capital*. Unlike antediluvian subsumption, which bridges feudalism and capitalism, this 'postdiluvian' form bridges capitalism with socialism. The existence of this transitional mode is important, because it further supports my broad definition of capital as monetary title to alien labour capacity. The idea is that, if capital is labour subsumed in the transition *to capitalism*, then it must also be labour subsumed in the transition *to socialism*.

I proceed as follows: first, I show that Marx does indeed think there is a set of capitalist relations of production that provide a bridge between capitalism and socialism. I then offer an argument that this set of relations engenders a mode of subsumption distinct from the ones canvassed so far: hybrid, formal, real. The argument, roughly, is that if petty commodity production can be subsumed by capital through market dependence on usurers or merchants, then it can be subsumed by capital through market dependence *tout court*, that is, without usurers or merchants. In other words, capital can subsume labour through *mere exchange*. I will call this mode of subsumption *abstract subsumption*. Consider some textual evidence for the existence of this mode.

In discussion of the cooperative factories, Marx writes:

> These factories show how [...] a new mode of production develops and is formed naturally out of the old. Without the factory system that arises from the capitalist mode of production, cooperative factories could not develop. Nor could they do so without the credit system that develops from the same mode of production. This credit system, since it forms the principal basis for the gradual transformation of capitalist private enterprises into capitalist joint stock companies, presents in the same way the means for the gradual extension of cooperative enterprises on a more or less national scale. Capitalist joint-stock companies as much as cooperative factories should be viewed as transition forms from the capitalist mode of production to the associated one, simply that in the one case the opposition is abolished in a negative way, and in the other in a positive way.   (Marx 1981, p. 571)

The putative connections between the positivity of the 'cooperative enterprise' and the negativity of the 'capitalist joint stock company' are opaque

CAPITAL AFTER WAGE-LABOUR   133

unless juxtaposed with Marx's critique of the ideological conflation of 'profits of management' with 'wages of supervision':

> With the development of cooperatives on the workers' part, and joint-stock companies on the part of the bourgeoisie, the last pretext for confusing profit of enterprise with the wages of management was removed, and profit came to appear in practice as what is undeniably was in theory, mere surplus-value, value for which no equivalent was paid.   (Marx 1981, pp. 513–14)

This contrast is further illuminated by Marx's famous orchestra analogy:

> A musical conductor need in no way be the owner of the instruments in his orchestra, nor does it form part of his function as conductor that he should have any part in paying the 'wages' of the other musicians. Cooperative factories provide the proof that the capitalist has become just as superfluous as a functionary in production as he himself, from his superior vantage point, finds the large landlord.   (Marx 1981, p. 511)

Through a characteristically Marxian dialectic of self-abolition, the capitalist system generates a credit system, which makes possible the separation of ownership from control, which, if realized, paves the way for worker-controlled factories under a system of social ownership of the means of production.[25] But suppose all factories were turned into cooperatives. Would *that* suffice to abolish the domination of labour by capital? No. For then worker-controlled, socially owned, market-operating cooperatives are not a mere *transitional* form towards socialism; they *are* socialism. Marx rejects this conclusion. He writes:

> The cooperative factories run by workers themselves are, within the old form, the first examples of the emergence of a new form, even though they naturally reproduce in all cases, in their present organization, all the defects of the existing system, and must reproduce them. But the opposition between capital and labour is abolished here, even if at first only in the form that the

---

[25] Marx (1981, p. 503) draws a distinction between the capitalist as *owner* and as *function*. In the former role, the capitalist earns a return equal to the rate of interest. In the latter role, she organizes production and thereby earns a return in excess of the rate of interest. According to Marx, the existence of joint stock companies is evidence that the capitalist is no longer indispensable in her performance of the functional role.

134 CAPITALIST EXPLOITATION: ITS FORMS, ORIGIN, AND FATE

workers in association become their own capitalist, i.e. they use the means of production to valorize their own labour. (Marx 1981, p. 571)

There is much debate as to exactly what Marx means by workers becoming 'their own capitalist'.[26] But the conjunction of this passage with passages where Marx claims that *both* workers *and* capitalists are dominated under capitalism (see e.g. Marx 1976, p. 990) seems to entail that the reciprocal pressures of competition cause workers-turned-capitalists to suffer some form of domination, or 'enslavement' *even where all factories are profit-maximizing cooperatives.*

Is this claim defensible? It is, I believe, defensible, but not for the widely held reason that market-operating cooperatives 'self-exploit'.[27] Section 5.6 refutes the 'self-exploitation' idea and suggests a reading of what 'valorize their own labour' means, one based on the idea of the abstract subsumption of labour to capital.

5.6 The Case Against Market Socialism

How does capital subsume labour in the transition to socialism? This section elaborates on the possibility that capital-using workers' cooperatives can subsume each other's labour. To do this, I will first identify the nature of subjection of productive purposiveness—labour subsumption—in the transition to socialism. I will then explain the relevance of this form of subsumption for contemporary debates on the 'gig economy' and precarious labour.

5.6.1 Against self-exploitation

Market socialism has been proposed as a half-way institutional remedy to exploitation that is neither based on central planning nor completely decentralized, as in some syndicalist theories. Instead, market socialism represents a decentralized form of worker management based on profit maximization, in which: (a) the means of production are jointly owned (either by workers

---

[26] See, for example, Jossa (2012) and Lebowitz (2010).

[27] Another common Marxist reaction is to treat this as a variant of petty commodity production and then dismiss it as economically unstable (see e.g. Cohen 1978, p. 186, Mandel 1974, pp. 7–41). But Marx does not say that workers become their own capitalists *after* competing cooperatives go bankrupt; they become capitalists the moment they 'use the means of production to valorize their own labour'. The question of instability is neither here nor there.

THE CASE AGAINST MARKET SOCIALISM   135

or by the state), (b) firms are democratically controlled by the workers in the firm, allowing them to share in the profit, and (c) production is for a market, in which values are determined by average or marginal cost. Economic democracy of the market socialist variety achieves inter-firm equilibrium through maximization of profit: the individual firm's maximand is revenue per worker. Thus in long-run competitive equilibrium the firms that survive are those, and only those, that make an economic profit greater than, or equal to, zero.[28]

A common complaint levelled against market socialism is that it encourages the 'self-exploitation' of workers. The idea seems to be that, since capitalists exploit workers, and since all workers are capitalists, capitalist-workers exploit capitalist-workers, that is, workers exploit themselves.[29] This complaint is incoherent. As a matter of conceptual necessity, to exploit is to benefit at someone else's expense (see Chapter 1). It follows that A cannot exploit A, and that A cannot exploit B if A does not extract a presumptive net benefit from some transaction with B. So even if it did make sense to say that workers somehow harm or degrade themselves under market socialism, it would still be false that they self-*exploit*. I now explain the real case against market socialism, which further illustrates the subsumed-labour definition of capital.

5.6.2 The real case against market socialism

Suppose there is a system of commodity production without a labour or a credit market. Under such a market system, different firms will come to control differential assets, depending on how successful they are at accumulating capital. The whole point of allowing the existence of profit-seeking firms, after all, is to take advantage of the coordinating informational signals putatively furnished by competitive markets. Now, some firms will do badly and will have to lay people off. Others will do well and will need to hire people. More successful firms will accumulate more wealth. It is a short step from this inequality to the claim that one firm can exploit another. The *Horizontal* case, already canvassed in Chapter 4, shows how this is possible:

---

[28] The most well-developed account of workers' cooperatives under market socialism is due to David Schweickart (1996, 2011). I discuss the Schweickart model, juxtaposed to Roemer's, in Chapter 7.

[29] This complaint does not describe *intra-firm* exploitation—for example, the exploitation of cooperative workers by cooperative managers. Rather, the idea is that a capital-subsumed economic unit can exploit itself even if it has only one member. Post (2011, p. 28) attributes self-exploitation to petty commodity producers—competition-subsumed individuals or family farms—in the antebellum USA.

136   CAPITALIST EXPLOITATION: ITS FORMS, ORIGIN, AND FATE

Horizontal—There are two cooperatives, Robinson Inc. and Friday Inc., trading only in final goods. Each firm has five employees and is operated democratically. Robinson Inc. is capital-rich, Friday Inc. is capital-poor. The economy-wide net product is worth $80 and the monetary expression of labour time is unity. In equilibrium, each member of the Robinson Inc. coop works 4 hours and receives 8 hours of labour time (expressed in her individual income of $8), while each member of the Friday Inc. coop works 12 hours and consumes 8 hours (expressed in her individual income of $8).

In Chapter 4, I called this horizontal exploitation.[30] That is, as long as Friday Inc. unilaterally appropriates surplus in value form, there is extraction of *surplus value*: having worked for four hours, the members of Robinson Inc. can relax for the rest of the day, while the members of Friday Inc. toil to produce what the former would otherwise have produced only with an extra four hours of work.

Now, insofar as it involves monetized control over alien labour capacity, the *Horizontal* case is a capitalist relation of production. I want to argue that such transactions, obtaining through mere trade in goods and in the absence of labour and credit markets, constitute abstract subsumption of labour by capital. Subsumption, I said at the outset, is a *freedom term*: it describes the way capital dominates labour. In the present example, Robinson Inc. clearly possesses a power over Friday Inc. The evidence for this is the discrepancy in the number of hours worked, engendered by a power that gets Friday Inc. to unilaterally serve Robinson Inc. for a full eight hours.[31] This subsumption of purposiveness is abstract in the sense that, unlike formal and real subsumption, it does not depend on the existence of a labour market and, unlike hybrid subsumption, it does not depend on the existence of a credit or money market. It is a capitalist relation of production that is, for all present purposes, abstracted from these institutions.

It is, now, but a short step to the claim that some forms of market socialism involve abstract subsumption. For cooperatives, even the most successful ones, will need access to raw materials, machinery, and other objective conditions of labour. Under market socialism, by assumption, these can only be purchased from other cooperatives. So the process of accumulation will eventually

---

[30] 'The relationship between labour days of different countries may be similar to that existing between skilled, complex labour and unskilled, simple labour within a country. In this case, the richer country exploits the poorer one, even where the latter gains by the exchange.' (Marx 1972, p. 106). It follows that the rich can exploit the poor in the absence of a labour or credit market.

[31] In Chapter 2 I argued that insofar as these inequalities are not independently justified they constitute servitude.

THE CASE AGAINST MARKET SOCIALISM   137

manifest itself in unequal exchanges of the *Horizontal* variety.[32] Such exchanges are capital-positing, insofar as they involve monetized extraction of surplus labour—an expression of unilateral control over alien purposiveness.[33]

I now explain in what sense abstract subsumption is a distinctive form of capitalist domination.

5.6.3 How abstract subsumption is distinctive

Capitalist power, in the form of abstract subsumption, does not presuppose credit or labour markets. I now illustrate the differences between abstract subsumption and the other modes of subsumption discussed so far: hybrid, formal, and real. Take hybrid subsumption first. There are some relationships between cooperatives that satisfy the usury circuit (first row of Table 5.2). Vanek's (1970) labour-managed firms, for example, have this form. Vanekian cooperatives are funded by loans from profit-seeking cooperative banks. They are therefore subject not to abstract but to *hybrid* subsumption: bank and cooperative occupy the same positions in the capitalist structure as usurer and peasant, respectively. Of course Vanekian labour-managed firms might be an excellent idea, as far as the medium-term freedom and autonomy of producers is concerned,[34] but that does not implicate these structures any less in hybrid subsumption. So abstract subsumption does not obtain in Vanek-type cooperative relations; it only obtains where a cooperative exploits another in the absence of a credit or labour market.

Now take formal and real subsumption. As I argued earlier, both of these presuppose a labour market. Abstract subsumption, like hybrid subsumption, does not presuppose a labour market. To illustrate the contrast, suppose there is a system of profit-seeking, worker-managed cooperatives that can freely hire and fire workers. Whenever there is a layoff, the state acts as employer of last resort (see Schweickart 2011). In this institutional setting, all unemployment is frictional and wage-labour is abolished, in the sense that wages and employment are no longer determined by the cost of reproducing the worker (however that cost is determined). Suppose, further, that there is a publicly

---

[32] The success of some cooperatives will sometimes depend solely on the superior talents of their members. When that happens, abstract subsumption obtains due to mere talent inequality, or, more generally, what Roemer (1988) calls inequality of *inalienable* assets. In Chapter 7 I discuss this idea in connection with the related notion of the labour epistocracy.

[33] In the Appendix I discuss horizontal exploitation across cooperatives with different capital–labour ratios.

[34] See Ellerman (2007) for an elegant recent defence of the Vanekian account.

138   CAPITALIST EXPLOITATION: ITS FORMS, ORIGIN, AND FATE

owned bank that provides loans to cooperatives without extracting surplus value from them. There is therefore no usury-type relation between banks and Vanekian cooperatives. For all practical purposes, no capital-positing credit or labour markets exist. There is, by implication, no hybrid, formal, or real subsumption of the worker. Yet horizontal exploitation may survive; cooperatives can 'valorize their own labour' by subjecting one another to unilateral control over that labour. These relations constitute abstract subsumption, referred to in Chapter 2 as domination at work.

It is worth pointing out, finally, that the abstract subsumption of labour, unlike formal and real subsumption, does not presuppose *bossing*, the domination of direct producers by capitalist bosses.[35] Abolishing bossing removes an intra-firm relation of servitude—*vertical capitalist exploitation*. But if there is such a thing as the abstract subsumption of labour by capital, then the abolition of bossing does not suffice to abolish inter-firm servitude—*horizontal capitalist exploitation*. Only democratic control over aggregate investment can do that.[36]

So the case for abstract subsumption is defensible. On the view I have defended, Marx's account of cooperative workers as 'valorizing their own labour' has critical force. I conclude by discussing some corollaries of the main theses defended in this chapter.

5.7 How Capitalists Dominate

This section summarizes the argument of the previous sections and draws some tentative conclusions. Capital, I have argued, can dominate workers in a number of distinct ways, each falling under the four genera of hybrid, formal, real, and abstract subsumption. Both Mercedes-Benz and Uber, for example, could be said to exploit their workers. They differ, however, in the kind of dominating power they possess. On the view defended in this book, subsumption *categorizes* capitalist exploitation. Table 5.3 illustrates the relevant positions, along with a historical instance of each.

All four modes of subsumption survive under contemporary capitalism. Take, for example, hybrid subsumption, and more specifically interest-bearing capital, the contemporary incarnation of usury capital. On a widely held view, credit institutions—hereafter 'banks'—do not extract surplus value directly

---

[35] Marglin (1975) claims that bossing is *a* source of domination under capitalist relations of production. My account is compatible with Marglin's.

[36] I discuss this conclusion in Chapter 7 and defend it in Vrousalis (2019a).

HOW CAPITALISTS DOMINATE   139

Table 5.3 How capitalists dominate

	Antediluvian			Postdiluvian
Subsumption mode	Hybrid	Formal	Real	Abstract
Example	Putting-out	Manufacturing	Industry	Cooperatives
Transitional	Yes	No	No	Yes

from producers (see e.g. Fine and Saad-Filho 2004, pp. 137, 145). Rather, they extract surplus value from industrial capitalists who, in turn, extract it from wage-labourers. So hybrid subsumption does not survive under industrial capitalism. This argument is demonstrably unsound.

Consider the case of B, who is self-employed and has bought a house with a mortgage from bank A. B uses her home office to work; in this sense her office is equivalent to the handicraftsman's workshop. Suppose, further, that B produces value added in the office, just like the handicraftsman produces value added in the workshop. In lending to B for interest, A unilaterally controls and appropriates newly-created surplus *value*, along the lines represented by the first row of Table 5.2. Therefore A's relation to B is a capitalist relation of production. The traditional view that surplus extraction must be mediated by wage-labour cannot make sense of this conclusion. For, by failing to acknowledge *nonwage* modes of labour subsumption as capitalist, it misconstrues the relationship between A and B as wage-labour 'in disguise' (Fine and Saad-Filho 2004, p. 140). As I showed in the case of Banaji in section 5.4, this is a common misconception, which makes for bad theory and incoherent politics.

The politics of 'disguised-wage-labour' is incoherent because its suppressed premiss—that wage-labour is the only source of surplus value—implies that wage labour is the unique object of capitalist exploitation. And now it follows that, if this class shrinks—due to, say, deindustrialization, an exogenous increase in self-employment, or spontaneous growth in the 'gig economy'— then the scope of capitalist exploitation shrinks. No opponent of capitalist exploitation today would accept this pro-capitalist conclusion. But many of those who do reject it do not realize that it follows validly from claim (1). Hence their appeals to 'forms of disguised wage-labour' and similar gimmicks. Opponents of capitalist exploitation must either drop claim (1), along the lines canvassed earlier, or accept the pro-capitalist conclusion.

I conclude this chapter by considering some implications of abstract subsumption for market socialism. Defenders of market socialism deny that cooperatives, such as Mondragon's, can exploit (see e.g. Schweickart 2011).

140   CAPITALIST EXPLOITATION: ITS FORMS, ORIGIN, AND FATE

That is, whether or not Mondragon-type cooperatives are capitalistically dominated by banks and other credit institutions, they do not themselves exploit, or dominate, other firms. That belief is false. Despite the huge benefits that accrue to the advancement of human freedom from democratizing the workplace, cooperatives implicated in capitalist structures are destined to 'reproduce in all cases, in their present organization, all the defects of the existing system'. Absent democratic control over the bulk of aggregate investment, cooperatives can extract surplus value from each other. They thereby subject other cooperating humans to their own ends *through mere trade*. So the subsumption of labour to capital—monetized control over alien productive purposiveness—can linger in the absence of wage-labour.

Conclusion

The chapter has studied the problem of how capital performs and generalizes a historically specific form of exploitation. It argued that wage-labour is not a necessary condition for capitalist relations of production. Capital, I have been insisting, is monetary title to unilateral control over alien labour capacity. So capitalist production relations should be construed more broadly than wage-labour, as forms of subsumption of labour to capital. The chapter defended the idea of two distinctive forms of subsumption which unite Marx's writings on the transition to and from capitalism. It concluded by using these definitions to develop a critique of market socialism. Chapter 6 extends the domination account of exploitation to international relations and the institutions of capitalist globalization.

Appendix: Exploitation across heterogenuous firms

This Appendix studies the implications of differing capital intensities for horizontal capitalist exploitation—exploitation across firms. In volume III of *Capital*, Marx introduces the famous 'transformation problem', dealing with the transformation of values into prices. Although this problem is beyond the scope of this book, Marx's proposed solution has some bearing on whether he thought abstract subsumption possible. I now argue that, Marx's solution— whether sound or not—entails horizontal exploitation of cooperatives by cooperatives.

HOW CAPITALISTS DOMINATE 141

The transformation problem arises because different capitalist firms or industries have different organic compositions of capital.[37] If prices and values are assumed proportional and if the ratio between surplus value and the wage bill is assumed constant—Marx calls this ratio the *rate of exploitation*—then firms with higher than average organic composition (call them F_{high}) will tend to earn lower than average profits, whereas firms with lower than average organic composition (call them F_{low}) will earn higher than average profits. But if there is a uniform rate of profit, which Marx (1981, pp. 254–301) assumes, then the excess surplus value extracted in F_{low} will be redistributed from F_{low} to F_{high} until profit rates are equal. The only way this transfer can be effected is if relative prices satisfy: $p_{F_{high}}/p_{F_{low}}>1$. And this, in turn, implies that relative prices will not be proportional to relative values at the level of the individual commodities. The set of prices formed out of the equalization of the rates of profit Marx calls *prices of production*.

Now, Marx's argument implies that F_{high} draws surplus labour from F_{low} *à la* Roemer, such that capital-intensive cooperatives exploit labour-intensive cooperatives. This is the horizontal mechanism we were looking for, which corroborates the abstract subsumption view of section 5.6. What we have here, in other words, is the horizontal power-induced extraction of unilateral labour flow: exploitation.

What does this imply for market socialism? Suppose the allocation of investment were made to depend exclusively on the market-mediated private decisions of worker-owned cooperatives. It would follow that some firms accumulate more capital than others, either due to the technical nature of their production process or due to success in competition. This implies differences in organic composition between F_{high} and F_{low}, generating transfers of surplus value from the latter to the former. If there is no independent justification for this transfer, workers in labour-intensive cooperatives will become the unhired servants of workers in capital-intensive cooperatives. And this is how cooperatives can exploit cooperatives through mere market exchange.

---

[37] Marx distinguishes between the *technical*, the *value*, and the *organic composition of capital*. The technical composition is simply the ratio of the mass of the means of production to the mass of labour necessary to set them into motion. The value composition is the value of the means of production, or *constant capital*, to the value of labour power, or *variable capital*. The organic composition is the value composition expressed as an increasing function of the technical composition (Marx 1976, pp. 762–3). See Howard and King (1975, pp. 196–8) for a simple model.

6

Exploitation and International Relations

This book argues that exploitation is a form of domination, the dividend the powerful extract from the servitude of the vulnerable. This chapter undertakes to extend the domination theory to international relations. The domination of one political community or state by another is called imperialism.[1] So if there is exploitation in international relations, and if my domination account is sound, then international exploitation must take the form of imperialism. As I will try to show, the conceptual toolkit of imperialism is useful, indeed indispensable, to understanding salient aspects of contemporary capitalist globalization.

In what follows, I use the critical resources of previous chapters to buttress an account of imperialism that makes the inference from international exploitation to imperialism palatable. Section 6.1 offers some definitions. Section 6.2 argues that there is a useful and defensible distinction between colonial and liberal imperialism, which maps on to a distinction between what I will call coercive and liberal domination. Section 6.3 argues that the main institutions of capitalist globalization, such as the WTO, the IMF, the World Bank, and so on, are largely the instruments of liberal imperialism; they are a reincarnation of what Karl Kautsky once called 'ultraimperialism'. Section 6.4 argues that resistance to imperialism is not, fundamentally, about a right to national self-determination. Such a right, it turns out, is conditional upon and derivative of the demands of working-class internationalism.

6.1 Domination in International Relations

This section distinguishes between two forms of domination, coercive and liberal, which map on to the distinction between colonial and liberal imperialism. Domination, I argued in Chapter 2, is unilateral or arbitrary or misrecognitive

---

[1] Although exploitation is not part of the definition of imperialism, it does seem to be a necessary condition for its reproduction. One important task is to explain how imperial exploitation under capitalism differs in *form* from imperial exploitation under pre-capitalist economic formations. The answer must have something to do with the historical novelty of so-called *informal empire*, which I discuss in this chapter.

Exploitation as Domination: What Makes Capitalism Unjust. Nicholas Vrousalis, Oxford University Press.
© Nicholas Vrousalis 2023. DOI: 10.1093/oso/9780192867698.003.0007

DOMINATION IN INTERNATIONAL RELATIONS   143

control over alien purposiveness. That unilateralism is clearly exemplified in the mundane space of the school playground. Here, the menace of the playground bully cuts a distinctive figure. The bully, P, engages in *coercive domination* when she physically forces Q to do what she wants, or issues credible threats to that effect. This is the bully at her thuggish best: she beats the kids who will not hand over their toys, threatens their friends, builds alliances with other kids to obtain access to the toys of the weaker kids, and keeps in shape so she can make the threat of force credible.

Now, coercive domination is unjust because it is a form of domination, not because it is a form of coercion. Coercion, in this sense, merely *categorizes* domination, but is neither necessary nor sufficient for the latter.[2] For there is a distinct form of domination, which I will call *liberal domination*,[3] and which does not involve coercion. Liberal domination involves P getting Q to do things in noncoercive but dominating ways. P might manipulate or deceive Q, bribe Q, or simply brainwash Q to want what P wants. Manipulation, deception and bribery are undue inducements, all of which normally imply domination. The most subtle form of liberal domination, in this sense, is *hegemony*: P's ability to get Q to want what P wants, by going to work directly on Q's preferences.[4]

The liberal bully is a true master of the subtler forms of thuggery: she manipulates other kids into handing over their toys, manipulates her friends into abstaining from sharing their toys unless she gets the lion's share, gets her friends not to lend to those who do not share with her, and accumulates toys just so she can deny access to the kids who will benefit most from playing with them. The liberal bully bullies because she unilaterally subjects the purposiveness of others to her ends.[5] This concludes my taxonomy of two forms of domination.

---

[2] Indeed, coercion sometimes *prevents* domination, as when the teacher coerces P to protect Q from domination. In exercising her coercive power, the teacher does not dominate P: insofar as her power over P is geared towards making available free actions for Q, it is only a 'hindering of a hindrance to freedom' (Kant 1996, p. 388).

[3] I call it 'liberal' just because the term resonates with the liberal form of imperialism I discuss in section 6.2.

[4] Hegemony, in this sense, is equivalent to what Nye (2005) has underhandedly called 'soft power'. See Lukes (1974, 2005) for discussion of this 'third dimension' of power.

[5] In Chapter 2, I discussed diverse justifications of the Non-Servitude Proviso—Kantian, republican, and recognitional. Some republicans construe domination as failure to track the interests of the vulnerable (see, for discussion, Pettit 2010, Gädeke 2016). The case has been made that the 'imperial liberalism' of the British Empire mobilized an institutional framework designed to track the interests of colonized peoples, and sometimes explicitly avowed such a commitment (see Pitts 2006 and section 6.3). But even if it is granted that colonialism sometimes tracked indigenous interests—'what did the Romans ever do for us?'—the Proviso itself envisages no incompatibility between tracking your interests and dominating you.

144 EXPLOITATION AND INTERNATIONAL RELATIONS

Note that the coercive and liberal forms of domination are strategic complements. In the context of international relations, the sometimes alternating, sometimes overlapping deployment of coercive and liberal modes of bullying is called 'diplomacy'. I begin by offering definitions that extend this taxonomy to international relations.

6.2 Colonial and Liberal Imperialism

Imperialism is the domination of one political community or state by another. A political community is any large-scale association of people capable of self-rule that claims a *de jure* right to self-rule through monopoly over the means of violence in its territory. A state is a political community whose right to self-rule is *de facto*.

Historians of imperialism, especially of the British Empire, have defended a distinction between 'formal' and 'informal' empire. The distinction was popularized by John Gallagher and Ronald Robinson in a celebrated 1953 paper entitled 'The Imperialism of Free Trade'. The term has also been used by Hobsbawm in his famous tetralogy of the ages of revolution, capital, empire, and extremes, and has gained currency among imperial historians such as Cain, Hopkins, and others. I will argue that this distinction is still useful, in a world where colonies are much less ubiquitous than they used to be, but where imperialism of the informal variety, embodied in the institutions of capitalist globalization, is no less ubiquitous. I discuss these institutions in Section 6.3. In this section I sketch the connections between formal and informal empire, or *colonial* and *liberal imperialism*.[6] I will argue that the former presupposes coercive and the latter liberal domination.

Gallagher and Robinson (1953) contrast British overseas expansion during the 19th century through 'informal empire' with 'dominion in the strict constitutional sense' (Gallagher and Robinson 1953, p. 1). Hobsbawm likewise asserts that Britain's informal empire consisted of 'independent states which were in effect [its] satellite economies' (Hobsbawm 1989, p. 74), but is not troubled by the joint ascription of independence and satellitehood to these states. In a similar vein, Ernest Mandel writes:

---

[6] Liberal imperialism contrasts with what Pitts (2006) calls *imperial liberalism*, which was, in fact, the form of *colonial* imperialism advocated by liberals such as J.S. Mill. Lichteim (1971) provides an informal introduction to the variants of imperialism discussed in this chapter.

On the morrow of the Second World War, the colonial revolution shook the foundations of the imperialist system. In order to continue to exploit the colonial countries, the capitalists of the metropolitan countries were increasingly obliged to go over from direct to indirect methods of domination. One after another the colonial countries were transformed into semi-colonial countries, that is, they attained political independence.

(Mandel 1962, p. 480)

Formal empire, according to Mandel, consists in state A's domination of B, through the direct exercise of both political and economic control by A over B. Informal empire does not involve exercise of political control. But what is 'political control'? In response to this question, A.G. Hopkins appeals to the related notion of 'sovereignty':

the concept of informal empire...is in principle a valuable means of categorising conditions of domination and subordination whereby a major state acts as an integrative force, exercising power in ways that infringe the sovereignty of smaller countries.   (Hopkins 1994, p. 483)

On any set of definitions of imperialism, India at the end of the 19th century must count as part of Britain's formal empire, whereas Argentina must come under the ambit of its informal empire (Hopkins 1994, p. 476. Cf. Hobsbawm 1999, Marichal 1989). But what is this 'sovereignty' that looms large in these definitions? Crucially, how does its violation under colonial imperialism contrast with its violation under liberal imperialism? The historians' answer seems to be that liberal imperialism is just colonial imperialism minus 'sovereignty'. That is, state A exercises liberal imperialism over state B only if A controls a substantial proportion of B's means of production, but not B's political process, including the appointment and operation of government. By contrast, A exercises colonial imperialism over B only if A controls *both* B's means of production and B's political process.

This way of drawing the distinction is misleading. For liberal imperialism *also* involves a measure of control over B's political process, albeit *through A's control over B's scarce productive assets*. In other words, loss of 'sovereignty' is insufficient for distinguishing between colonial and liberal imperialism, for it is common to them both.

If sovereignty cannot buttress the distinction, then perhaps it is existentially dependent on the *mode* of domination, coercive or liberal, that I sketched earlier. The rest of this section defends this claim. I will first discuss pure cases of colonial and liberal imperialism and then bring in hybrid cases.

146 EXPLOITATION AND INTERNATIONAL RELATIONS

6.2.1 Colonial imperialism

Colonial imperialism, in its purest form, entails coercive domination. The maintenance of the British colony in India during the 19th century, for example, involved unilateral control over the latter through occupation, blockades, and engineered famines, initially at the behest of the East India Company, and eventually of the British Crown. The fact that some Indian leaders, and a portion of the population, were loyal to the Empire does not disculpate the latter of domination. In light of these examples, one might object that colonial imperialism is simply *alien territorial control* and that, as a consequence, the concept of coercive domination is superfluous.

There are conceptual and normative problems with this suggestion. First, the concept of alien territorial control is itself slippery. Suppose state A withdraws armies from B's territory, but maintains a credible threat of, say, invading B. Has state B regained control over its own territory? Or suppose state A issues a credible threat to starve the residents of B, unless B hands over half of its annual silver production. Does B possess control over its own territory?

More importantly, insofar as imperialism is a form of domination, what makes it unjust is not captured, without remainder, by appeal to mere *territorial* entitlement. Suppose individual P owns the only well in the territory, Q needs access to water, and Q has access to no water source other than P's well. As it happens, P has a moral right to *exclusive* use of the well, either because her original appropriation of it was morally legitimate, or because Q has waived or forfeited a right of access. It is still unjust for P to use this ownership-conferred power to convert Q into a lifetime servant in return for access to the well.[7] So mere territorial entitlement does not accurately describe the colonial predicament. A more compelling hypothesis as to what makes that predicament unjust appeals instead to domination, as defined by the Non-Servitude Proviso of Chapter 2.[8]

Now, coercive domination is necessary but not sufficient for colonial imperialism, since state A can coerce B in order to *eschew* colonization. Suppose that A wants or needs access to B's silver, which B is unwilling to provide. A uses coercion to throw B's door open, thus obtaining unimpeded access to B's silver thereafter. Forcing a door open is a convenient way of ensuring unforced traffic—in people or goods—that serves A's interests at the expense of B's. The open door analogy suggests that it is possible to enlist coercion in the interest

---

[7] I defend this claim in Chapter 3, section 3.4.1.

[8] For an account of the injustice of colonialism congenial to this conclusion, see Ypi (2013).

COLONIAL AND LIBERAL IMPERIALISM   147

of *not* having to use coercion. When this is the case, A enlists an army but installs no viceroy; coercion merely clears the path to exploitative extraction.[9]

So these are instances of coercive domination that are not tantamount to colonial imperialism. What completes the set of sufficient conditions for the latter is some form of enduring and direct political control of one state by another: A enlists an army *and* installs a viceroy in B's territory. Restriction of sovereignty, in this sense, only helps complete the set of sufficient conditions. I now explain how colonial contrasts with liberal imperialism.

6.2.2 Liberal imperialism

By contrast with colonial imperialism, liberal imperialism presupposes liberal domination. This sometimes involves the addition of genuine options, such as a lucrative trade deal, leading to improvement in the situation of the subaltern state. Recall that the liberal bully never gets her hands dirty: all she does is provide inducements that promote her interests through exercise of unilateral control over a share of the subaltern's net product. So liberal domination sometimes involves the dominator promoting her servant's interests in a way that increases her hold over that servant, much like the drug pusher who increases her hold over the addict by offering drugs.[10]

One well-known paradigm of liberal imperialism is Britain's relation to Latin America from 1870 to 1914. This is the era of free trade and the 'gentlemanly capitalism' of the City of London.[11] Here 'the very process which weakened British production—the rise of new industrial powers, the enfeeblement of the British competitive power—reinforced the triumph of finance and trade' (Hobsbawm 1999, p. 110. See also Barratt Brown 1963, p. 63). Consider, as an instance of this general phenomenon, the British Empire's relationship with Argentina.

---

[9] The US post-war policy of the 'open door' had already been put to good use by the British Empire in its 19th-century dealings with China and Egypt. For a wealth of examples from recent history supporting the view that the international economic order has a strongly coercive dimension, see Cavallero (2010).

[10] The underdevelopment literature seems to have gone awry precisely in its assumption that imperialism is *incompatible* with economic development. See Frank (1976) and Wallerstein (2011) for exposition on the main underdevelopment themes and Lichtheim (1971) for trenchant criticism. Hopkins (1994) offers an illuminating defence of the case for informal empire, while rejecting the main conclusions of underdevelopment and dependency theory.

[11] The term 'gentlemanly capitalism' is due to Cain and Hopkins (2001, pp. 135–50), who track the ascendancy of British liberal imperialism in Latin America through the rise of finance capital.

148 EXPLOITATION AND INTERNATIONAL RELATIONS

Prior to the sovereign debt crisis of 1890 (the 'Barings' crisis), Argentina had embarked on an ambitious debt-financed railway-building programme. Its largest creditor was the London-based Barings Bank. When the Argentinian state became unable to finance its debt obligations to Barings, the Bank of England intervened by orchestrating an international rescue for Barings, with the direct involvement of prominent British bankers. British and Argentinian banks raised interest rates and the Argentinian government embarked on a decade-long recessionary programme of debt refinancing. The country's national income only recovered to its pre-crisis levels by the turn of the century; the recovery itself was fueled by intensified exploitation of workers and peasants, significant reductions in real wages and pensions, and a surge in unemployment and poverty. An integral part of this 'structural adjustment' programme *avant la lettre* was the full resumption of interest payments to British banks and a return to the Gold Standard by 1898. A.G. Hopkins elaborates:

> This reaction was fully in accord with London's judgement, which was formed in the knowledge that Argentina had no alternative sources of external capital and was managed by an elite that ... could be trusted in the end to conform to the rules of the game. This was not a deal between peers: the parties had joint interests, but not equal power in pursuing them. (Hopkins 1994, p. 481)

So the British Empire dominated Argentina without coercing it; this was an instance of liberal imperialism. More generally, if state A possesses a sufficient degree of control over B's scarce productive assets, either through A's financial institutions or through foreign direct investment, then A possesses unilateral control over B's powers of self-determination, which grounds its domination of B.

These distinctions generate three conceptual possibilities. First, colonial imperialism, involving army and viceroy. Second, liberal imperialism, involving neither army nor viceroy. Third, hybrid imperialism, which is a combination of coercive domination—A forces B's door open—and liberal domination—A buys B's factories for a pittance once the door is open. Schematically, the possibilities are:

(a) Colonial imperialism = unilateral alien control over another state's scarce productive assets with direct political control through (threats of) force.

GLOBALIZATION AND INTERNATIONAL EXPLOITATION   149

(b) Liberal imperialism = unilateral control without direct political control or (threats of) force.
(c) Hybrid imperialism = unilateral control with (threats of) force but without direct political control.

The social theory of liberal imperialism I have laid out has important implications for our understanding of the contemporary institutions of globalization. I turn to these presently.

6.3 Globalization and International Exploitation

A necessary condition for the reproduction of imperialism is the exploitation of *indigenous* by *metropolitan* states. The metropolis dominates, with a view to appropriating a share of the indigenous net product, thereby facilitating its own enrichment. This section has two parts. The first sketches the relevant exploitative connections between states and classes. The second sets out a simple model that purports to answer the 'who exploits whom?' question in international relations.

6.3.1 States and classes

This section clarifies some assumptions underlying the class analysis of imperialism under globalized capitalism.

Suppose there are two states, rich (S_R) and poor (S_P). On a rudimentary model of domination under capitalism, each state comprises two classes: capitalists C_i and workers L_i, $i = R, P$. In S_R, for example, C_R exploits and thereby dominates L_R; this is a structural fact entailed by the relative position of C_R and L_R in S_R, in conjunction with the definition of domination as subsumption of one's powers of self-determination. In the case that exercises exploitation theorists, C_R's control over scarce productive assets gives C_R unilateral control over the several labour powers of L_R and therefore over the social surplus that L_R alone produces. This generates six variables, where:

$$C_R, S_R, C_P, S_P, L_R, L_P$$

stand for capitalists, states, and workers in states R and P, respectively. On the assumption that states can themselves exploit other states and classes, the

150 EXPLOITATION AND INTERNATIONAL RELATIONS

Table 6.1 Who dominates whom (full logical partition)

	C_R	S_R	C_P	S_P	L_R
Dominates	S_R, C_P, S_P, L_R, L_P	C_P, S_P, L_R, L_P	S_P, L_R, L_P	L_R, L_P	L_P

aforementioned variables are ordered such that, for any group i, any group to its left dominates i and any group to its right is dominated by i. The idea is that capitalists in the rich state can dominate everyone else; rich states themselves can, in turn, dominate everyone else, minus the rich capitalists; the capitalists of the poor states can dominate everyone minus rich states and capitalists; and so on. This generates a total of fifteen possibilities, presented in Table 6.1.

For the purposes of exposition, Table 6.1 contains too many variables. To make the exposition manageable, I will assume a reductive view of the state, namely *instrumentalism*. Instrumentalists maintain that the state is but a weapon in the hands of a class. The instrumentalist assumption is unrealistic and relies on an agential view of the state. But unrealistic assumptions are admissible if they help to generate novel predictions. The classical theories of imperialism developed by John Hobson and Rudolf Hilferding in the early 20th century did generate such predictions.[12] In the Appendix to this chapter I loosen the instrumentalist assumption and explain which of the bilateral relationships of Table 6.1 are exploitative and why.

Now, on the instrumentalist assumption, the agency of S_i is simply absorbed by C_i, for all i: capitalists use the state as a battering ram for the extraction of surplus labour. The schema of Table 6.1 therefore simplifies to the special-case schema of Table 6.2.

Table 6.2 Who dominates whom (instrumentalist partition)

	C_R	C_P	L_R
Dominates	C_P, L_R, L_P	L_R, L_P	L_P

We are now in a position to discuss the basics of a sociology of imperialism and its implications for international exploitation.

---

[12] Those theories predicted the rise of colonial imperialism and how it would lead to war. They went something like this: capital has an inherent tendency to expand beyond the borders of the state. But the state always follows capital in the pursuit of market share as its guardian and protector; it is capital's bouncer. Clashes between different capitalist states are therefore inevitable, and so is war. Thus capitalism reaches its 'highest stage' when it makes world war inevitable. That stage Lenin calls 'imperialism' (note that Lenin *by definition* precludes the possibility of liberal imperialism). An alternative to instrumentalism sees the state as capable of some degree of autonomy, indeed sufficient autonomy to dominate non-state agents, including certain types of capitalist. I discuss these possibilities in the Appendix.

GLOBALIZATION AND INTERNATIONAL EXPLOITATION   151

6.3.2 How imperialists exploit

How do C_R, the capitalists of the rich state, exploit L_P, the workers of the poor state? The case that preoccupied classical theories of imperialism was capital exports. Here, the source of surplus-extraction is activities like Foreign Direct Investment (FDI): by investing directly in P's land, equipment and machinery, and by offering higher wages than C_P, C_R is able to directly exploit L_P. If the central argument of this book is sound, C_R thereby dominates L_P. This is what sweatshops are all about, for example. But C_R's exploitation of L_P—sweatshop labour—does not suffice for imperialism proper. As long as the rich capitalists, C_R, are playing by the independently determined rules of the poor state, S_P, they are not engaged in an imperial project. Call the activities of these capitalists *transnational exploitation*.

Contrast a case where C_R gets S_P, the poor state, to enforce capitalist private property in favour of C_R's exploitation of L_P. This is beginning to look like imperialism proper. So *international exploitation*, in contrast to transnational exploitation, is the exploitation of indigenous workers by metropolitan capitalists, facilitated by the institutions of the indigenous state through the intervention of metropolitan states or capitalists. The rest of this chapter studies the sources and forms of international exploitation.

FDI is only one source of international exploitation. Another is the terms of trade. Here, unilateral labour flow may obtain through the market exchange of a unit metropolitan labour for an increasing amount of indigenous labour. For example, £1 worth of Indian wool contains more labour than £1 worth of a British Blu-ray.[13] It follows that British Blu-ray industrialists benefit at the expense of Indian wool producers from every £1 of trade. Deteriorating terms of trade for India increase this gain at the Indian producer's expense.[14] And insofar as the institutional setup of a deteriorating balance of trade reflects the power of the rich state, it is an instance of liberal imperialism.

So different answers to the source-of-surplus question imply different answers to the 'who exploits whom?' question. In the case of capital exports, the answer is straightforward, indeed equivalent to the domestic case: C_R exploits L_R by setting up shop in R and having S_R enforce C_R's property rights; C_R exploits L_P by setting up shop in P and having S_P enforce C_R's property rights. In the case of pure trade, it is possible, moreover, that

---

[13] See Chapter 3 for a discussion of the centrality of surplus labour to exploitation.
[14] There is considerable evidence to corroborate this phenomenon in the case of primary commodities (the so-called Prebisch-Singer hypothesis). See, for example, Harvey et al. (2010).

152 EXPLOITATION AND INTERNATIONAL RELATIONS

Table 6.3 Mode of surplus-extraction

Source of surplus	Colonial imperialism	Liberal imperialism
Capital export	1	3
Trade	2	4

metropolitan capitalists exploit indigenous capitalists. This is one of the main sources of exploitation of poor countries, particularly those specializing in manufacturing and primary commodities.

Table 6.3 sets out the different modes of surplus extraction under colonial and liberal imperialism. The classical theories of imperialism, due to Hilferding and Hobson, are exhausted in the first column (cells 1 and 2). The exploitation of India under British rule, for example, took place through coercive enforcement of preferential treatment for British investment and Britain's trading partners. British capitalism's exploitation of Argentina, by contrast, was marked by that variant of liberal imperialism that Kautsky (1914) called 'ultraimperialism'. This was a form of liberal domination by a catallaxy of industrial and financial interests under the aegis of the British Empire, riding on the golden chariot of the Gold Standard. The rest of this section discusses international exploitation under liberal imperialism (cells 3 and 4). I discuss free trade first and capital exports second. Both cases, I argue, fit naturally into the domination account of exploitation defended in this book.

6.3.2.1 Free trade

How is international exploitation through genuinely free trade possible? Suppose that the playground bully owns all the cool toys. You want to play with them, so the bully makes you an offer: 'You can play with one of my cool toys. But I demand, in return, all of your less cool toys. Take it or leave it.' The upshot is that you find yourself with an ever-diminishing rate of exchange between your toys and the bully's. The bully is in a position to demand this just because she controls scarce productive resources which confer on her power over your purposiveness. So she exploits you. Now imagine that the bully and the rest of her cool-toy-possessing friends make the following offer to the less-cool-toy-possessing kids: 'You can all play with our cool toys. But we demand, in return, all of your less cool toys. Take it or leave it.' Again, the bullying faction can benefit asymmetrically in virtue of its possession of an ownership-conferred power over the others, indeed a power that dominates those others. The bullies exploit.

GLOBALIZATION AND INTERNATIONAL EXPLOITATION   153

This is the playground equivalent of the World Trade Organization (WTO): by enforcing the rules of free trade, rules that include bilateral free trade agreements between states with large markets and states with small markets, the WTO perpetuates a deterioration in the terms of trade of the poor. It thereby underwrites international exploitation, surplus-extraction by the rich through unilateral control over the labour capacities of the poor. Since this is an instance of liberal domination of state by state, the WTO sometimes functions as an instrument of liberal imperialism.[15]

It is worth noting that this anti-WTO argument is independent of the claims popularized by Thomas Pogge (2008), to the effect that WTO rules violate the negative rights of the poor, by encouraging rent-seeking and dictatorial extraction in developing countries. For suppose Pogge is right. Suppose, further, that global trade is completely denuded of pro-rich export subsidies, pro-rich institutions of technological transfer and the like. Insofar as superior economic power can still be brought to bear on terms of trade and investment, as well as the internal structure of subaltern economies, the WTO will continue to embody liberal imperialism. Note, finally, that this argument is orthogonal to the positive-rights thesis of Peter Singer (2004). The WTO institutionalizes the international exploitation of the poor by the rich on a global scale, whether or not such exploitation violates positive rights, and whether or not it improves the condition of the poor.[16] This concludes my discussion of liberal imperialism through free trade.[17]

6.3.2.2 Capital exports

I turn now to liberal imperialism through capital exports. Lenin's (1951) attempted synthesis of Hilferding (1910) and Hobson (1902) assumes that the international exploitation of indigenous workers by metropolitan capitalists will occur mainly through the proliferation of formal empires. The vehicle of that proliferation was assumed to be 'finance capital', that is, 'capital controlled by banks and employed by industrialists'.[18] How does financial capital exploit?

---

[15] Richard Miller (2010) defends a version of this argument. He suggests that when the USA brings its market size and level of development to bear on openness to trade by the poor, it illegitimately uses its superior bargaining power at their expense. In allowing such agreements, the WTO rules are intrinsically exploitative. Ha-Joon Chang (2002) arrives at a similar conclusion, starting from a premiss about first-mover-advantage.

[16] It bears noting that if exploitation is Pareto superior to nonexploitation, then the injustice of exploitation may be all-things-considered justified. This concession does not, however, make the injustice of exploitation go away.

[17] Under what conditions would free trade not be exploitative? An interesting and comprehensive answer is provided by Risse and Wollner (2019).

[18] Although the level of synergy between banks and industry envisaged by Hilferding and Lenin never materialized, the dominance of financial capital, broadly construed, is with us today more than ever before.

154 EXPLOITATION AND INTERNATIONAL RELATIONS

The case of Argentina, discussed earlier, exemplifies such exploitation. In that case, metropolitan financial institutions came to unilaterally control indigenous productive powers by either offering loans to indigenous capitalists or directly to indigenous workers. Metropolitan banks can offer loans at more attractive rates than indigenous banks, having better access to risk-pooling instruments and collateral. In the case of loans to indigenous capitalists, the situation is subtly different, for finance capitalists do not control means of production. They only own money capital, the means to mobilize those means that indigenous capitalists control. The metropolitan finance capitalist is therefore relevantly like the kid who owns the stick and lends it to the bully, on condition that she receives a return on her loan. That makes the stick kid into a bully. Bullies exploit in packs, and so do capitalists (see Chapter 4, section 4.6 for a structural argument to that effect). This concludes my discussion of liberal imperialism through capital exports.

To sum up the argument so far: international exploitation presupposes the domination of states, which constitutes either colonial or liberal imperialism. Liberal imperialism, in turn, can enlist a variety of channels, including trade and capital flows, to effect the domination of indigenous states. I conclude this section with a note on globalization. Contrary to Lenin's prognoses, finance and liberal imperialism go well together.

Why would metropolitan capitalists go to war when their banks unilaterally control a substantial proportion of indigenous assets and debt (and therefore of the surplus product)? All they need is an economic architecture that includes a bailiff for the international financial system; enter the International Monetary Fund (IMF), the World Bank, and related vehicles of capitalist globalization. Insofar as these vehicles facilitate the international exploitation of poorer states through mechanisms like the ones I have outlined, they are vehicles of liberal imperialism. If this is correct, then Kautsky was right to insist on the possibility of *ultraimperialism*: contemporary 'flat-earth' globalization is, in this sense, ultraimperialism writ large.[19] And it also follows that Lenin was wrong to think it inevitable that inter-imperialist rivalry will lead to inter-imperialist war (which is not to say that inter-imperialist war won't occur).[20]

The rest of this chapter studies resistance to imperialism and its internationalist grounds.

---

[19] Hardt and Negri (2001) are here simply following Kautsky.
[20] None of this implies, of course, that a genuinely democratic globalization is infeasible or undesirable. All that follows is that such a globalization is impossible under the existing institutional setup.

6.4 Resistance and Working-Class Internationalism

If there is such a thing as international exploitation, then states must dominate states. This conditional is a corollary of the central thesis of this book, namely that exploitation is a form of domination. And since domination in international relations is called imperialism, international exploitation presupposes imperialism. How should imperialism be resisted? This section argues that there is a right to resist imperialism, a right entailed by the more general right to resist domination. The former right does not, however, entail an unconditional right to national self-determination, as some anti-imperialists maintain. Rather, according to the domination account, the existence of a right to national self-determination is derivative and conditional upon that more general right of resistance. This section defends this claim and its internationalist pedigree.

6.4.1 The right to resist

It is uncontroversial that persons and groups have a moral right to resist domination.[21] In the most general case, they can permissibly resist those who (attempt to) dominate them. Suppose, for example, that Q has a moral right not to hand over her wallet at gunpoint. P violates that right by threatening Q at gunpoint. In the course of P's attempt to violate Q's right, Q can permissibly take steps to prevent its violation. When this happens, it is normally the case that (i) Q permissibly employs certain means to resist P's threat and (ii) third parties have an obligation not to interfere with Q's employment of these means.[22] This is the kind of right justified resistance needs. I now elaborate on some implications of that right for anti-imperialism.

If there is a moral right to resist domination and if imperialism is a form of domination, then there is a moral right to resist imperialism. Any community or state capable of rightfully wielding such a right has it. Moreover, dominators normally forfeit not just the right to do what constitutes domination, but also

---

[21] The best philosophical treatment of that right is Finlay (2015).

[22] What means Q can permissibly employ is in part constrained by proportionality considerations. In some cases, the only steps that Q can permissibly take consist in shouting for help, calling the police, and so on. But if there is reason to think that such measures are unlikely to succeed in thwarting P's bullying, then Q can permissibly take steps to resist it directly. Caney (2015) and Finlay (2015) discuss proportionality and related issues.

156　EXPLOITATION AND INTERNATIONAL RELATIONS

the right to resist those whom they dominate.[23] For consider the following: the perpetrator of a crime normally forfeits certain rights, including the right to freedom of movement. She thereby also forfeits the right to resist being deprived of freedom of movement. So if, as a matter of structural necessity, capitalists dominate workers, then capitalists forfeit any rights to resist workers. And if metropolitan capitalists dominate indigenous workers as a matter of *global* structural necessity, then the former also forfeit any rights to resist the latter. In other words, international exploiters forfeit both the right to conduct business as usual and to hinder hindrances to such conduct.

The most controversial part of this argument says that metropolitan workers can exploit indigenous workers. This is the assumption, in Table 6.1, that L_R exploits L_P, the old idea of a 'labour aristocracy'. This situation arises when C_R internationally exploits L_P, and a small part of that surplus redounds to L_R. Then C_R and L_R are jointly implicated in the international exploitation of L_P.[24] And if it is thereby granted that L_R exploits L_P, then the metropolitan working class forfeits any rights of resistance vis-à-vis the indigenous working class. But this might just be another way of saying that *metropolitan workers have obligations of solidarity to indigenous workers that indigenous workers themselves lack.*

These conclusions about rightful resistance are consistent with widespread practices of divide and rule. Consider, for example, C_R's structural disposition to deprive L_R of jobs through capital flight, when doing so is conducive to profitability. That is, being possessed of the metropolitan means of production, C_R has a number of options. C_R can exploit L_P through FDI or trade, and then throw L_R some breadcrumbs. Alternatively, if L_R becomes too unruly, C_R can threaten to hire L_P, whose wages are lower. That threat is sometimes credible. It is therefore sufficient to rein in on L_R. When the threat itself does not suffice, its consequent (of capital flight) is carried out. In these cases, L_R will suffer unemployment and poverty. This is how the free international movement of capital stacks the deck against the workers: it gives metropolitan capitalists room to play L_R against L_P, while maintaining the inequality between them

---

[23] The objects of a rights-forfeiture might vary: P might forfeit her claim-right not to be bullied in her relations with Q, but might retain that right in her relations with R. Consider the criminal, P, who forfeits her right to freedom of movement vis-à-vis political community Q, but not vis-à-vis political community R. By the same token, the bully might forfeit her right not to be bullied vis-à-vis subordinates without forfeiting her right vis-à-vis other bullies.

[24] Whether this is an instance of joint action, complicity, or mere benefit from injustice is a difficult question. On complicity and its differences from joint action and mere benefit from injustice, see Lepora and Goodin (2013).

RESISTANCE AND WORKING-CLASS INTERNATIONALISM   157

within the limits circumscribed by C_R's profitability. This is a basic structural feature of liberal imperialism (see Galtung 1971 for a simple model).

I have, so far, sketched the idea of a right to resist imperialism as a form of domination. I now use the critical resources of the previous sections to argue that national self-determination is not an unconditional or fundamental right. Rather, resistance to imperialism draws its justification from a broader internationalist response to domination.

6.4.2 Against national self-determination

The main post-Westphalian vehicle of resistance to imperialism has been the nation-state. This section rejects a widely held justification of that resistance, premissed on the idea of national self-determination. According to that justification, L_P's right to resist international exploitation is only rightfully realized in a right of national self-determination for S_P. Advocates of the domination account of exploitation, I argue, should not accept national self-determination as the content of a fundamental or nonderivative right.[25] To do so would be inconsistent with their opposition to domination, which nationalism countenances. Instead, advocates of the domination account can only draw on an internationalist justification for anti-imperialism.

In 1909, Rosa Luxemburg wrote:

> The duty of the class party of the proletariat to protest and resist national oppression arises not from any special rights of nations, just as, for example, its striving for social and political equality of the sexes does not at all stem from any special rights of women which the movement of bourgeois emancipation refers to. *This duty arises solely from the general opposition to the class regime and to every form of social inequality and social domination,* in a word, from the basic position of socialism.
>
> (Luxemburg 1976, p. 110, emphasis added)

Luxemburg's argument was a response to Lenin and those opponents of imperialism who defended a fundamental 'right of nations to self-determination'. The polemic was symptomatic of a deep ambivalence among

---

[25] To keep things simple, I preserve the instrumentalist assumption that, if S_R engages in imperialism vis-à-vis S_P, then the class relations of Table 6.2, and only those relations, hold.

158   EXPLOITATION AND INTERNATIONAL RELATIONS

Marxists, including Marx himself, on the national question.[26] Lenin's view consisted in drawing a distinction between 'oppressed' and 'oppressor' nations,[27] assigning a right of national self-determination to the former.[28]

There are at least two problems with Lenin's view. The first is that state B can be dominated by A while itself dominating C: a bully in one relation may be bullied in another.[29] The conditions of ascription of the right to national self-determination are therefore less determinate than its defenders assume. Second, unlike the right to *popular* sovereignty, a right to *national* sovereignty is more amenable to morally arbitrary exclusion; it easily lends itself to the domination of minorities through segregation, xenophobia, or outright racism, *especially* within dominated states. This is why, after decades of experimentation with the Leninist strategy, its overall balance sheet seems to be in the negative. As Hobsbawm put it:

> There is no denying the fact that only in a few cases have Marxists suc-ceeded in establishing or maintaining themselves as the leading force in their national movement. In most cases, especially when such movements were already in existence as serious political forces or under the auspices of state governments, they have either become subordinate to, or been absorbed by, or pushed aside by non-Marxist or anti-Marxist nationalism.
>
> (Hobsbawm 1977, pp. 10–11)

Hobsbawm adds that the disappearance of colonies 'has snapped the main link between anti-imperialism and the slogan of national self-determination' (Hobsbawm 1977, p. 11). If this is true, then it remains doubtful that L_P's right of resistance against C_R is rightfully realized in a right to national self-determination.

Now, an important question lurking in the background of this debate is the relevant account of the 'nation'. Nationalists of every stripe claim that a people has a—possibly defeasible—moral claim to self-determination, where

---

[26] See Avineri (1991) and Hobsbawm (1977) for a summary of these debates.

[27] 'Oppression' is too generic a concept. I shall refer instead to domination, which is part of the definition of imperialism offered in this chapter.

[28] Lenin's position contradicts the views of Marx and Engels, who were vocally opposed to the self-determination of 'reactionary' nationalisms, such as the Czech and Croatian nationalisms of the Austro-Hungarian empire (see Avineri 1991, p. 641). To take some contemporary examples, no case can be made that Wallonia dominates Flanders in contemporary Belgium, or that Southern Italy dominates Northern Italy. There is no justice to these claims for national self-determination, such as they are.

[29] In 1975, when Vietnam beat the US invader, the international anti-imperialist movement cele-brated one of its greatest victories. Three years later, Vietnam invaded Cambodia, staying there for thirteen years.

a 'people' may be ethnically, culturally, or politically constituted. Hobsbawm seems to have in mind the ethnic nationalisms of the 20th century, all of which entail a broad-scope right to exclude. Such nationalisms are practically certain to run afoul of the anti-imperialist emphasis on nonexploitation and equal freedom for metropolitan and indigenous workers alike.[30] In other words, if the exercise of a right to national self-determination promotes the long-term interests of L_R at the expense of L_P, then that right does not serve the cause of rightful resistance in the right way.

There are, however, forms of nationalism that emphasize merely political collective self-determination, as opposed to ethnic or cultural identity (see, for example, Stilz 2011). Such views ground the right to exclude on contingent and nonascriptive characteristics of affected groups. On the political view, immigrants who share neither ethnic nor cultural background with other members of a state, but are subject to its laws, are not permissibly excludable from the rights and obligations of citizenship. So members of L_P, such as workers of the poor country who have migrated into S_R, are not permissibly excludable from S_R as long as they are subject to S_R's laws.

Even this inclusive view, however, makes the demands of nonexploitation contingent upon membership of a political community: L_P can still be internationally exploited by C_R through sweatshops, predatory trade rules, and other forms of liberal imperialism. This is, again, to run afoul of the anti-exploitation commitments defended in this book. So the ascription of a right to national self-determination must be *subject to* these commitments. That is, victims of imperialism enjoy a right to national self-determination *if and only if the ascription of such a right strengthens the hand of the victims of imperialism as a whole*. It follows that the right to national self-determination is conditional upon, and derivative from, the more general right to resist domination. I now explain what this conditionality means.

6.4.3 The burdens of working-class internationalism

The development of human individuality presupposes human interdependence, so a division of labour, and therefore globalized production. But capitalism only globalizes production by globalizing value-constituted domination. So what is the form of 'the general opposition to ... social domination' alluded

---

[30] These considerations also seem to rule out cultural nationalisms of the variety defended by Margalit and Raz (1990).

160   EXPLOITATION AND INTERNATIONAL RELATIONS

to by Luxemburg? The answer must have something to do with the nature of the general right to resist domination. In what follows, I sketch some features of that right.

A right is *derivative* if its ascription is part of a conclusion to a syllogism that has a non-derivative right as a premiss. P's derivative right to swear in the centre of town, for example, is ascribed to P as a conclusion to a syllogism that has P's non-derivative right to free speech as a premiss. The right to national self-determination is similarly derivative of a fundamental right to resist domination. And it is conditional, in that its ascription depends on whether it promotes the overall cause of nondomination *for the whole class of the dominated.*[31]

What is it to promote the cause of nondomination for the *whole class* of the dominated? Suppose A is bullying B and C. If the amount of bullying suffered by each of B and C is reduced when they independently barricade themselves in their own homes, then the whole class of the dominated suffers less domination. In this case, self-determination for each of B and C succeeds in fending off domination. What the anti-imperialist defender of a right to national self-determination must show, however, is that the self-determination strategy (B and C individually barricading in their own homes) makes their resistance more effective—that is, reduces domination by more—than jointly barricading in the *same* home.[32] As Hobsbawm and many others have pointed out, the balance of evidence from the recent history of nationalism is far from conclusive that this is the case.

I now summarize the argument so far. I have argued that international exploitation is a specific form of exploitation involving states. The domination of states is imperialism. And if the central thesis of this book is sound, such that exploitation is enrichment through the domination of others, then international exploitation entails imperialism. Being a form of domination, moreover, imperialism gives rise to rights of resistance. So, like the proverbial bully, imperialist states forfeit their rights to act in imperialism-constituting ways, including their rights to national self-determination. It follows that imperialist states can be permissibly compelled—whether through coercive

---

[31] In the earlier quote, Luxemburg defines that cause as socialism. Nothing of substance hinges on that proviso. Indeed, if capitalism is defined as the generalized domination of labour by capital, then nondomination trivially implies socialism.

[32] This reduction may be more important the worse off one is. Suppose that C is worse off than B and a joint resistance strategy leaves B slightly worse off and C slightly better off compared to the sectarian alternative. Then B may be obligated to accept the joint strategy. These tradeoffs are discussed by Finlay (2015, chapter 5).

or noncoercive proportional means—to do things that contradict (what they perceive to be in) their national interests.[33]

Who can permissibly compel imperialists to do these things? One answer might be: dominated states, or coalitions thereof. This response is unstable, for the victims of imperialism might simply prioritize their own interests or even turn imperialist (see footnotes 28 and 29). Removing this kind of instability requires that any counter-imperialist coalition be sufficiently inclusive across its resisters, metropolitan and indigenous workers, and their allies. More precisely: only a coalition of anti-imperialist states, whose democratic goals and structure are constitutively anti-domination, would guarantee that their use of power against imperialism counts as anti-domination only. Their resistance would then amount to a mere hindrance to a hindrance to freedom, the moral equivalent of a coalition of anti-bullies disarming the playground bully.

I conclude that working-class internationalism is morally prior to national self-determination, such that any permissible use of the latter is derivative and conditional upon the former. This does not mean there is no right to national self-determination, but only that such a right is conditional upon and derivative from a more general right to resist international exploitation.

Conclusion

If exploitation is a form of domination and if there is exploitation in international relations, then there is domination in international relations. This form of domination is called imperialism. This chapter used the critical resources of previous chapters to buttress an account of imperialism that makes this set of inferences palatable. After arguing for the cogency of the concept of imperialism, I argued for the distinction between colonial and liberal imperialism. That distinction, I claimed, maps on to a distinction between coercive and liberal domination. I then argued that some of the institutions of contemporary globalization, such as the WTO, the IMF, the World Bank, and so on, are largely the instruments of liberal imperialism; a reincarnation of what Karl Kautsky once called 'ultraimperialism'. I concluded by arguing that resistance to imperialism does not, in general, ground a right to national

---

[33] Imperialist states, can, for example, be permissibly compelled to abstain from engaging in war, to join international institutions, to enter into binding environmental treaties, to drop export subsidies or protectionism, to acquiesce to export subsidies, protectionism and capital controls abroad, and so on.

162 EXPLOITATION AND INTERNATIONAL RELATIONS

self-determination. Such a right, it turns out, is conditional upon and derivative of a more general right to resist domination.

Appendix: Who exploits whom?

Who can exploit whom in international relations? This appendix discusses
the full logical partition of fifteen possibilities broached in Table 6.1. Note
that dropping state instrumentalism makes both agential and relational views
of the state eligible. States might, for example, be agentially or relationally
constituted and still possess relative autonomy from the interests of any social
class. This relative autonomy would go some way towards explaining political
heterogeneity across states, depending on the nature of class division there and
the mode of subsumption of labour by capital underlying it.

(a) C_R exploits C_P: TRUE.

The simplest illustration of (a) is trade flow. The source of surplus extraction,
in this case, is the terms of trade. This is an instance of horizontal capitalist
exploitation: one capitalist (or group thereof) exploiting another.

(b) C_R exploits S_R: FALSE.

Consider the case of debt: finance capitalists from the rich state (C_R) lend
money to that state (S_R) by buying cheap bonds at interest. Suppose that C_R
thereby exploit. Do they exploit S_R? Or do they exploit S_R's main funders, tax-
paying workers L_R? The answer is not obvious.

Suppose Z gives money to Y for safekeeping. Y falls into a pit. X comes over
and asks for Z's money, in return for costless rescue. Y obliges. Does X exploit Y
or Z? It might seem that Y is exploited here. But this presumption is mistaken.
For Y acts as a mere middleman for Z: it is as if Z found herself in the pit,
X asked for the money, and Y acted as Z's lawyer. X exploits Z. If this is correct,
then C_R does not exploit S_R, but only the tax-payer L_R. So (b) is false.

(c) C_R exploits S_P: FALSE.

By reasoning similar to (b).

(d) C_R exploits L_R: TRUE.

RESISTANCE AND WORKING-CLASS INTERNATIONALISM 163

This is a corollary of the argument about the nature of the relationship between capital and labour, discussed in Chapters 2–5 of this book.

(e) C_R exploits L_P: TRUE.

This is the theme that preoccupied classical theories of imperialism: capital flow. The main channel through which C_R exploits L_P is state-backed foreign direct investment (FDI). So the only difference between (d) and (e) is that C_R's investments take place outside of their country of origin. By investing directly in land, equipment, and machinery, and by offering better wages than C_P, C_R is able to exploit L_P. This is what sweatshops are all about, for example.

(f) S_R exploits C_P: TRUE.

Suppose S_R bureaucrats demand large bribes in return for furnishing C_P with advanced technology. If the bribe is accepted and a share of the net product redounds to S_R, then S_R exploits C_P. This is an instance of liberal imperialism.

(g) S_R exploits S_P: TRUE.

The main channel here is debt. Suppose S_R charges very high interest rates for a low-cost loan that S_P needs. Insofar as this leads to power-induced extraction of unilateral labour flow from S_P, this is exploitative and another instance of liberal imperialism.

(h) S_R exploits L_R: TRUE.

By levying taxes on workers, S_R can exploit and thereby dominate L_R. Some of these taxes might redound to L_R in the form of public good provision, but a good deal will go to the coffers of banks and capitalists to repay the national debt (see (b)). When this happens, S_R exploits L_R.

(i) S_R exploits L_P: TRUE.

Imagine a large state-owned company that charges foreign workers an exorbitant amount for some basic necessity, such as oil or gas, with the blessing of S_P. This seems to be the standard practice of Gazprom, for instance. S_R exploits L_P, an instance of liberal imperialism.

164 EXPLOITATION AND INTERNATIONAL RELATIONS

(j) C_P exploits S_P: FALSE.

By reasoning similar to (b).

(k) C_P exploits L_R: TRUE.

By reasoning similar to (e). Note that FDI flows overwhelmingly between metropolitan areas, and not between rich and poor countries (perhaps with the exception of China; see Harvey 2005). So even though (e) and (k) are conceptually possible, they are not widely observed.

(l) C_P exploits L_P: TRUE.

By reasoning similar to (d).

(m) S_P exploits L_R: TRUE.

By reasoning similar to (i).

(n) S_P exploits L_P: TRUE.

By reasoning similar to (h).

(o) L_R exploits L_P: TRUE.

This is the labour aristocracy argument. L_R benefits from unilateral labour flow from L_P, by enlisting the superior power of C_R to benefit at L_P's expense. It is an open question whether L_R exploits jointly with C_R, is complicit with C_R without exploiting, or merely benefits from L_P's exploitation without exploiting.

PART IV
ALTERNATIVES

PART B

ALTERNATIVES

7

The Emancipated Economy

This book has argued that exploitation is a dividend of servitude, the servitude of having one's purposiveness subjected to the ends and dispositions of the powerful. Applied to work, this servitude consists in unilateral control over the labour capacity of others. Furthermore, capital is an instance of such control: it is monetized control over alien labour capacity. So capitalism, the mode of production in which capital predominates, is a form of structural servitude. This servitude, in turn, structurally facilitates exploitation, which buttresses and reproduces the subjection of purposiveness. In a word, capitalism is a cage. The cage's bars extend vertically, in exploitative authority relations between capitalists and workers, and horizontally, in exploitative market relations between (possibly democratic) firms. Finally, the capitalist cage has global and temporal girth, expressed in varieties of colonial and liberal imperialism.

This chapter sketches alternatives to capitalist subjection. It considers three important theories of emancipated production: unconditional basic income (UBI), property-owning democracy (POD), and workplace democracy (WD). It argues that only POD and WD are eligible candidates for the abolition of exploitation. POD does better attenuating horizontal exploitation, whereas WD does better in terms of vertical exploitation. It is therefore possible that a hybrid theory would do better than each by itself. 'Doing better', I argue, is a matter of finding an efficient form of free, undominated, cooperative activity under universal laws. I then show that this form is democratic socialism: worker control under strongly predistributive public ownership. I conclude by outlining a problem faced by democratic socialists which I will call the socialization dilemma. Opponents of exploitation, I argue, must constantly wage a war on two fronts, quite independently of capitalism: against statism, from above, and against a labour epistocracy, from below.

The chapter is structured as follows. Section 7.1 criticizes UBI. Section 7.2 discusses a recent attempt to defend POD, due to John Roemer. I argue that POD does well in terms of attenuating horizontal exploitation, the exploitation of firms by firms. In section 7.3, I argue that WD does better in terms of vertical exploitation, the exploitation of workers by bosses. It is therefore possible that a hybrid theory could do better than each institutional setup

Exploitation as Domination: What Makes Capitalism Unjust. Nicholas Vrousalis, Oxford University Press.
© Nicholas Vrousalis 2023. DOI: 10.1093/oso/9780192867698.003.0008

168   THE EMANCIPATED ECONOMY

taken by itself. In section 7.4, I discuss the hybrid model: worker control plus a strongly predistributive form of public ownership. In section 7.5 I take up the relationship between the democratic socialization of the means of production and the state.

7.1 Against Unconditional Basic Income

The exploitation objection to unconditional basic income (UBI) is well-known.[1] According to that objection, it is exploitative for able-bodied people to serve other able-bodied people without receiving reciprocal effortful contribution from the latter. To focus intuitions, consider the following:

> *Crazy and Lazy*—Crazy and Lazy live on an abandoned island with two coconut trees. Each owns one tree and each enjoys consuming coconuts. Fetching the coconuts requires labour, which Crazy loves to perform, but Lazy hates. So Lazy provides Crazy with access to her tree, in return for a share in the coconuts fetched. The final distribution (in the relevant metric) across Crazy and Lazy—taking into account both the utility of coconut consumption and the (dis)utility of labour—is equal.

Van Parijs (1995) uses examples like this to attack the idea that unreciprocated labour flow is exploitative. He argues that the final distribution in *Crazy and Lazy* is just, precisely *because* there is unequal exchange of labour or effort. That is, given the work/leisure preferences of Crazy and Lazy, an egalitarian planner can legitimately distribute rights to worldly resources such that Crazy unilaterally serves Lazy, thereby providing Lazy with—what is effectively—an unconditional basic income. This is, in rough outline, Van Parijs' argument for why distributive justice allows that Lazy, as well as the proverbial Malibu surfer, should be fed from the labour of others. What are we to make of this argument?

The domination account of exploitation defended in this book does not deem the *Crazy and Lazy* case as exploitative.[2] Recall that, to count as exploitative, any given transaction must violate the Non-Servitude Proviso.

---

[1] It has been studied at length by Van Parijs (1995), White (2004), and Van Donselaar (2009).
[2] The case is analogous to the *Rich and Poor* case of Chapter 3, section 3.1.3.

AGAINST UNCONDITIONAL BASIC INCOME 169

Non-Servitude Proviso—For any agents or groups engaged in mandatory mutually affecting cooperation under a division of labour, and barring any special justification that exempts them, none should possess unilateral control over the labour capacity of any other.

To show that Lazy exploits Crazy, two further conditions would need to be safisfied. First, the case would have to involve mandatory cooperation for the establishment of mutual independence. Second, it would have to be shown that Lazy possesses and exercises unilateral or arbitrary control over Crazy's purposiveness. So if Lazy's effortful contribution is mandatory and if Lazy can unilaterally or arbitrarily control Crazy's labour performance, then Lazy exploits Crazy. This remains the case even if Lazy appropriates a distributively just share of the net product.[3]

But things could be worse for the justification of Lazy's behaviour. Schweickart (2017) argues that, in any dynamic scenario involving accumulation, the introduction of a UBI would lead to higher overall consumption and fewer people working—some will quit their jobs and live on the UBI. This means that fewer people will be doing more work, possibly for higher wages. And this, in turn, makes it difficult to sustain UBI as a requirement of justice. To illustrate, consider a variant of the *Ant and Grasshopper* example (discussed in Chapter 3).

Grasshopper's Blackmail—Grasshopper sings and dances all summer, failing to accumulate provisions. She does this in the expectation that, come winter, she will be in a position to emotionally blackmail Ant into offering costless shelter. Grasshopper's ploy succeeds.

In *Grasshopper's Blackmail* Grasshopper's behaviour may not result in an *act* of exploitation, if, say, Grasshopper's attempt to blackmail is unsuccessful. But Grasshopper's *behaviour* is still exploitative: it is a ploy to extract unilateral labour flow from Ant by subjecting Ant to Grasshopper's ends. And if UBI evinces a similar disposition—a disposition, on the part of the Lazies, to emotionally blackmail the Crazies into bailing them out—then, by the definition of exploitation offered in this book, the behaviour of the Lazies is exploitative.

This complaint is amplified once coercive institutions come into play. By the Proviso, Lazy cannot rely on the background structure of power relations to effect a unilateral transfer of labour from Crazy. For this would be tantamount

---

[3] I defend this conclusion in Chapter 3.

170 THE EMANCIPATED ECONOMY

not only to exploitative behaviour but to an act of exploitation proper.[4] It would be equivalent to Grasshopper singing and dancing all summer in the expectation that her Leviathan buddy would bail her out in winter, by compelling Ant to provide a basic income.

Now, I do not know of evidence that a UBI would encourage exploitative behaviour on the part of the Lazies. There is, moreover, scant evidence that the Lazies can mobilize Leviathan to facilitate their ends—unless the Lazies include high-ranking politicians, CEOs, and corporate officials who live off the labour of others. But that may be less important than the categorically *anti-solidaristic* nature of UBI. In an economy with a UBI, much like in any capitalist economy, everyone lacks the (publicly promulgated) assurance that others lack a Grasshopper-like exploitative disposition, that is, a disposition to free ride on the effortful contribution of others by dint of power over them. This is the core disposition of patrimonial capitalists and corporate welfare bums. So, even if one grants that it ameliorates capitalist exploitation, UBI capitalism preserves a regrettable, indeed contemptible, feature of capitalist civilization.

The rest of this chapter applies the domination account of exploitation to theories of the institutions of socialism, excluding UBI. I begin by showing how marketable resources other than alienable capital can function as vehicles of labour subordination. I then use this conclusion to argue for workplace democracy plus a predistributive form of public ownership.

7.2 Ambiguities of Property-Owning Democracy

John Rawls famously argued that only two institutional proposals exemplify his theory of justice as fairness: 'liberal socialism' and 'property-owning democracy' (POD) (Rawls 2001, pp. 136–8). I will discuss POD in this section and liberal socialism in section 7.3.

Defenders of POD believe that the power of capital should be attenuated through egalitarian *predistribution*, that is, through publicly funded health and education, progressive taxation of real-estate and capital-gains, demogrants, and possibly coupon-ownership of the major means of production.[5] This section criticizes the most egalitarian version of POD in the recent literature, Roemer's model of coupons socialism.

---

[4] I discuss this distinction and its relevance in Chapter 1.
[5] See O'Neill and Williamson (2012) for different variants of POD.

AMBIGUITIES OF PROPERTY-OWNING DEMOCRACY   171

7.2.1 Roemer's POD

According to Roemer (1982, 1996), capitalism evinces three sources of exploitation:

(a) inequalities in marketable *worldly resources*,
(b) inequalities in marketable *knowledge resources* and control over organizational processes, and
(c) inequalities in marketable *talents* and 'personal' resources.

Roemer (1996) dubs exploitation that issues from (a) *capitalist exploitation* and exploitation that issues from (b) and (c) *socialist exploitation*. (b) includes the knowledge workers attain through education and vocational training, in addition to tacit knowledge obtained exclusively in the workplace. (c) includes abilities and transferable talents due to genetic factors.[6] The last two dimensions are plainly relevant to the domination account of exploitation. For, on that account, all of (a) to (c) are possible sources of unilateral surplus extraction, insofar as they involve *marketable* resources conferring, on some, unilateral control over the labour capacity of others.

To deal with capitalist exploitation, Roemer (1994) develops and defends a market socialist model based on pure public ownership. Roemer's model would give every citizen an equal and tradeable share in the beneficial ownership of the means of production. There is a coupon stockmarket, a socialist imitation of the capital market, in which coupons are freely tradeable but not monetizeable or bequeathable. Every year, each worker receives a dividend from her share of the stocks, worth several thousands of dollars, as a matter of right. This is a model of *pure* public ownership, in that it does not include worker participation or worker control.[7]

Roemer thinks that his model preserves the allocative efficiency of the capitalist capital market, while the non-bequeathable and non-monetizable nature of his coupon stockmarket immunizes labour from capitalist exploitation. The model raises a host of questions about industrial organization, the role of socialized banks and finance, and the role of the state. But it suffers

---

[6] Unlike Roemer (1982), Roemer (1996) is largely uninterested in exploitation, because the domination-based, non-distributive considerations mooted in section 7.1, are no longer on his radar. This is why his main objections to (a)–(c) are couched in terms of 'equal opportunity for political influence' and 'equality of social status' (see the first two chapters of Dworkin 2000, for the main inspiration behind Roemer's change of mind). See Chapter 3 for discussion.
[7] See Roemer (1996, pp. 50–1). For similar models, see Bardhan and Roemer (1992) and Weisskopf (1992).

172   THE EMANCIPATED ECONOMY

from a glaring blind spot, namely inequalities across firms in terms of their members' marketable knowledge, know-how, and talent, that is, (b) and (c). There is considerable evidence (see e.g. Piketty 2014, Roemer 2000) that these inequalities contribute to unilateral surplus extraction just as much as inequalities in alienable scarce productive assets. I now make this objection more precise.

7.2.2 Why POD is not enough

Roemerian managers organize production from above; they are engaged in 'managerial socialism'. Managerial socialism allows market norms of talent, knowledge and skill scarcity to determine the remuneration of the beneficiaries of the genetic lottery, along with those who possess scarce knowledge and technical skills. In that sense, Roemer fails to address the problem of socialist exploitation or, as I will call it, of the *labour epistocracy*: the existence of a class of workers who, by dint of higher epistemic credentials and talents, can subjugate the labour of those with lower epistemic credentials.[8] The labour epistocracy includes Piketty's (2014) 'supermanagers', but also the talented self-employed, whose extraction of scarcity rents in the market—think Justin Bieber and J.K. Rowling—enables them to unilaterally control the labour capacities of subordinate market agents.

Now, the Roemerian stockmarket gives everyone an equal share in the value of, say, Apple stocks. These stocks presumably include the value of Apple's human capital capitalized. But *this says nothing about the determination of the (pre-profit) rents extracted by the labour epistocracy in the form of positions, perks, and wages inside socialized firms*. These rents will partly determine the size of the coupon dividend, which, according to Roemer, is to be shared equally across all members of society.[9] More worryingly, insofar as epistocratic inequalities ramify beyond inequalities of income and wealth—for example, are expressed in hierarchies in the organization and meaningfulness of work— a highly progressive tax system will not suffice to attenuate them. Even a 100

---

[8] The labour epistocracy is distinct from Kautsky's (1901) and Lenin's (1951) labour *aristo*cracy, in that the former is a coalition of direct producers who exploit other producers by leveraging their scarce knowledge and talents in the market. For an account of the epistocracy in a different context, see Estlund (2009).

[9] It is precisely for this reason that G.A. Cohen's famous critique of unequalizing incentives in Rawls' political philosophy focuses on 'certain forms of market socialism' (Cohen 2008, p. 34); Cohen does not only have Rawls in his sights. I discuss Cohen's position in Vrousalis (2015).

AMBIGUITIES OF PROPERTY-OWNING DEMOCRACY   173

percent marginal tax rate on income and wealth is compatible with a labour epistocracy.

So pure public ownership models of market socialism, like Roemer's, are blind to epistocratic, (b)- and (c)-, forms of exploitation. They are also, for that reason, likely to be unstable:

> The changes proposed in this tradition are merely distributional, and, apart from the disappearance of powerful tycoons, the bulk of the social differences between CEOs and ordinary employees is left untouched... One can even question the stability of the property arrangements of market-socialist models, because the ruling class of managers would have very strong incentives to push toward the restoration of capitalism, with little popular resistance.
>
> (Fleurbaey 1993, p. 274)

One possible rejoinder to these epistocratic objections, recently broached by Thomas (2017), consists in supplementing Roemer's model with the full panoply of *re-* and *pre-*distributive liberal institutions, such as free access to health care, education, training, and so on. This supplementation, call it *Roemer+*, promises to attenuate (b)-type inequalities in knowledge and skills and therefore remove an important source of epistocratic exploitation.

Unfortunately, this rejoinder will not take us very far, since substantial epistocratic exploitation will persist, even after re- and pre-distribution have worked their magic. For one, tacit knowledge and sector-specific skills can only be obtained in the workplace; substantial (b)-type inter-firm inequalities are therefore likely to persist under Roemer+.[10]

More importantly, Salieri cannot be Mozart; I cannot be Lebron James. On the domination account of exploitation, natural inequalities as such are unproblematic,[11] as long as they do not translate into unilateral control over alien purposiveness. But if (c)-type inequalities are pervasive, and if there is a labour market, as in Roemer+, then they will almost certainly translate into epistocratic exploitation inside firms. That is, for as long as there are humans like Beauvoir and Dostoyevsky and Mozart and Lebron, a subset of whom are able and willing to leverage their scarce talents in the market, they will be able to extract monopoly rents or get high-ranking jobs managing the labour

---

[10] For a more extensive argument that the Thomist extension of the Roemer model does not suffice to attenuate exploitation, see Vrousalis (2018b).

[11] Indeed, they are a brute fact about this world that make it an unambiguously better place.

174   THE EMANCIPATED ECONOMY

of others.[12] As Howard and King (1975, p. 131) point out, epistocratic rents must be understood along the lines of the monopolistic models that Ricardo and Marx reserved for agriculture. It follows that even the predistributive version of pure public ownership, Roemer+, is unlikely to sufficiently attenuate exploitation, as understood in this book. Stronger vertical egalitarianism is needed to deal with that.

To sum up the argument so far: capital is a monetary claim to unilateral control over alien labour capacity. That control, moreover, is conferred on the basis of ownership not just of alienable but also of inalienable assets, such as one's talents. In other words, inequality in marketable talents is a source of unilateral control over alien labour within the firm and therefore of vertical exploitation. Managerial socialism, the most egalitarian version of POD, does little to attenuate vertical exploitation and may even exacerbate it. So those concerned with exploitation need to supplement POD with vertically nonexploitative institutions.

7.3 Trepidations of Workplace Democracy

I now explain how the domination account of exploitation subsumes garden-variety objections against vertical exploitation under a more general critique of capitalism. These objections hold that capitalism is objectionable insofar as it vitiates worker autonomy[13] or degrades worker creativity and skills.[14] According to the domination account, the source of such oppression is not the capitalist workplace as such, but the nature of the capital relation itself. It is, in other words, the market-conferred power of the capitalist that enables her to oppress and exploit the worker, not her control over the *actual* labour process. The kindly capitalist who never exploits her workers (e.g. by distributing profits to the workers at the end of each year) still *dominates* them, insofar as the form of the labour process is *up to her*. So, although she does not strictly exploit, she does structurally relate to her workers as exploitable and therefore as subordinates.

---

[12] In the latter case, they are likely to be exploiting the labour of those others. Note that the distinction between 'can't' and 'won't' is relevant here. That Lebron *won't* perform socially beneficial work without extracting a scarcity rent does not exempt him from the ambit of the Non-Servitude Proviso, which censures such extraction as exploitative. But if he *can't* perform that work without a scarcity rent (e.g. to compensate him for increased labour burden or difficulty), then that might exempt him from the Proviso's requirements.

[13] See, for example, Anderson (2015), Breen (2015), and Gonzalez-Ricoy (2014).

[14] The classic here is Braverman (1974). See Chapter 2, section 2.6.

Starting from this normative premiss, a preliminary case for workplace democracy (WD) has been made on the following grounds:

> We speak of the co-operative movement, especially of the co-operative factories raised by the unassisted efforts of a few bold 'hands' ... [T]hey have shown that production on a large scale, and in accord with the behest of modern science, may be carried on without the existence of a class of masters employing a class of hands; that to bear fruit, the means of labour need not be monopolised as a means of dominion over, and of extortion against, the labouring man himself; and that, like slave labour, like serf labour, hired labour is but a transitory and inferior form, destined to disappear before associated labour plying its toil with a willing hand, a ready mind, and a joyous heart.   (MECW 20, p. 11)

Marx extolled the cooperative movement by appeal to something like the Non-Servitude Proviso. Cooperatives, he argued, are necessary to ensure 'the means of labour' are not 'means of dominion over, and of extortion against' the worker herself. Dominion over labour disappears when and because she can bind any other worker, from shop floor to top floor, to performing as much and as good labour as he can bind her. So, barring some independent justification for unequal control, she must have an equal say, one person, one vote, on all matters that subject her labour to the decisions of others. I now describe this argument for WD, as a remedy to vertical exploitation, in some depth.

7.3.1 The general case for WD

Some philosophers have argued that hierarchical workplace relations can only be legitimated by WD. Gonzalez-Ricoy (2014), for example, emphasizes the arbitrary power of bosses, noting that bossing power may not bother opponents of domination, 'as long as it is adequately checked' (Gonzalez-Ricoy 2014, p. 238; see also Breen 2015).

This argument against the power of bosses does not, however, seem to uniquely favour WD. Workplace constitutionalists, for example, maintain that an adequate remedy to workplace domination implements and enforces stringent pro-labour labour legislation (Hsieh 2005, Dagger 2006). In response to domination-type complaints, the workplace constitutionalist insists on comprehensive enforcement of such laws. Workplace democracy, she infers, is not the sole remedy for vertical exploitation. The rest of this section rebuts this position.

176   THE EMANCIPATED ECONOMY

The advocate of WD has two rebuttals to the workplace constitutionalist. The first goes as follows: exclusively legal remedies to workplace domination, however well designed, are both infeasible and undesirable. They are infeasible because not every possible contingency of the employer–employee relation can be written into a contract. And even if it could, such minute specification would deprive both parties of dealing effectively with contingencies.

This argument can be generalized. Bowles and Gintis (1990, 1992) suggest that labour markets are characterized by what they call 'contested exchange', that is, exchange in which one agent possesses power over another in virtue of incomplete markets or contracts. According to Bowles and Gintis, all contested exchange is subject to 'endogenous enforcement'; that is, contested exchange engenders a principal–agent relationship such that parties external to the contract—courts, for example—cannot fully enforce its terms. Bowles and Gintis maintain, further, that contested exchange pervades labour markets. This is the main contrast between their account and Walrasian economic models, in which all enforcement is exogenous, that is, implemented by parties external to the contract:

> While the employer's promise to pay the wage is legally enforceable, the worker's promise to bestow an adequate level of effort and care upon the tasks assigned, even if offered, is not. At the level of effort expected by management, work is subjectively costly for the worker to provide, valuable to the employer, and costly to measure. The manager-worker relationship thus is contested exchange.   (Bowles and Gintis 1992, p. 333)

It follows that the anti-domination ameliorative ambitions of workplace constitutionalism are severely circumscribed. To sum up the anti-constitutionalist argument: contested exchange engenders power relations. These relations, in turn, arise 'from wealth-holders' structural location in nonclearing markets, which allows them to use sanctions to elicit managerial compliance with the objectives of profit maximization, or through their analogous use of sanctions to control workers directly' (Bowles and Gintis 1992, p. 330). If A is the employer, and B the employee, then:

> [I]n equilibrium there will exist unemployed workers identical to B who would prefer to be employed. Thus A's threat to dismiss B is credible and dismissal is costly to B. Hence A can apply sanctions to B . . . Thus A has power over B.   (Bowles and Gintis 1992, p. 338)

Bowles and Gintis thus conclude that unemployment is both necessary and sufficient for workplace domination; it is, as they put it, a 'worker disciplining device'. In these circumstances, the workplace constitutionalist's responses are severely limited.

The second argument for WD—and against workplace constitutionalism—does not turn on Bowles/Gintis-type assumptions. According to that argument, the costs of leaving a job, or abandoning work altogether, are nearly always considerable, even under full employment. Worker control over the workplace attenuates this domination by giving workers control rights over their conditions of production. So, if markets fail to clear, or if the costs of exit are considerable, then WD offers a better remedy to vertical exploitation than workplace constitutionalism.

Now suppose that these arguments are sound, such that worker control prevails over worker constitutionalism. A lingering concern for WD's anti-exploitation credentials is the labour epistocracy. Sections 7.3.2 and 7.3.3 explain how WD deals with epistocratic exploitation.

7.3.2 The labour epistocracy

How does WD deal with the labour epistocracy? And does it do a better job than POD? This section discusses the first question; section 7.3.3 addresses the second.

The labour epistocracy, I have argued, exacerbates market frictions. By adding heterogeneity to the employers' monitoring practices it adds to their costs; it also tends to raise efficiency wages as a disciplinary response to shirking (Bowles and Gintis 1992). Furthermore, insofar as epistocratic rents raise the exit costs from specialized firms, they strengthen the hold of bosses over workers. In all of these cases, the labour epistocracy exacerbates vertical exploitation, the exploitation of workers by capitalist bosses and owners.

WD seems capable of attenuating these concerns: instead of turning the workplace into a dictatorship of experts, one might ensure that knowledge, especially skills and tacit knowledge, is shared as equally as possible through democratically elected managers, optional job rotation and training, and the full panoply of constitutional protections afforded by a pro-labour labour law.[15] These policies are likely to compress epistocratic inequalities

---

[15] Terminological sidenote: although worker control over the firm may have positive or negative predistributive effects, it is not a *form* of predistribution, any more than capitalist control is a form of

178 THE EMANCIPATED ECONOMY

within firms and inject an ethos of solidarity into the economy. The most sophisticated model in this literature is due to David Schweickart.

In the Schweickart (2002, 2011) model, workers operate and manage profit-maximizing state-owned firms. The Schweickartian firm is not a marketable commodity, but a *community of producers*, membership of which entitles each to equal voting rights—one person, one vote. Every firm keeps a depreciation fund, which ensures it can procure repairs and capital replacement. Aggregate investment in the economy, as a whole, is funded by a capital tax on worker-controlled firms and is socially administered by regional and national legislatures, through the banking system. So Schweickart's is a *hybrid model* of market socialism, in that it combines public ownership of the firm with universal worker control.[16] How does this model fare compared to POD?

7.3.3 Why WD is not enough

Compared to Roemer's, Schweickart's model does well attenuating vertical inequalities, especially vertical (b)-type inequalities in skills and tacit knowledge. The model's Achilles heel is its treatment of market-generated, horizontal inequalities. For differences in profitability across cooperatives are likely to generate inequalities in alienable assets.[17] Insofar as these inequalities reflect differences in labour input, effort, or adaptability to new technology, they are not necessarily sources of exploitation. But if they reflect power-conferring differences in the capital/labour ratio, or in talent and innate skill, then they are possible sources of exploitation.[18]

Things get worse for the Schweickart model. Suppose that higher (a)-type inequalities in alienable assets across democratic firms will, other things equal, exacerbate (c)-type inequalities in marketable talents. Burdin (2015) argues that there is such a tendency, which is largely due to the substantial expected relative gains, for the talented, of exit over voice. Then, given that the

---

predistribution. Issues of control over the workplace pertain to the mode and relations of production, not to forms of distribution of their product.

[16] For similar accounts, see Ellerman (2007) and Vanek (1970). Rawls (2001) broaches a version of the hybrid model but does not defend it.

[17] On the assumption that exploitation can obtain through mere trade across firms with different capital-to-labour ratios (whether of physical or human capital), cooperatives can exploit cooperatives. For a defence of this claim, see Roemer (1982) and Chapter 5, section 5.6.2.

[18] Schweickart (2012) admits that his account does worse than the Roemer model on that count. Now, Schweikart's flat-rate tax on the firm's capital assets might go some way towards attenuating (a)-type inequalities. But the whole point of that tax is to generate state revenue with minimal distortion to accumulation incentives. Significantly raising the tax rate or making it highly progressive would defeat that purpose.

'LIBERAL SOCIALISM:' THE HYBRID MODEL   179

Schweickart model does worse than Roemer+ in terms of (a)-type inequalities, it is likely to do worse, other things equal, in terms of (c)-type inequalities.

One might object, in Schweickart's defence, that a democratic firm would endogenously compress the extent of vertical inequalities, subject to efficiency constraints. But even if the objection is granted, it does not follow that horizontal inequalities, which originate from the labour market itself, will fail to create conditions of exploitation, especially epistocratic exploitation. A democratic workplace, in other words, does not guarantee a democratic economy.[19] I now show that the Scweickart and Roemer+ models are complementary.

7.4 'Liberal Socialism:' The Hybrid Model

To sum up the argument so far: by dint of their emphasis on the egalitarian (p)redistribution of capital, POD models, such as Roemer+, tend to do better in terms of horizontal, (a)-type and possibly of (c)-type, inequalities.[20] By dint of their emphasis on workplace democracy, on a solidaristic ethos, and on shared informal and tacit knowledge, WD models tend to do better in terms of vertical, (b)-type, inequalities. Table 7.1 summarizes the pros and cons of the two theories, in terms of different sources of exploitation.

Given the pros and cons of each model, it would seem that a worker control model with a stronger predistributive component (POD plus WD) than Schweickart's could do better, in terms of exploitation, than each model

Table 7.1 Exploitation under POD and WD

Source of exploitation	Roemer+	Schweickart
Alienable assets: intra-firm	n/a	n/a
Alienable assets: inter-firm	+	−
Knowledge: intra-firm	−	+
Knowledge: inter-firm	?	?
Talents: intra-firm	−	+
Talents: inter-firm	+	−

[19] See J. Cohen (1989) and Vrousalis (2019a). Of course, a competitive market composed of democratic firms contrasts with a market composed of capitalist firms in that the former do not face a 'grow or die' imperative. Market competition is therefore likely to be less intense under worker control. But epistocratic inequalities are *labour-market-conferred powers over the labour capacities of others*, that is, sources of rents originating from the segmented structure of the *labour market*, not the product market.

[20] 'Possibly', that is, on the assumption that the lucrativeness of exit for the talented dominates the integrity of voice. But if exit does not dominate voice or if the talented do not change employment much, and if the distribution of talents across firms is uniform and relatively wide, then the Schweickart model might do better in terms of (c), by compressing *intra*-firm inequality. The question of the workers' ethos (Cohen 2008, Casal 2013) is paramount here.

180   THE EMANCIPATED ECONOMY

by itself. Roughly speaking, POD deals with horizontal exploitation and WD with vertical exploitation. One obvious way to do this would be to convert the capital value of Schweickartian worker-controlled firms, or, more narrowly, of their depreciation funds, into Roemerian coupons. This would produce a more strongly predistributive version of public ownership than Schweickart allows, keeping worker control in place. It would thereby make room for a non-capitalist capital market, Roemer-style, which might also generate important efficiency gains (Fleurbaey 1993, Dow 2003).[21]

Would this form of liberal socialism—coupons + worker control—suffice to abolish the exploitation and monetized servitude of human beings? A lingering and important concern pertains to the role of investment finance in the hybrid model. Financial institutions, whether state-owned mutual funds holding Roemerian coupons or Schweickartian loan-making investment banks, have power over firms. They therefore have power over the labour performance of their workers. The question is whether that power is independently justified or whether it runs afoul of the Non-Servitude Proviso, and is therefore exploitative. In the rest of this section, I broach three possible descriptions of a democratic socialist banking system. I then raise some questions about their exploitation properties.

In the Roemer model, socialized firms are owned by large consortia akin to the japanese *keiretsu* system. Their investment is funded by public banks, whose performance is dependent on the consortium's share price. In the Schweickart model, by contrast, public banks are funded by general taxation, not individual savings. The income from the flat-rate tax on the cooperatives' capital assets forms a 'national investment fund', controlled by public banks. These banks are, in turn, controlled by 'national, regional and local legislatures' (Schweickart 2011, p. 56), which determine the remuneration of bank managers. Finally, in a cognate model of economic democracy developed by Marc Fleurbaey, there are private and public investment banks, all of which could be worker-owned. As in the Roemer model, there is competition between banks, but not all banks are public. The possibilities are depicted in Table 7.2.

Fleurbaey (1993) argues that the relationship between bank ownership and control in the Schweickart model gives rise to a principal–agent problem.[22] What incentive do national and local legislatures have to fund the best available

---

[21] Note that the existence of worker control does not, as such, remove the stick of financial discipline furnished by the Roemer model, since the banking sector may be legally responsible for monitoring the worker-elected management of democratic firms.

[22] Principal–agent relationships arise in situations where a principal (e.g. the owner) needs an agent (e.g. the manager) to maximize some objective function, but lacks complete control over the agent's actions.

'LIBERAL SOCIALISM:' THE HYBRID MODEL   181

Table 7.2 Banking structure under market socialism

Banking structure	Roemer model	Schweickart model	Fleurbaey model
Ownership	Public	Public	Mixed
Control	Managers	State	Workers
Competition	Yes	No	Yes

national and local investments? And how does the appointment and remuneration of state-owned bank managers conduce to the most socially desirable
allocation of investment funds? These are questions I cannot address here.
More relevant to my purposes is the objection that the absence of competition in the Schweickartian banking sector allows epistocratic exploitation of
workers by banks. The argument for that objection is as follows.

By the Non-Servitude Proviso, the only way the individual worker will fail
to be exploited is if she can bind any other worker in the economy, *whether
in her own firm or in any other*, to performing as much and as good labour
as he can bind her. This is why, barring some independent justification for
unilateral control over the labour capacity of others, even unilateral labour
transfers *across* democratic firms may be exploitative.[23] On this view, there
will normally be no exploitation within the Schweickartian *firm*, since each
worker has an equal say on all matters that subject her labour to the decisions
of another. But there may still be exploitation in the Schweickartian *economy* if
the banks have too much power over the cooperative labour of their borrowers,
such that they can extract epistocratic rents.

When that is the case,[24] it would make sense to introduce more competition
between banks, binding their behaviour more closely to market signals. That is,
it would make sense to link the allocation of investment or of firm depreciation
funds to a noncapitalist capital market along Roemerian lines.

These are questions with a strong empirical component, which cannot be
addressed without the contribution of economists and economic sociologists.
However, all of these models immediately invite normative questions: what
structure would the *state* need to have for these models to be workable?
I conclude this book by explaining why the question of the state and its
justification is unavoidable in the context of an emancipated economy.

---

[23] See Chapters 2 and 4 for an argument to that effect.
[24] For an argument that banks will, in general, have too much power in the Schweickart model, see
Fleurbaey (1993, p. 275f) and Chapter 2, section 2.4. A bank can extract surplus value through loans to
surplus-value-extracting capitalists, but also through direct loans to the direct producers, for example,
workers' cooperatives and the self-employed. Schweickartian socialism does away with the former, but
not necessarily with the latter form of extraction.

182   THE EMANCIPATED ECONOMY

7.5 The Black Box of the State

In Chapters 2 and 4, I argued that the problem of exploitation for the economy as a whole is conceptually entangled with the problem of the legitimacy of private property and therefore of the state. The hybrid model I defended earlier (coupons+worker control) immediately invites questions about the relationship between the socialized sector and the state. To whom are socialized banks answerable, for example? And who appoints their managers? In the Schweickart model, social control over the 'national investment fund' is assigned to state-owned banks. These are, in turn, controlled by 'national and regional legislatures'. Roemer envisages a similar form of control over his public banks. But therein lies the rub. These state-administered national investment funds are liable to replacing capitalist oligarchies by state oligarchies. Both models, in other words, are liable to conferring too much power on state bureaucrats, even if these are appointed by and held accountable to 'national and regional legislatures'. I now consider the parallel between capitalist and bureaucratic domination more closely.

The main argument for WD, rehearsed in section 7.3, is opposition to vertical exploitation: a worker subject to the extractive dispositions of her capitalist boss is exploited when these dispositions are realized. She is thereby dominated. But much the same remains true if her boss gets chosen for her disposition to maximize bureaucratic value—maximally grow the bureaucracy—or for her disposition to placate parliamentary leaders. State-appointed officials are often no less purveyors of exploitation than shareholder-appointed officials.[25] So, insofar as the argument from vertical exploitation counts against capitalist bosses, it also counts against state-appointed or trade-union-appointed bosses.[26] I now explore one way that the hybrid model might deal with these possible sources of domination, whether from above or from below.

---

[25] This roughly describes the parliamentary statism of European social democracy during the *Trente Glorieuses*. Under the auspicious economic circumstances of post-war reconstruction, high-ranking trade union officials colluded with high-ranking politicians and state officials to keep industrial democracy at bay. In return, workers were provided with better welfare, wages, and work conditions. The stratagem is potentially exploitative, for it implies that state officials, not capitalists, can dominate workers. See Miliband (1972) for a seminal treatment.

[26] It will not do to object that the optimizing decisions of individual bureaucrats do not constitute credible *threats* because they are decentralized and uncoordinated. Suppose there is a democratically authorized decision to reduce the remuneration of already privileged public officials with scarce talents. These officials threaten to quit in light of that decision. Their decentralized and uncoordinated threats, let us suppose, help overturn the decision. These bureaucrats behave no different from capitalists who engage in lockouts in order to preserve profits.

7.5.1 Worker control, bottom-up

If the hybrid model is liable to collapsing into some form of statism, further democratic checks and balances may be required to keep its socialized sectors democratic. One way to do that would be to create an independently elected labour parliament, that is, a federation of workers' councils, elected from below, endowed with control rights over the socialized sector as a whole. How might that work?

The requisite institutional setup is provided by an old model of worker control. The idea is simple: workers own and manage their workplace conditions of production through democratically elected workplace councils. Each council then elects representatives to a regional workers' council. Regional councils elect national councils, which are, in turn, entrusted with control over aggregate investment in the economy. In this model, workplace councils are the building blocks of economy-wide councils, which exercise direct control over economy-wide conditions of production. This 'social' parliament would, in turn, be responsible for the election, appointment, and supervision of the heads of banks and other socialized enterprizes.[27]

The argument of this book has been that the desirability of such an institutional setup depends on whether it undermines servitude, which is unilateral control over alien purposiveness. Now suppose there is a system of 'dual power', in which political parliaments and independently constituted labour parliaments share control over the means of production in the economy as a whole. Suppose that, as a result, the power of capitalist, manager, or bureaucrat does not hold sway; their structural dispositions are largely aligned with the independent exercise of productive purposivenesses under just laws. Then the envisaged partial transfer of power from state institutions to workers' councils is not incongruent with the commitment to nondomination. Indeed, it is required by the core Enlightenment value of individual independence in free community with others. But there is a catch.

7.5.2 Dilemmas of socialization

Most past attempts at the democratic socialization of production through workers' councils were disastrous failures. They include 1917 Russia, 1918 Germany, 1920 Italy, 1936 Spain, 1956 Hungary, 1973 Argentina, 1974 Portugal, and so on. Some explanations for these failures have less to do with the workings of the council system itself and more with external

[27] I discuss this institutional setup and its history more extensively in Vrousalis (2019b).

184   THE EMANCIPATED ECONOMY

circumstances, including bourgeois hostility, or war. Other explanations emphasize the system itself. According to one such explanation, exclusive council control over the workplace tends to lead to a full-fledged dictatorship of experts, as in the former totalitarian dictatorships of Eastern Europe. The ground of this concentration of power is control over organizational and knowledge resources—what I called epistocratic exploitation.

If this is correct, then socialists seem to be faced with a *socialization dilemma*. On the one hand, when control over the means of production is vested exclusively in state officials, or even in democratic parliaments, then the best we can hope for is a parliamentary system served by an unaccountable and undemocratic state bureaucracy running the economy. On the other hand, when control over the means of production is vested exclusively in workers' councils, then the likely outcome is a dictatorship of managers and experts, a labour epistocracy (see Korsch 1975, pp. 70–8, Poulantzas 2008, p. 366, Vrousalis 2019b, Wright 1985). Opponents of exploitation must therefore constantly wage a war on two fronts, quite independently of capitalism: against *statism*, from above, and against a *labour epistocracy*, from below.

By what institutional means might they wage that war? This is a difficult, even daunting, question in institutional design, which is beyond the scope of this book. It is a question that no critic of exploitation can ignore.

Conclusion

This chapter sketched three important theories of the emancipated economy: unconditional basic income (UBI), property-owning democracy (POD), and workplace democracy (WD). It argued that only POD and WD are eligible candidates for the abolition of exploitation. POD does better in terms of horizontal exploitation; WD does better in terms of vertical exploitation. It is therefore possible that a hybrid theory could do better than each institutional setup taken by itself: a system of worker control coupled with a strongly predistributive form of public ownership. The chapter concluded by outlining the socialization dilemma, whose two horns are statism—rule by state bureaucrats—and a labour epistocracy—rule by those who control knowledge and organizational resources. Opponents of exploitation have yet to describe an institutional setup that deals appositely with that dilemma.

References

Anderson, E. 2015. 'Equality and Freedom in the Workplace'. *Social Philosophy and Policy* 31: 48–69.

Anderson, P. 1974. *Passages from Antiquity to Feudalism*. London: Verso.

Arneson, R. 1981. 'What's Wrong with Exploitation?', *Ethics* 91: 202–27.

Arneson, R. 1989. 'Equality and Equal Opportunity for Welfare'. *Philosophical Studies* 56: 77–93.

Arneson, R. 2016a. 'Exploitation, Domination, Competitive Markets, and Unfair Division'. *Southern Journal of Philosophy* 54 (supplement): 9–30.

Arneson, R. 2016b. 'Comment on Vrousalis, How Exploiters Dominate'. Unpublished.

Attas, D. 2000. 'The Case of Guest Workers: Exploitation, Citizenship and Economic Rights'. *Res Publica* 6: 73–92.

Avineri, S. 1991. 'Marxism and Nationalism'. *Journal of Contemporary History* 26: 637–57.

Banaji, J. 1975. 'India and the Colonial Mode of Production: Comment'. *Economic and Political Weekly* 10(49): 1887–9; 1891–2.

Banaji, J. 2010. *Theory as History*. London: Haymarket Books.

Bardhan, P. 1999. *The Political Economy of Development in India*. Oxford: Oxford University Press.

Bardhan, P. and J. Roemer. 1992. 'Market Socialism: A Case for Rejuvenation'. *Journal of Economic Perspectives* 6: 101–16.

Bardhan, P. and J. Roemer (eds.) 1993. *Market Socialism: The Current Debate*. New York: Oxford University Press.

Barratt-Brown, M. 1963. *After Imperialism*. London: Hillary House.

Basu, K. 1986. 'One Kind of Power'. *Oxford Economic Papers* 38: 259–82.

Bazard, E. 1831. *Doctrine de Saint-Simon*. Université de Lausanne, mimeo.

Benn, S. 1988. *A Theory of Freedom*. Cambridge: Cambridge University Press.

Bertram, C. 2007. 'Exploitation and Future Generations'. *Imprints* 10: 69–92.

Bhandari, R. 2008. 'The Disguises of Wage-Labour: Juridical Illusions, Unfree Conditions and Novel Extensions'. *Historical Materialism* 16: 71–99.

Bowles, S. and H. Gintis. 1990. 'Contested Exchange'. *Politics and Society* 18(2): 165–222.

Bowles, S. and H. Gintis. 1992. 'Power and Wealth in a Competitive Capitalist Economy'. *Philosophy and Public Affairs* 21: 324–53.

Bratman, M. 2014. *Shared Agency: A Planning Theory of Acting Together*. New York: Oxford University Press.

Breen, K. 2015. 'Freedom, Republicanism, and Workplace Democracy'. *Critical Review of International Social and Political Philosophy* 18: 470–85.

Brewer, A. 1996. *Marxist Theories of Imperialism: A Critical Survey*. London: Routledge.

Brenner, R. 1976. 'Agrarian class structure and economic development in pre-industrial Europe'. *Past and Present* 70: 30–75.

Brenner, R. 1977. 'The Origins of Capitalist Development: A Critique of Neo-Smithian Marxism'. *New Left Review* 104: 25–92.

186 REFERENCES

Brenner, R. and C. Isett. 2002. 'England's Divergence from China's Yangzi Delta: Property Relations, Microeconomics, and Patterns of Development'. *The Journal of Asian Studies* 61: 609–62.

Buchanan, A. 1984. *Marx and Justice*. Totowa: NJ: Rowman and Littlefield.

Byres, T. 2006. 'Differentiation of the Peasantry Under Feudalism and the Transition to Capitalism: In Defence of Rodney Hilton'. *Journal of Agrarian Change* 6: 17–68.

Cain, P.G. and A.G. Hopkins. 2001. *British Imperialism*. London: Routledge.

Callinicos, A. 2014. *Deciphering Capital*. London: Bookmarks.

Caney, S. 2015. 'Responding to Global Injustice: On the Right of Resistance'. *Social Philosophy and Policy* 32: 51–73.

Cavallero, E. 2010. 'Coercion, Inequality and the International Property Regime'. *Journal of Political Philosophy* 18: 16–31.

Casal, P. 2013. 'Occupational Choice and the Egalitarian Ethos'. *Economics and Philosophy* 29: 3–20.

Chang, H.-J. 2002. *Throwing Away the Ladder*. New York: Anthem Press.

China Bureau of National Statistics. 2015. *China Statistical Yearbook*. https://www.stats.gov.cn/ (Accessed 15 November, 2020).

Clark, J.B. 1902. *The Distribution of Wealth*. New York: Macmillan.

Cohen, G.A. 1978. *Karl Marx's Theory of History: A Defence*. Oxford: Oxford University Press.

Cohen, G.A. 1979. 'The Labor Theory of Value and the Concept of Exploitation'. *Philosophy and Public Affairs* 84: 338–360.

Cohen, G.A. 1988. *History Labour and Freedom*. Oxford: Oxford University Press.

Cohen, G.A. 1989. 'On the Currency of Egalitarian Justice'. *Ethics* 99, 906–944.

Cohen, G.A. 1995. *Self-Ownership, Freedom and Equality*. Cambridge: Cambridge University Press.

Cohen, G.A. 2011. *On the Currency of Egalitarian Justice*. Otsuka, M. (ed.) Princeton: Princeton University Press.

Cohen, J. 1989. 'The Economic Basis of Deliberative Democracy'. *Social Philosophy and Policy* 6: 25–50.

Cudd, A. 2006. *Analyzing Oppression*. Oxford: Oxford University Press.

Dagger, R. 2006. 'Neo-republicanism and the Civic Economy'. *Politics, Philosophy and Economics* 5: 151–73.

De-Shalit, A., 1998. 'Transnational and International Exploitation'. *Political Studies* 46: 693–708.

Donselaar, G. van. 2009. *The Right to Exploit*. Oxford: Oxford University Press.

Dow, G. 2003. *Governing the Firm*. Cambridge: Cambridge University Press.

Dumenil, G. 1984. 'The So-Called "Transformation Problem" Revisited: A Brief Comment'. *Journal of Economic Theory* 33: 340–48.

Dworkin, R. 2000. *Sovereign Virtue*. Cambridge, MA: Harvard University Press.

Einspahr, J. 2010. 'Structural Domination and Structural Freedom: A Feminist Perspective'. *Feminist Review* 94: 1–19.

Ellerman, D. 2007. 'On the Role of Capital in "Capitalist" and in Labor-Managed Firms'. *Review of Radical Political Economics* 39: 5–26.

Elster, J. 1982. 'Roemer against Roemer: A Comment on "New Directions" in the Marxian Theory of Exploitation and Class'. *Politics & Society* 11: 363–73.

Elster, J. 1985. *Making Sense of Marx*. Cambridge: Cambridge University Press.

Feinberg, J. 1987. *Harm to Others*. Oxford: Oxford University Press.

Feinberg, J. 1988. *Harmless Wrongdoing*. Oxford: Oxford University Press.

REFERENCES 187

Ferguson, B. 2016. 'The Paradox of Exploitation'. *Erkentnnis* 81: 951–72.

Fine, B. and Saad-Filho, M. 2004. *Marx's Capital*. London: Verso.

Fleurbaey, M. 1993. 'Economic Democracy and Equality: A Proposal'. In Bardhan and Roemer (eds.). *Market Socialism: The Current Debate*, pp. 240–58.

Foley, D. 1982. 'The Value of Money the Value of Labor Power and the Marxian Transformation Problem'. *Review of Radical Political Economics* 14: 37–47.

Frank, A.G. 1967. *Capitalism and Underdevelopment in Latin America*. New York: Monthly Review Press.

Frye, M. 1983. *The Politics of Reality: Essays in Feminist Theory*. Trumansburg, NY: The Crossing Press.

Gaedeke, D. 2016. 'The Domination of States: Towards an Inclusice Republican Law of Peoples'. *Global Justice: Theory Practice Rhetoric* 9: 15–34.

Gaedeke, D. 2020. 'Does a Mugger Dominate? Episodic Power and the Structural Dimension of Domination'. *Journal of Political Philosophy* 28: 199–221.

Gallagher, J. and R. Robinson. 1953. 'The Imperialism of Free Trade'. *Economic History Review* 6: 1–15.

Galtung, J. 1971. 'A Structural Theory of Imperialism'. *Journal of Peace Research* 8: 81–117.

Gauthier, D. 1985. *Morals by Agreement*. Oxford: Oxford University Press.

Geras, N. 1986. 'The Controversy about Marx and Justice'. New Left Review 150: 47–85.

Gilbert, M. 1996. *Living Together*. Lanham, MD: Rowman & Littlefield.

Gonzalez-Ricoy, I. 2014. 'The Republican Case for Workplace Democracy'. *Social Theory and Practice* 40: 232–54.

Goodin, R. 1985. *Protecting the Vulnerable*. Chicago: University of Chicago Press.

Goodin, R. 1987. 'Exploiting a Situation and Exploiting a Person'. In Reeve 1987, pp. 166–200.

Gordon, R.J. 2012. 'Is U.S. Economic Growth Over?'. NBER Working Paper.

Gosseries, A. and L. Meyer. 2009. *Intergenerational Justice*. Oxford: Oxford University Press.

Gould, C. 1988. *Rethinking Democracy*. Cambridge: Cambridge University Press.

Greasley, K. 2012. 'A Legal Market in Organs: The Problem of Exploitation'. *Journal of Medical Ethics* 40: 51–6.

Hardt, M. and A. Negri. 2001. *Empire*. Cambridge, MA: Harvard University Press.

Harvey, D. 2005. *A Brief History of Neoliberalism*. Oxford: Oxford University Press.

Harvey, D. 2010. *A Companion to Marx's Capital*. London: Verso.

Harvey, I., N. Kellard, J. Madsen, and M. Wohar 2010. 'The Prebisch-Singer Hypothesis: Four Centuries of Evidence'. *Review of Economics and Statistics* 92: 367–77.

Haslanger, S. 2012. *Resisting Reality*. Oxford: Oxford University Press.

Havel, V. 1985. *The Power of the Powerless*. London: Routledge.

Hilferding, R. 1910. *Das Finanzkapital*. Berlin: Marx-Studien, vol. III.

Hindriks, F. 2018. 'Collective Agency: Moral and Amoral'. *Dialectica* 72: 3–23.

Hobbes, T. 1994. *Leviathan*. Curley, E. (ed.). London: Hackett.

Hobsbawm, E. 1977. 'Some Reflections on *The Break-Up of Britain*'. *New Left Review* 105: 3–23.

Hobsbawm, E. 1989. *The Age of Empire: 1875–1914*. London: Vintage Books.

Hobsbawm, E. 1999. *Industry and Empire*. London: New Press.

Hobson, J. 2015 [1902]. *Imperialism: A Study*. New York: Albion Press.

Hodgskin, T. 1832. *The Natural and Artificial Right of Property Contrasted*. London: B. Steil.

Hohfeld, W.N. 1919. *Fundamental Legal Conceptions*. New Haven, CT: Yale University Press.

Holmstrom, N., 1977, 'Exploitation'. *Canadian Journal of Philosophy*, 72: 353–69.

188 REFERENCES

Hopkins, A.G. 1994. 'Informal Empire in Argentina: An Alternative View'. *Journal of Latin American Studies* 26: 469–84.

Howard, M.C. and J.E. King. 1975. *The Political Economy of Marx*. London: Longman Publishers.

Hsieh, N. 2005. 'Rawlsian Justice and Workplace Republicanism'. *Social Theory and Practice* 31: 115–42.

Hussain, W. 2023. *Living with the Invisible Hand: Corporations, Markets, and Human Freedom*. Ripstein, A. and N. Vrousalis (eds.). New York, NY: Oxford University Press.

Jossa, B. 2012. 'Cooperative Firms as a New Mode of Production'. *Review of Political Economy* 24: 399–416.

Julius, A.J. 2016. 'Mutual recognition'. *Jurisprudence* 7: 193–209.

Kagan, S. 1991. *The Limits of Morality*. Oxford: Oxford University Press.

Kant, I. 1996. *Practical Philosophy*. Gregor, M. (trans.). Cambridge: Cambridge University Press.

Kautsky, K. 1902. *The Social Revolution*. London: Charles Kerr.

Kautsky, K. 1914. 'Der Imperialismus'. *Die Neue Zeit* 32: September 11, 1914.

Korsch, K. 1977. *Revolutionary Theory*. Kellner, D. (ed.). Austin: University of Texas Press.

Laborde, C. and J. Maynor (eds.). 2008. *Republicanism and Political Theory*. Malden, MA: Blackwell Publishing.

Lawford-Smith, H. and S. Collins. 2017. 'Responsibility for States' Actions: Normative Issues at the Intersection of Collective Agency and State Responsibility'. *Philosophy Compass* 12 https://doi.org/10.1111/phc3.12456. (Accessed 15 November 2020).

Lebowitz, M. 2010. *The Socialist Alternative*. New York, NY: Monthly Review Press.

Lenin, V.I. 1951. *Imperialism: The Highest Stage of Capitalism*. London: Routledge.

Lepora, C. and R. Goodin. 2013. *On Complicity and Compromise*. Oxford: Oxford University Press.

Levine, A. 1988. *Arguing for Socialism*. London: Verso.

Liberto, H. 2014. 'Exploitation and the Vulnerability Clause'. *Ethical Theory and Moral Practice* 17: 619–29.

Lichtheim, G. 1971. *Imperialism*. London: Allen Lane.

List, C. and P. Pettit. 2011. *Group Agents*. Oxford: Oxford University Press. Lovett, F. 2010. *A General Theory of Domination and Justice*. Oxford: Oxford University Press.

Lukacs, G. 1923. *History and Class Consciousness*. London: Merlin Press.

Lukes, S. 1974. *Power: A Radical View*. London: Macmillan.

Lukes, S. 2005. *Power: A Radical View*. 2nd edition. London: Palgrave.

Luxemburg, R. 1976. *The National Question: Selected Writings*. Horace B. Davis (ed.). Monthly Review Press.

MacKinnon, C. 1989. *Towards a Feminist Theory of the State*. Cambridge, MA: Harvard University Press.

Mandel, E. 1962. *Marxist Economic Theory*. Brussels: Merlin Press.

Mandel, E. 1974. *An Introduction to Marxist Economic Theory*. London: Pathfinder Press.

Margalit, A. and J. Raz. 1990. 'National Self-Determination'. *Journal of Philosophy* 87: 439–61.

Marglin, S. 1975. 'What Do Bosses Do?'. *Review of Radical Political Economics* 6: 60–112.

Marichal, C. 1989. *A Century of Debt Crises in Latin America*. Princeton, NJ: Princeton University Press.

Marin, M. 2018. 'What Domination Can and Cannot Do'. Mimeo.

Marshall, A. 1890. *Principles of Economics*. London: Macmillan.

Marx, K. 1969. *Theories of Surplus Value*. vol. 1. Moscow: Progress Publishers.

REFERENCES 189

Marx, K. 1972. *Theories of Surplus Value*. vol. 3. Moscow: Progress Publishers.

Marx, K. 1973. *Grundrisse*. Harmondsworth: Penguin.

Marx, K. 1976. *Capital*. vol. 1. Harmondsworth: Penguin.

Marx, K. 1981. *Capital*. vol. 3. Harmondsworth: Penguin.

Marx, K. 2004. *The German Ideology*. Harmondsworth: Penguin.

Marx, K. and F. Engels, 1988. *Collected Works* (MECW). vol. 20. Moscow: Progress Publishers.

Marx, K. and F. Engels, 1988. *Collected Works*. vol. 28. Moscow: Progress Publishers.

Marx, K. and F. Engels, 1988. *Collected Works*. vol. 30. Moscow: Progress Publishers.

Marx, K. and F. Engels, 1989. *Collected Works*. vol. 32. Moscow: Progress Publishers.

Marx, K. and F. Engels, 1994. *Collected Works*. vol. 34. Moscow: Progress Publishers.

Marx, K. and F. Engels, 1994. *Collected Works*. vol. 35. Moscow: Progress Publishers.

Marx, K. and F. Engels, 1992. *Selected Works*. London: Lawrence and Wishart.

Mayer, R. 2005. 'Guestworkers and Exploitation'. *The Review of Politics* 67: 311–34.

Mayer, R. 2007. 'Sweatshops, Exploitation, and Moral Responsibility'. *Journal of Social Philosophy* 38: 605–19.

McKeown, M. 2016. 'Global Structural Exploitation: Towards an Intersectional Definition'. *Global Justice: Theory Practice Rhetoric* 9: 155–77.

Miliband, R. 1972. *Parliamentary Socialism*. London: Merlin Press.

Mills, C. 2017. *Black Rights, White Wrongs*. Oxford: Oxford University Press.

Miller, R. 2010. *Globalizing Justice*. Oxford: Oxford University Press.

Miller, R. 2017. 'Unequal Bargaining Power and Economic Justice: How Workers Are Exploited and Why It Matters'. In Monique Deveaux and Vida Panitch (eds.), *Exploitation: From Practice to Theory*. New York, NY: Rowman & Littlefield. 15–34.

Morishima, M. 1973. *Marx's Economics*. Cambridge: Cambridge University Press.

Murray, P. 2004. 'The Social and Material Transformation of Production by Capital'. In Bellofiore, R. and N. Taylor (eds.), *The Constitution of Capital*. London: Palgrave.

Nozick, R. 1974. *Anarchy, State and Utopia*. New York, NY: Basic Books.

Nye, J. 2005. *Soft Power*. New York: Public Affairs Publishers.

O'Neill, M. and J. Williamson (eds.). 2012. *Property-Owning Democracy: Rawls and Beyond*. Chichester: Wiley.

Ogilvie, S. 2008. 'Protoindustrialization'. In Durlauf, S. and Blume, E. (eds.), *The New Palgrave Dictionary of Economics*. London: Palgrave.

Otsuka, M. 2005. *Libertarianism without Inequality*. Oxford: Oxford University Press.

Parfit, D. 1981. *Reasons and Persons*. Oxford: Oxford University Press.

Parijs, P. van 1983. 'What (If Anything) is Intrinsically Wrong With Capitalism?' *Philosophica* 34: 85–102.

Parijs, P. van 1995. *Real Freedom for All*. Oxford: Oxford University Press.

Pateman, C. 1988. *The Sexual Contract*. London: Polity.

Peffer, R. 1990. *Marxism, Morality and Social Justice*. Princeton, NJ: Princeton University Press.

Pettit, P. 1999. *Republicanism*. Oxford: Oxford University Press.

Pettit, P. 2010. 'A Republican Law of Peoples'. *European Journal of Political Theory* 9: 70–94.

Pettit, P. and D. Schweikard, 2006. 'Joint Actions and Group Agents'. *Philosophy of the Social Sciences* 36: 18–39.

Piketty, T. 2014. *Capital in the Twenty-First Century*. Cambridge, MA: Harvard University Press.

Pitts, J. 2006. *A Turn to Empire: The Rise of Imperial Liberalism in Britain and France*. Princeton, NJ: Princeton University Press.

190 REFERENCES

Pogge, T. 2008. *World Poverty and Human Rights*. New York, NY: Polity Press.

Pomeranz, K. 2000. *The Great Divergence*. Princeton, NJ: Princeton University Press.

Post, C. 2013. 'Capitalism, Laws of Motion and Social Relations of Production'. *Historical Materialism* 21: 71–91.

Poulantzas, N. 2008. *The Poulantzas Reader*. Martin, J. (ed.). London: Verso.

Rajan, R. and L. Zingales. 'The Firm as a Dedicated Hierarchy: A Theory of the Origins and Growth of Firms'. *The Quarterly Journal of Economics* 116: 805–51.

Rawls, J. 1955. 'Two Concepts of Rules'. *The Philosophical Review* 64: 3–32.

Rawls, J. 1971. *A Theory of Justice*. Oxford: Oxford University Press.

Rawls, J. 2001. *Justice as Fairness: A Restatement*. Cambridge, MA: Harvard University Press.

Reeve, A. (ed.)., 1987. *Modern Theories of Exploitation*. London: Sage.

Reiff, M. 2013. *Exploitation and Economic Justice in the Liberal Capitalist State*. Oxford: Oxford University Press.

Reiman, J. 1987. 'Exploitation, Force, and the Moral Assessment of Capitalism: Thoughts on Roemer and Cohen'. *Philosophy and Public Affairs* 16: 3–41.

Ripstein, A. 2009. *Force and Freedom*. Cambridge, MA: Harvard University Press.

Risse, M. and G. Wollner. 2013. 'Three Images of Trade: On the Place of Trade in a Theory of Global Justice'. *Moral Philosophy and Politics* 1: 201–25.

Risse, M. and G. Wollner. 2019. On Trade Justice. Oxford: Oxford University Press.

Roemer, J. 1982. *A General Theory of Exploitation and Class*. Cambridge, MA: Harvard University Press.

Roemer, J. 1985. 'Should Marxists be Interested in Exploitation?'. *Philosophy and Public Affairs* 14: 30–65.

Roemer, J. 1986. 'New Directions in the Marxian Theory of Exploitation and Class'. In Roemer, J. (ed.), *Analytical Marxism*. Cambridge: Cambridge University Press.

Roemer, J. 1988. *Free to Lose*. Cambridge, MA: Harvard University Press.

Roemer, J. 1994. *A Future for Socialism*. Cambridge, MA: Harvard University Press.

Roemer, J. 1996. *Egalitarian Perspectives*. Cambridge: Cambridge University Press.

Roemer, J. 2017. 'Socialism Revised'. *Philosophy and Public Affairs* 45: 261–315.

Roemer, J. and E. Trannoy. 2016. 'Equality of Opportunity: Theory and Measurement'. *Journal of Economic Literature* 54: 1288–332.

Rousseau, J.-J. 1968. *The Social Contract*, Victor Gourevitch (ed.). Hardmonsworth: Penguin.

Sample, R. 2003. *Exploitation: What It is and Why It's Wrong*. London: Rowman and Littlefield.

Schouten, G. 2019. *Liberalism, Neutrality, and the Gendered Division of Labour*. Oxford: Oxford University Press.

Schweickart, D. 1996. *Against Capitalism*. London: Westview Press.

Schweickart, D. 2002. *After Capitalism*. London: Rowman and Littlefield.

Schweickart, D. 2011. *After Capitalism*. 2nd edition. London: Rowman and Littlefield.

Schweickart, D. 2012. 'Property-Owning Democracy or Economic Democracy?'. In O'Neill and Williamson (eds.) *Property-Owning Democracy: Rawls and Beyond*. Chichester: Wiley.

Schweickart, D. 2017. 'If We Want a Sustainable and Equitable Economy, We Need to Abandon Capitalism'. In Mary Mellor (ed.), *Money for the People*. https://www.greattransition.org/publication/roundtable-money.

Scott, J. 1987. *Weapons of the Weak: Everyday Forms of Peasant Resistance*.

Scott, J. 1990. *Domination and the Arts of Resistance*. Cambridge: Cambridge University Press.

REFERENCES 191

Screpanti, E. 2018. *Labour and Value*. London: Open Book Publishers.

Searle, J. 1964. 'How to Derive "Ought" From "Is" '. *The Philosophical Review* 73: 43–58.

Searle, J. 2009. *The Making of the Social World*. Oxford: Oxford University Press.

Sen, A. 1992. *Inequality Reexamined*. Cambridge, MA: Harvard University Press.

Shelby, T., 2002. 'Parasites, Pimps and Capitalists: A Naturalistic Conception of Exploitation'. *Social Theory and Practice* 28: 381–418.

Singer, P. 2004. *One World*. New Haven, CT: Yale University Press.

Skillman, G. 2007. 'Value Theory vs. Historical Analysis in Marx's Account of Capitalist Exploitation'. *Science and Society* 71: 203–26.

Skillman, G. 2022. 'Domination and Exploitation in Economic Relationships'. *Economics and Philosophy*, forthcoming.

Skinner, Q. 1997. *Liberty before Liberalism*. Cambridge: Cambridge University Press.

Snyder, J., 2008. 'Needs Exploitation'. *Ethical Theory and Moral Practice* 11: 389–405.

Steiner, H., 1984. 'A Liberal Theory of Exploitation'. *Ethics* 94: 225–41.

Stiglitz, J. 2012. *The Price of Inequality*. New York: W.W. Norton.

Stilz, A. 2011. *Liberal Loyalty*. Oxford: Oxford University Press.

Sweezy, P. 1942. *The Theory of Capitalist Development*. Cambridge, MA: Monthly Review Press.

Szigeti, A. and E. Malmqvist. 2019. 'Exploitation and Joint Action'. *Journal of Social Philosophy* 50: 280–300.

Taylor, A. 2016. *Exit Left*. Oxford: Oxford University Press.

Thomas, A. 2017. *Republic of Equals*. Oxford: Oxford University Press.

Thompson, W. 1824. *An Inquiry into the Principles of the Distribution of Wealth*. London: Longman.

Valdman, M. 2009. 'A Theory of Wrongful Exploitation'. *Philosophers' Imprint* 9: 1–14.

Veneziani, R. and N. Yoshihara. 2018. 'The Theory of Exploitation as the Unequal Exchange of Labour'. *Economics and Philosophy* 34: 381–409.

Vanek, J. 1970. *The General Theory of the Labor-Managed Economies*. Ithanca, NY: Cornell University Press.

Vrousalis, N. 2013. 'Exploitation, Vulnerability and Social Domination'. *Philosophy and Public Affairs* 41: 131–57.

Vrousalis, N. 2015. *The Political Philosophy of G.A. Cohen*. London: Bloomsbury Academic.

Vrousalis, N. 2016. 'Exploitation as Domination: A Response to Arneson'. *Southern Journal of Philosophy* 54: 527–538.

Vrousalis, N. 2018a. 'Exploitation: A Primer'. *Philosophy Compass* 19 https://doi.org/10.1111/phc3.12486 (Accessed 15 November 2020).

Vrousalis, N. 2018b. 'Review of Thomas, *Republic of Equals*'. *The Philosophical Review* 128: 125–30.

Vrousalis, N. 2019a. 'Workplace Democracy Implies Economic Democracy'. *Journal of Social Philosophy* 50: 259–79.

Vrousalis, N. 2019b. 'Erfurt plus Councils: The Distinctive Relevance of the German Revolution of 1918–19.' *Socialist History* 55: 27–46.

Vrousalis, N. 2020a. 'Review of Screpanti, *Labour and Value*'. *Erasmus Journal for Philosophy and Economics* 13: 102–9.

Vrousalis, N. 2020b. 'Free Productive Agency: Reasons, Recognition, Socialism'. *Philosophical Topics* 48: 265–84.

Vrousalis, N. 2021. 'Socialism Unrevised: A Reply to John Roemer on Marx, Exploitation, Solidarity, Worker Control'. *Philosophy & Public Affairs* 49: 78–109.

192 REFERENCES

Vrousalis, N. 2022. 'Interdependent Independence: Civil Self-Sufficiency and Productive Community in Kant's Theory of Citizenship'. *Kantian Review* 27: 443–460.

Wallerstein, I. 2004. *World-Systems Analysis*. Durham: Duke University Press.

Wartenberg, T. 1988. *Forms Of Power: From Domination to Transformation*. Philadelphia, PA: Temple University Press.

Weisskopf, T. 1992. 'Toward a Socialism for the Future, in the Wake of the Demise of the Socialism of the Past'. *Review of Radical Political Economics* 24: 9–30.

Wenner, D. 2015. 'Against Permitted Exploitation in Developing World Research Agreements'. *Developing World Bioethics* 16: 36–44.

Wertheimer, A. 1999. *Exploitation*. Princeton: Princeton University Press.

Wertheimer, A. 2011. *Rethinking the Ethics of Clinical Research*. Oxford: Oxford University Press.

White, S. 2004. 'The Citizen's Stake and Paternalism'. *Politics and Society* 32: 61–78.

Wollner, G. 2018. 'Anonymous Exploitation: Non-individual, Non-agential and Structural'. *Review of Social Economy* 76: 143–62.

Wood, A.W. 1972. 'The Marxian Critique of Justice'. *Philosophy and Public Affairs* 1: 244–82.

Wood, A.W. 1995. 'Exploitation'. *Social Philosophy and Policy* 12: 136–158.

Wood, A.W. 2004. *Karl Marx*. London: Routledge.

Wood, A.W. 2014. *The Free Development of Each*. Oxford: Oxford University Press.

Wood, E.M. 1999. *The Origin of Capitalism*. London: Verson.

Wood, E.M. 2002. 'The Question of Market Dependence'. *Journal of Agrarian Change* 2: 50–87.

World Bank. 2011. *World Development Report 2011*. Washington, DC: World Bank.

Wright, E.O. 1985. *Classes*. London: Verso.

Yoshihara, N. 2017. 'A Progress Report on Marxian Economic Theory: On the Controversies in Exploitation Theory Since Okishio'. *Journal of Economic Surveys* 31: 1421–48.

Young, I.M. 1990. *Justice and Politics of Difference*. Princeton, NJ: Princeton University Press.

Young, I.M. 2011. *Responsibility for Justice*. Oxford: Oxford University Press.

Ypi, L. 2013. 'What's Wrong With Colonialism'. *Philosophy and Public Affairs* 41: 158–91.

Zwolinski, M. 2007. 'Sweatshops, Choice, and Exploitation'. *Business Ethics Quarterly* 17: 689–727.

Zwolinski, M. 2012. 'Structural Exploitation'. *Social Philosophy and Policy* 29: 154–79.

Zwolinski, M. and A. Wertheimer. 2016. 'Exploitation'. *Stanford Encyclopedia of Philosophy* (Accessed 15 November 2020).

Index

1 percent 46–51, 70–2, 105–8, 159–61, 179–84; as exploitable 77–8

absolutism 2–3, 22
abundance 40–1
accumulation 69–72, 86–7, 127–30; clean capitalist 48–50, 65
advantage 13–15; and barganing power 29–3, 55–9, 70–5; and mutual benefit 11–12, 18–19, 38–42, 78–80, 155–160; and globalization 152–4; and polygamy 41–2, 62; and vulnerability 29–30, 73–5
agency 38–43, individual 59–62; group 105–8, 150, 162; see also domination
alienation 59–62, 117–21; see also reification, perfectionism
Anderson, E. 86–7
Ant and Grasshopper 25–6, 84–7; see also accumulation, leisure-work tradeoff
Arneson, R. xi, 27–8, 84–90
assets 12–13, 27–8, 84–90; alienable 171–2; inalienable 171–2, 178–9; see also inequality, talents, labour epistocracy
autocracy: in the workplace 55–9, 174–9; in the state 182–4

badness 11–12, 16–20; and globalization 147–9; see also harm, justice
Banaji, J. 128–9
bargaining power 29–33, and advantage 48–52; and exploitation 30–3, 51–2, 74–5
Barings crisis of 1890 147–8, 154
basic needs 77–8
benefit 12–13, 53–4; see also advantage, exploitation
Bertram, C. 112–13

biopolitics 97n.11
Bowles, S. 176–7
Brecht, B. 60
Brenner, R. 130–1
British Empire 146–9; see also imperialism
bureaucracy 182–4; see also socialization dilemma

capabilities 11–12, 68–9
capital exports 151–4, 162–3
capitalism 12, agrarian 128–31; cleanly-generated 48–51, 85–7; definition of 46, 118–19; People's 51–2; American 131; British 48, 150–1; Russian 131; and historical materialism 100, 104; and injustice 12, 59–65, 101–3; and money 53–4; and private property 27–8, 69–71; see also freedom, invisible hand, market, ownership
care 41, 80–1, and gestational labour 81; and contract pregnancy 81
catallaxy 48–50; see also invisible hand
Catallaxy Prison 106
Charlotte and Werther 18
China 113–14
civil society 48–50; see also market
class 46–8, 69–70, 109–11, 123–7, 149–54, 171–2, 182–4; cleanly-generated 48–50; ruling 50–1, 169
coercion 22–5; and capitalism 46–7, 69–71, 103–5, 151–2; see also force
Cohen, G.A. 11, 27–8, 49, 71, 84–8, 119
Cohen, J. 179
collective action 46–8
collective intentionality 105–7
Comeupance 83
commercial surrogacy: see contract
commodification 53–4; and sex work 78–80

194 INDEX

commodities 90–1

communism 45–6, 132–4, 159–61, 179–81; forms of 170–82; *see also* socialism, Marx, Marxism

consent 17–18, 78–80

contract 2–3, 18–19, 84–8; pregnancy 80–1; *see also* consent

cooperation 11–13, 45–8; mandatory 38–42, 88–90, 101–3, 169–70; and globalization 159–60

cooperative firms 60, 132–40, 174–7

corn economy 45–52, 118

coverture 42

Crazy and Lazy 168

David and Goliath 76

debt 148, 154, 163, slavery 129n.20

democracy 38, 107, 182–4; and workplace 60, 132–40, 174–7; and globalization 59–61

difference principle 37, 170; and globalization 159–60; *see also* Rawls, John, incentives, inequality

division of labour 45–8, gendered 42–3, 98–100, global 1–2, 159–60; *see also* capitalism, labour, patriarchy

discrimination. 95–6

Domestic Servant 69, 79

domination 30–3, 38–45, 73–5, 125–8, coercive vs. liberal 142–4; interpersonal vs. structural 95–101; intergenerational 111–13; Kantian 43; republican 44; recognitional 44; and labour 58–61, 125–8; without exploitation 51–2; and servitude 38–41; at work vs. at workplace 54–9

Donselaar, G. Van 21

duress 77–8

Dworkin, R. 37, 87

efficiency 45–6, 179–81; *see also* Pareto principle

effort 48–9, 67–9, relative 68; as contribution 48, 50–1, 168–70

egalitarianism: relational 29, 87–91; *see also* luck egalitarianism

Ellerman, D. 44

Elster, J. 60

empire 142–9; *see also* imperialism

Enclosure 17

epistocracy: *see* labour epistocracy

equality 12–13, 17, 41–3, 49; in assets 26–8, 69–70, 171–3; in political power 182; *see also* assets, exploitation, justice

exclusion 46–8, 103

exit 42–3, 60, 177–9

exploitation: capitalist vs. socialist 171; epistocratic 171, 177–8; horizontal vs. vertical 109–11; structural 95–8, 151–4; and distributive justice 26–8, 84–8; and libertarianism 22–6; international vs. transnational 151–2; intergenerational 111–13; metric of 67–72; and alienation 59–60; and consent 17–19; and family 41–3, 80–1; and Pareto efficiency 19, 62n.48, 153n.16; and race 97, 108; and respect 22–8; and sexism 42, 95; and social surplus 11, 45–51, 109–11, 120–3; and teleology 16–21; and vulnerability 29–30, 73–5, 81–4; at work vs. at workplace 54–9; of billionaires 77–8

exploitation-first theory 75

explomination 89

externality 58

factory: as archetype of modernity 125; and capitalism 57–9, 106; and socialism 60, 139–40, 179–81; *see also* cooperation, cooperative firms

false consciousness 60n.41, 99–103, 108n.37; *see also* alienation, reification

family: farms 131; *see also* patriarchy, sexism

feasibility 13–14, 45–8, 62–3

Feinberg, J. 78

feminism 42, 98–101; *see also* patriarchy, sexism

feudalism 2–3, 19, 22n.21; and transition to capitalism 122–32

finance 53–4; and usury 122–9; under market socialism 180–1

flourishing 60, 61n.45

Fleurbaey, M. 173, 181

force 22, 103–5; *see also* coercion

INDEX   195

Free Riders 88
freedom and unfreedom 29–31, 38, 42–3, 59–61, proletarian 22–3, 77–8; and property 47, 57–8, 69–70; *see also* capitalism, coercion, domination, inequality, socialism
French Revolution 38
Friday and Robinson 56, 110–11, 136–7
functionalism 100n.19

Gates, W. 77–8
Gauthier, D. 21
gift-giving 20–1, 62–4
Gintis, H. 177–9
globalization 149–54, benefits of 159–61; and exploitation 151–3; and capitalism 144–6; and state 149–50; and working class 155–61
good life 16–21, 61n.45
Goodin, R. 14
Grasshopper's Blackmail 169

harm 11, 16–19, 53; *see also* exploitation, good life
Haslanger, S. 99–101
Havel, V. 98
Hayek, F. 106
Hegel, G.W.F. 106
hegemony 143
Hilferding, R. 153–4
historical materialism 94–5, and economic structure 118–20; mode of production interpretation of 42–3, 120–1; and superstructure 94–5
Hobsbawm, E. 145, 168
Hohfeld, W. 73n.9
Hopkins, A.G. 145, 148

ideology 60n.41, 97–100
imperialism 151–4, colonial 144–6; liberal 147–9; *see also* British Empire, empire
incentives 174; moral 179; *see also* Rawls, John
inequality: in assets 26–8, 69–70, 171–3; in political power 182; *see also* assets, exploitation, justice
independence 39, 59–60, 144–9
India 146

industry 125–7, 132–4, 138–40
intentions: individual 51–3; shared 105–7
interest rate 47n.24, 53–4, 122–9
interdependence 38–9, 159–60; as interdependent independence 38n.1
intergenerational justice 112–13
international exploitation 151–4
International Monetary Fund (IMF) 152–4
internationalism 159–61
interpersonal exploitation: *see* exploitation
investment planning 179–84
invisible hand: as process 48–51; *see also* market, Nozick, R.

justice 38–43, in acquisition 39–45; circumstances of 45–8; distributive 26–8; non-distributive 29–31, 38–45; metric of 66–9; in transfer 48–50, 53–4

Kant, I. 22–6, 38–9, 143n.2, 143n.5
Kantianism 43–4, and respect theories 22–6; and servitude 38–45
Kautsky, K. 154, 172n.8
keiretsu system 180
Kibney 80–1
kidney markets 80–1

labour 39–43, 111–13, epistocracy 172–3, 177–9; flow 67–72; -managed firms 60, 132–40, 174; market 46–8, 121–31, 174–80; meaningful 102n.24; sexual 78–80; gestational 80–1; social 41; and general equilibrium 45n.18, 68
labour theory of value 68n.4, 70–1, 79n.16
labour union 42
Latin America 147–8
Lenin, V.I. 129n.21, 150n.12, 154
leisure-work tradeoff 25–6, 84–7
liberal domination 143
liberal imperialism 147–9, 151–4
liberal neutrality 61
liberal socialism 179–81
liberalism 22–5, 37, 143; *see also* Rawls, J.
libertarianism 19, 25–6; *see also* Nozick, R.

196 INDEX

love 18, 59–60
luck egalitarianism 27–8, 69–70, 84–7;
  lenience objection to 84–7;
  trivialization objection to 88–90
Lukács, G. 105
Lukes, S. 143n.4
Luxemburg, R. 157–61

MacKinnon, C. 99nn.15,17
managers: as supermanagers 172; and
  socialism 172, 177–9
manufacturing 124–31
marginal productivity theory 19–20
market: for labour 48–52; for
  gestation 80–1; for sex 78–80; for
  organs 80; as baseline 26, 31–3; as
  simple commodity production
  122–4; Walrasian 58, 176–7;
  see also capitalism, commodification,
  socialism
market proceduralism 31–3, see also
  Wertheimer, A.
market socialism: in Roemer 171–2; in
  Schweickart 178–9; the case
  against 134–8
Marx, K. 3, 19, 20, 22, 24–5, 27, 49–50,
  58–62, 68, 75, 90–1; and Capital, 117–40;
  and Communist Manifesto 62, 104–5;
  and Non-Servitude Proviso 61–2; and
  horizontal exploitation 136; see also
  capitalism, communism, socialism
Marxism: analytical 27–8, 45, classical 62,
  150; see also socialism, communism
Master and Servant 76–7
meaningful work 102n.24
might vs. right 2–3, 38–43
Mill, J.S. 3, 173–4
Miller, R. 82, 153n.15
Mondragon cooperative 139–40
money: as capital 153–4; as means of
  exchange 53; monetized servitude 4, 52
monopoly 15–16, 21, 26, 52, 85
moral responsibility 100–1
Morishima, M. 50n.31
Mozart and Salieri 173

national self-determination 157–9
needs 77–8
neoclassical economics 19–20, 45

Non-Servitude Proviso 38–45, 49–55,
  67–9, 72–83, 88, 105, 109–11, 143,
  168–70, 174–82
Nozick, R. 22–5; and cleanly-generated
  capitalism 48–51; and G.A.
  Cohen 49n.28

offers 42–3, 78–80
oppression: see domination
opportunity costs 49n.29, 87
organ markets 80–1
ownership: collective 45–6; private 46–8;
  public 171–2, 179–82; see also
  capitalism, ownership, socialism,
  property-relations definition

Pareto principle 46, 62n.48
Parfit, D. 112
Parijs, P. Van 168–70
Pateman, C. 42n.10
patriarchy 42–3, 81, 99–101
perfectionism 61n.45
Pettit, P. 44n.14, 52, 107
Piketty, T. 3, 172
Pit 15, 39, 49–50, 53–4, 66–7, 70,
  86, 95–8
Platonism, methodological 62–3
political morality 62, 103–5, 167
polygamy 41–2, 62
power: economic vs. market 59n.40;
  effective 41n.7, 118–19; political 144–9,
  162–4
preferences 48–9; expensive 85–7
prices: just 26–7; of production 140–1;
  and market proceduralism 31–3
principles 62–3
prison guards 105–7, 110
Prison Warden 107
privatization 46–8, 179–82
production: see cooperation, labour
productivity: marginal 19–20; increase
  in 65; under capitalism
  46–50, 129–31
profit motive 19n.13, 46–8
prostitution: see labour, patriarchy
property: see ownership
property-relations definition 57–8, 69–70;
  see also Roemer, J.
property law 104

property-owning democracy (POD) 38–9, 170–4; contrasted with workplace democracy (WD) 174–81
putting-out 119, 124–31

race and racism 97, 108
Rawls, J. 22–5, 37, 143; and democratic equality 84–8; and liberal socialism 170, 179; *see also* incentives, inequality, difference principle, socialism
realism: of assumptions 45; and Marxism 49
reciprocity 19–21, 111–13
recognition 44
Regulated Domination 98
Reiff, M. 27
reification 60, 102; *see also* alienation, capitalism
reproduction: economic 45–8, 142n.1; social 78–81; *see also* labour
rescue, duty to 84–7
resistance 155–7; to imperialism 157–61
respect theories 22–8
responsibility: causal vs. moral 100–1
Ricardo, D. 3, 26–7, 68n.3
Rich and Poor 71, 90–1
rights 25–6, 85–7
Ripstein, A. 44n.13
Roemer, J. 27–8, 45–8, 67–9; and domination 55; and exploitation theory 69–79; socialism of 171–3
Rousseau, J.-J. 38n.1, 61–2

Saint-Simon, H. de 14
Sample, R. 22, 27n.27
scarcity 40–1
Schweickart, D. 178–82
Searle, J. 97n.11
secession 158–61
self-ownership 119; *see also* libertarianism
Sen, A. 11n.1
serfdom 2–3, 19, 22n.21, 113–14
service vs. servitude 38–41, 67–9
servitude 67–9; and Non-Servitude Proviso 38–43; monetized 52–4, 59–62; dividend of: *see* exploitation
sex market: *see* market

sexism 42–3, 81, 95–101
sexual labour: *see* labour
sexual exploitation 78–80
Skillman, G. 124–8
slavery 1–3, 119
Smith, A. 3, 20
social science 45, 62–3
socialism 45–6, coupons- 171–3; liberal 179–81; market 134–8, 171–2, 178–9; and investment planning 179–84; *see also* capitalism, communism
socialization dilemma 183–4
solidarity 38, international 156, 159–61
sovereignty 144–9
Soviet Union 131, 183
state 103–5, 107–8, forms of 150–1; and property rights 162; as a collective agent 105–8
Steiner, H. 25–6
Stiglitz, J. 12
structural: exploitation 48–51, 70–3, 109–11; power 93–8; vulnerability 98
subsumption of labour to capital 117–40, antediluvian 124–31; postdiluvian 132–40
superstructure 94–5
surplus: labour 11–14, 46–8, 67–73; material 11–12; value 131
sweatshops 39, 151–4, 163
Sweezy, P. 122

talents 171, 177–9; *see also* incentives, labour epistocracy
taxation 173
technology 12, in the corn model 45–7
teleological theories 16–21
trade 45–8, 56, 110–11, international 136–7, 151–3
transformation problem 20, 140–1

unconditional basic income (UBI) 42, 168–70
unconscionable contracts: *see* consent
underdevelopment theories 147n.10
unequal exchange: of value 122–9; of labour 69–72
using as mere means 11; *see also* Kantianism, respect theories
utopia 62–3, 167–84

198 INDEX

vaccines 1, 50n.29
Vanek, J. 137
Veneziani, R. 68n.4
voluntariness 17–18, 78–80; *see also* consent, responsibility
vulnerability 29–30, 73–5, 81–4, structural 97–8; and power 73

waived obligation or immunity 60–1
wage labour 46–8; and exploitation 59–60, 95–8, 109–11; and origins of capitalism 124–31; *see also* capitalism, commodification, exploitation, market
welfare 16–19
Wertheimer, A. 31–3
Wolff, J. 21n.20
women 42–3, and care 41, 80–1; and pregnancy contracts 81; and family 42, 99–101; *see also* sexism

Wood, A.W. 81
Wood, E.M. 129–31
work 39–43, 62–72, 111–13, domination at 54–9; meaningful 52, 102n.24; *see also* labour
worker control 178, and models of socialism 170–84
workers' councils 183
working-class internationalism 157–61
workplace: domination at 55–9
workplace democracy (WD) 60, 132–140, 174–7
World Bank 152–3
World Trade Organization (WTO) 152–3
Wright, E.O. 184

Yoshihara, N. 68n.4
Ypi, L. 146n.8

Zuckerberg, M. 77–8